M000036385

WORLDLY ACTS AND SENTIENT THINGS

WORLDLY ACTS AND SENTIENT THINGS

THE PERSISTENCE OF AGENCY
FROM STEIN TO DELILLO

ROBERT CHODAT

CORNELL UNIVERSITY PRESS
Ithaca and London

Publication of this book has been aided by a grant from the Boston University Humanities Foundation.

Copyright © 2008 by Cornell University

All rights reserved. Except for brief quotations in a review, this book, or parts thereof, must not be reproduced in any form without permission in writing from the publisher. For information, address Cornell University Press, Sage House, 512 East State Street, Ithaca, New York 14850.

First published 2008 by Cornell University

Printed in the United States of America

Library of Congress Cataloging-in-Publication Data

Chodat, Robert.
  Worldly acts and sentient things : the persistence of agency from Stein to DeLillo / Robert Chodat.
       p. cm.
  Includes bibliographical references and index.
  ISBN 978-0-8014-4678-8 (cloth : alk. paper)
  1. American literature—20th century—History and criticism. 2. Agent (Philosophy) in literature.
3. Consciousness in literature. 4. Subjectivity in literature. 5. Philosophy, Modern, in literature. I. Title

  PS288.A49C48 2008
  810.9'384—dc22

2008001243

Cornell University Press strives to use environmentally responsible suppliers and materials to the fullest extent possible in the publishing of its books. Such materials include vegetable-based, low-VOC inks and acid-free papers that are recycled, totally chlorine-free, or partly composed of nonwood fibers. For further information, visit our website at www.cornellpress.cornell.edu.

Cloth printing   10 9 8 7 6 5 4 3 2 1

❧ Contents

✍ ACKNOWLEDGMENTS

An argument running throughout this book is that our culture is marked by a widespread uncertainty about what kinds of things should be treated as sentient and sapient, as doers and thinkers, and hence as responsible beings. A version of this uncertainty has been felt throughout my own years of writing. A happy life and a finished book are typically ascribed to only a single agent, though neither could ever be achieved without the words and wisdom of a great many others. Nobody's life and nobody's book exemplify this more than my own.

To begin out west, gratitude should first be expressed to four advisers at Stanford University. David Halliburton encouraged my early intuitions that there was something to say about the American intellectual tradition, and Arnold Rampersad has always been abundantly trusting of my work, even when the original seeds of this book threatened to become an unmanageable thicket. Brett Bourbon's intellectual adventurousness I shall probably never encounter again, and many of the following pages can be traced to one or another bracing conversation with him. Last, Richard Rorty began to exert an influence on my thinking just before he arrived at Stanford, and in the years that I knew him he was remarkably generous both as an adviser and as a teacher. News of his death came just as I was completing the book, and while there are things here with which he may not have wholly agreed, I regret that I was never able to hear him voice objections in person. Warm thanks also to George Dekker and Art Strum, early mentors, as well as to Hilary Edwards, whose capacity for spying lazy sentences and ideas I will always cherish. Thanks, too, to three great friends from 21st and Valencia: Julia Beltsiou, Rebecca Groves, and Van Swearingen.

Moving eastward, I thank everyone in the English department of Boston University, which has welcomed me graciously over the last few years. Special gratitude should be expressed to James Winn for his guidance and leadership, and to John Paul Riquelme for his generosity, punning, and professional prodding. Bill Carroll, Laura Korobkin, Jim Siemon, Larry Breiner, and Bob Levine have been particularly benevolent counsels for a novice professor, and without Harriet Lane and Margaret Johnson I could never navigate the administrative labyrinths. Thanks also go to colleagues who have been audiences for this or related items: Mo Lee, Susan Mizruchi, Erin Murphy, Anita Patterson, Matt Smith, and Andy Stauffer. I'm enormously grateful also to the officers and staff at the American Academy of Arts and Sciences, which granted me a postdoctoral fellowship in 2003–4. While there I incurred many debts, especially to Jim Carroll and my fellow Visiting Scholars, in particular Ann Mikkelsen, Matthew Lindsay, and above all Jona Hansen, who with typical insight read the book as it was nearing completion. Among other friends in the Boston area, I thank Stephanie Akin, Stephanie Birdsall, Shawn Boburg, Jim Cahill, Sarah Duggan, Matt Meyer, and Husain Naqvi. Very special thanks as well to Bernie Rhie, whose intelligence and conversation are always immeasurably heartening. Finally, I can't leave the East Coast without paying tribute to a few teachers I was deeply fortunate to encounter years ago in Montreal: Peter Gibian, David Hensley, and last but by no means least, Kerry McSweeney, who one day asked a very good question.

A final setting for the work that went into this book has been Berlin, and while there I've been supported by various individuals and institutions. The Deutscher Akademischer Austauschdienst awarded me a fellowship in 1999 to begin what eventually became this book, and with artful symmetry a fellowship from the Alexander von Humboldt Stiftung in 2006–7 gave me time to finish it. I'm very grateful to Winfried Flück at the Freie Universität Berlin and Günter Abel at the Technische Universität Berlin for sponsoring these extended visits. Great thanks go as well to friends who over the years have made this frequently gray city into a sunny sanctuary: Carsten Beyer, Antonio Arroyo Gil, John Lambert, Max Meier, Stefan Seiterle, Allison Williams, and especially Anyssa Neumann, who scrupulously proofread the manuscript.

Peter J. Potter of Cornell University Press has been an ideal editor, supporting my work and guiding me smoothly through the publication process, and I thank Teresa Jesionowski and Herman Rapaport for their help editing the manuscript. The book has benefited greatly from the input of two readers for the press, John Gibson and Joseph Tabbi, who read the manuscript judiciously and made many thoughtful suggestions. A version of chapter 1 first saw the light of day as "Sense, Science, and the Interpretations of Gertrude Stein," in *Modernism/Modernity* 12.4 (November 2005): 581–605, and an earlier edition of chapter 3 appeared as "Beyond Science and Supermen: Bellow and Mind at Mid-Century," in *Texas Studies in Literature and Language* 45.4 (2003): 391–425. Copyright © 2003 by the University of Texas Press.

I am grateful to the editors and staff of these journals for allowing me to reprint these materials.

My final debt goes well beyond geography. Nothing attributable to my life or to this book would have been imaginable without my family: my brother Joseph, my mother Carolyn, and my father David.

R.C.

❧ Abbreviations

PI   Ludwig Wittgenstein, *Philosophical Investigations*, trans. G. E. M. Ans-
        combe (New York: Macmillan, 1953), followed by section number
        or page number where appropriate.
SPR   Wilfrid Sellars, *Science, Perception, and Reality* (London: Routledge
        and Kegan Paul, 1963).
HRK   Saul Bellow, *Henderson the Rain King* (1959; New York: Penguin,
        1996).
IM   Ralph Ellison, *Invisible Man* (1952; New York: Vintage, 1990).
U   Don DeLillo, *Underworld* (New York: Scribner's, 1997).

WORLDLY ACTS AND SENTIENT THINGS

INTRODUCTION

French Cathedrals and Other Forms of Life

How do you seduce a heap of chiseled stones? One person who tried, at least for a while, was Henry Adams. In the "Vis Nova" chapter of *The Education of Henry Adams,* Adams describes traveling around France at the turn of the last century, and he depicts himself as a lover infatuated with the facades and stained glass of the country's medieval cathedrals, whose beguiling spirit he pursues gallantly across the country.

> For him, the Virgin was an adorable mistress, who led the automobile and its owner where she would, to her wonderful palaces and chateaux, from Chartres to Rouen, and thence to Amiens and Laon, and a score of others, kindly receiving, amusing, charming and dazzling her lover, as though she were Aphrodite herself, worth all else that man ever dreamed. He never doubted her force, since he felt it to the last fibre of his being, and could no more dispute its mastery than he could dispute the force of gravitation of which he knew nothing but the formula....
>
> ...The Virgin had not...altogether gone; her fading away had been excessively slow. Her adorer had pursued her too long, too far, and into too many manifestations of her power, to admit that she had any equivalent either of quantity or kind, in the actual world, but he could still less admit her annihilation as energy.

So he went on wooing, happy in the thought that at last he had found a mistress who could see no difference in the age of her lovers.[1]

There is no indication here that Adams is speaking metaphorically or pulling our leg. Scrutinizing a map of the stars, the astrologer sees a spray of random lights no more than the palm reader sees a fluke arrangement of wrinkles on a hand, and the sexagenarian Adams, in a similarly earnest spirit, sees an expressive pattern in certain buildings scattered around France. Indeed, I've referred to the cathedrals as heaps of chiseled stone, but for the traveler Adams, this is precisely what the cathedrals were not. They were not even, as I have also implied, mere "buildings." In Adams's account, the cathedrals are "manifestations" of some power, not slabs of mute matter but things expressing attitudes and ideas—the body of his beloved, the sensuous lips and arms whose postures encourage his passion and charm his eyes. He stands before them not only as what Miguel Tamen has called a "friend," offering to speak for and represent them to whoever may fail to appreciate their dazzle.[2] He actually presents himself as having what today would be called an "intimate relationship" with them.

Adams's romance with the cathedrals proved not to be eternal. Touring Troyes one day, he hears a report that the Russian Minister of the Interior was assassinated in St. Petersburg. Adams is shaken by the news, and his memoir spends considerable time recording how he feels confronted suddenly by "chaos of time, place, morals, forces and motives" (*Education* 1050–51). Taking rest in the Church of St. Pantaleon, he contemplates a new "formula for the universe." A "Dynamic Theory of History," as he calls it, would be built upon a vastly different relation between humans and non-humans than the one that engenders his affair with the cathedrals.

A dynamic theory, assigning attractive force to opposing bodies in proportion to the law of mass, takes for granted that the forces of nature capture man. The sum of force attracts; the feeble atom or molecule called man is attracted; he suffers education or growth; he is the sum of the forces that attract him; his body and his thought are alike their product; the movement of the forces controls the progress of his mind, since he can know nothing but the motions which impinge on his senses, whose sum makes education. (*Education* 1153)

---

[1] *The Education of Henry Adams,* in *Novels, Mont Saint Michel, The Education* (New York: Library of America, 1983), 1148–49. Henceforth cited as *Education.*

[2] Miguel Tamen, *Friends of Interpretable Objects* (Cambridge: Harvard University Press, 2002), chap. 8.

The *vis nova,* he concludes, compels us to face the melancholy facts: not only do "forces, sensible and occult, physical and metaphysical, simple and complex, surround, traverse, vibrate, rotate, repel, attract, without stop," but "man's senses are conscious of few, and only in partial degree" (*Education* 1165).

Under this new dispensation, there is no room for the kind of erotic intimacy Adams displays with the cathedrals of Chartres and Rouen. To say now that the buildings are doing anything as complex as flirtation would be a disposable rhetorical flourish, mere personification. If we take the "Dynamic Theory" seriously, the cathedrals exhibit purposeful patterns no more than the barren dunes upon a beach. The seductive give-and-take of Adams's romance with the Virgin—his effort to "woo" and "pursue" her, her willingness to "kindly" receive and amuse him—reflect a participatory universe, one in which "mind" was "a mode of force directly derived from the intelligent prime motor," and which entailed a Thomistic "reconciliation between thought and mechanics" (*Education* 1112). Hence what Adams frequently refers to as medieval "Unity." But modernity, as Adams describes it, is characterized by an ever-broadening reduction of "thought" to "mechanics," the latter of which is now consistently described as lawlike purposeless motion rather than regular purposeful action. The "new unit" of modern science, he says, "would not be an intelligence—probably not even a consciousness" (*Education* 1113).[3]

It is this mounting fear that the universe is, in the phrase Max Weber was to circulate a few years later, "disenchanted" that has placed *The Education* among the foundational texts of modern thought and literature.[4] Adams was hardly the first to say that the *vis nova* had stripped the universe of its purposes. An ancient Greek mariner may have attributed the ocean storm to Poseidon's foul temper, but atmospheric states and other natural phenomena

---

[3] I've implied here that the outbreak of the Russo-Japanese War is the turning point in Adams's narrative, but the trajectory of *The Education* is of course far more tortuous. Disillusion marks Adams's experiences in virtually every chapter, and as a result of various events (reading Pearson, seeing the dynamo, etc.)—to the point that readers often have trouble identifying any narrative trajectory in the book at all. On the scientific and philosophical context of Adams's text, in particular its reading and misreading of Herbert Spencer, see Ronald E. Martin, *American Literature and the Universe of Force* (Durham: Duke University Press, 1981), chap. 3. For a different take on Adams and modern science, see N. Katherine Hayles, *Chaos Bound: Orderly Disorder in Contemporary Literature and Science* (Ithaca: Cornell University Press, 1990).

[4] For a sense of Adams's place in twentieth-century thought, see *Modernism: An Anthology of Sources and Documents,* ed. Vassiliki Kolocotroni, Jane Goldman, and Olga Taxidou (Chicago: University of Chicago Press, 1998), in which selections from *The Education* appear next to selections from Marx, Darwin, Nietzsche, and Freud. On Adams and modern literature generally, see John Carlos Rowe, *Henry James and Henry Adams: The Emergence of a Modern Consciousness* (Ithaca: Cornell University Press, 1976).

had long been barred from the class of things said to have minds and moods. What makes *The Education* seem central to modern accounts of ourselves is the insistence with which even this classification—the belief that at least *some* things have motives and morals—now seems dubious. The patterns of purposive "thought" are now less a part of our working ontology than the purposeless "mechanics" of the universe, which can no longer "be supposed to relax its energy to suit the convenience of man" (*Education* 1171). From this anxiety that his beliefs may be a mere tissue of fictions arises the famous third-person voice of Adams's narrative. His actions, as he says in his preface, can be presented only as those of a "manikin," a "geometrical figure" useful for study but, metaphysically, always to be taken with a grain of salt: "It must have the air of reality; must be taken for real; must be treated as though it had life;—Who knows? Possibly it had!" (*Education* 722). Not only can I no longer say that the heap of chiseled stones called "Chartres Cathedral" are "about" anything; I can no longer say this about the sounds that come from my own mouth. Not only do I begin to draw stares from other visitors when I address the cathedrals with warm devotion, but even my own self-descriptions come to seem empty terms of endearment.

The starting point of this book is that writers of the last century have most typically resembled not the Adams who fears the gradual evaporation of minds in modernity, but rather the earlier, lovestruck Adams who feels the intentional "force" of the cathedrals "to the last fibre of his being." Like Adams, modern and contemporary writers have treated a startling range of entities as sentient speakers and actors. Future generations, I'll be arguing, will see the last century's literature not as exhibiting the dissolution of agency, but the gradual displacement of it onto new and varied forms. They will regard recent writers as students of *The Education,* but more for the quixotic seductions it records than its collection of somber obituaries.

Such a starting point may seem a counter-intuitive place, today, to begin a discussion of agency in modern thought and literature. As I have said, Adams's accounts of the dynamo are often taken to be among the central statements of modernity, and one could object to my thumbnail characterization of modern and contemporary literature by pointing to the various strands of our intellectual culture that seem to descend from his "dynamic theory." One such strand is modern and contemporary literature itself. Readers have often distinguished the competing movements and schools of the last century's poetry and fiction: Imagism, Futurism, Surrealism, Avant-Garde, Pop, Minimalism, or—most broadly—Modernism and Postmodernism. But for all the very real differences identified in these labels, each of them refers, in part, to a deep suspicion about agency thematized and formalized throughout recent texts. One thinks, for instance, of Adams's French contemporary Sté-phane Mallarmé, whose experiments led Sartre to say that, in *Un coup de dés* and other texts, "reader and writer are canceled out simultaneously" until "the Word alone remains." One thinks also of T. S. Eliot, a reader of both Adams and Mallarmé whose early essays popularized an "escape from per-sonality," or Hemingway, who expunged descriptions of mental life in favor of, to cite an oft-cited sentence, "the numbers of roads, the names of roads, the numbers of regiments and the dates." Or one might recall Pynchon's first novel, *V.* (1963), whose mysterious shape-shifting title character grows so (the keyword of the text) "inanimate" that she is eventually disassembled piece by piece. Or one could cite Richard Powers's *Galatea 2.2* (1995), in which a young novelist spends a year working on an advanced computer with a connectionist cognitive scientist named Philip Lentz, a self-described "reductionist" who startles the narrator by claiming that "consciousness is a deception," "a glorified, fudged-up Turing machine."[5]

A second anti-intentionalist strand is less literary than philosophical, and it comprises the various forms of anti-humanism that in recent decades have had an enormous impact across the humanities. Separating "literature" and "philosophy" in this instance is of course an oversimplification, since what is called anti-humanism has its roots not only in post-Hegelian philosophy but also in a sustained engagement with modern writing: Derrida's encounters with Joyce, Foucault's readings of Blanchot and Borges, and so on. My point here, however, is less about the origins of such philosophy than about its dominant claims. As with the spectrum of modern literary movements, there are vital disagreements between Derrida, Foucault, and Barthes, or between Lacan, Althusser, and Bourdieu. But the basic impulse shared by all these figures is to demythologize the self-directing "I," the monarchical transcen-dental consciousness purporting to lord over the contingencies of history or unconscious desire. Younger theorists today stand on the shoulders of these giants, and, though often adding important nuances, take for granted most of their suspicions about meaning, mindedness, and other aspects of agency.[6]

---

[5] Jean-Paul Sartre's remark appears in Denis Donoghue, *Ferocious Alphabets* (London: Faber and Faber, 1981), 153. See T. S. Eliot, *Selected Prose of T. S. Eliot*, ed. Frank Kermode (London: Faber and Faber, 1975), 37–44; Ernest Hemingway, *A Farewell to Arms* (New York: Scribner's, 1957), 185; Thomas Pynchon, *V.* (New York: Perennial, 1990); Richard Powers, *Galatea 2.2* (New York: Picador, 1995), 88, 71 (henceforth cited parenthetically as *Galatea*).

[6] This isn't to underestimate the differences between, say, Fredric Jameson, Judith Butler, or Homi Bhabha. My point here is simply, and uncontroversially, that books like *The Political Unconscious, Gender Trouble,* or *The Location of Culture,* not to mention the numerous other studies these books have inspired in turn, would have been inconceivable without the work of the philosophical figures I've noted.

A third strand of modern intellectual culture that could be placed under the anti-intentionalist banner is the domain from which Richard Powers's cognitive scientist Lentz emerges. Lentz's brand of connectionism aligns him closely with eliminative materialism, the belief that the powers traditionally associated with mindedness can be explained (and eventually discarded) in the course of scientific inquiry. He accordingly has only contempt for what he sees as the voguish irrationalism among the literary critics across campus. But Lentz is allied to his literary and theoretical counterparts insofar as his "critique of intelligence" (*Galatea* 86) shares the basic thrust of Adams's "dynamic theory." The controlling "forces" for Lentz may be the neural systems modeled by connectionist Artificial Intelligence, rather than those of History or Language, and he may see meanings as the result of massively layered sub-systems in the brain, rather than the conventions imposed by variable forms of social power. But if Derrida and Foucault may not entirely share Lentz's hostility toward what he unassumingly refers to as "non-computational emergent Berkeley Zen bullshit" (*Galatea* 47), all these figures concur with Adams that some kind of "forces" "surround, traverse, vibrate, rotate, repel, attract" us "without stop," forces of which we "are conscious of few, and only in partial degree."[7]

A profound skepticism toward agency, then, bridges different philosophical traditions of the last century as well as literary and philosophical culture generally—more so than these frequently conflicting camps usually recognize.[8]

---

[7] Philip Lentz, we should note, doesn't represent the whole of cognitive science, and many cognitive scientists refuse to traffic in the connectionism and eliminative materialism that I've ascribed to him here. Jerry Fodor is one prominent case, but another is Steven Pinker, whom I'll discuss in chapter 2; for his take on connectionism, see *How the Mind Works* (New York: Norton, 1999), 112–31. The cognitive scientist who most approximates Lentz is perhaps Paul C. Churchland, whose *The Engine of Reason, the Seat of the Soul: A Philosophical Journey into the Brain* (Cambridge: MIT Press, 1995) appeared the same year as Powers's novel. For more on the links between connectionism and eliminativism, see William Ramsey, Steven Stich, and Joseph Garon, "Connectionism, Eliminativism, and the Future of Folk Psychology," *Philosophical Perspectives* 4 (1990): 499–533.

[8] That the commonalities between literary writers, continental anti-humanists, and scientific-minded reductionists have been so infrequently recognized is perhaps the clearest evidence for the persistence of the rift dividing continental and Anglo-American thought, and literary from philosophical debate in American intellectual life. The most powerful account bringing together continental and analytic forms of anti-intentionalism is the two-volume work of Vincent Descombes, *La Denrée Mentale* (Paris: Les Editions de Minuit, 1995) and *Les institutions du sens* (Paris: Les Editions de Minuit, 1996). For more passing remarks about these parallels, see David Lodge, *Consciousness and the Novel: Connected Essays* (Cambridge: Harvard University Press, 2002), 88–91; *Beyond Representation: Philosophy and Poetic Imagination,* ed. Richard Eldridge (Cambridge: Cambridge University Press, 1996), 3–5; Daniel C. Dennett, *Consciousness Explained* (Boston: Back Bay Books, 1992), 410–11; Charles Altieri, *Act and Quality: A Theory of Literary Meaning and Humanistic Understanding* (Amherst: University of Massachusetts Press, 1980), 99–102.

So why insist, as I have, that the point of contact with Adams in these texts and theories is not his "dynamic theory" of modernity and mechanization, but his tireless pursuit of "an adorable mistress" who kindly amuses her lover like the old Greek goddess of love? Why claim that the writers and philosophers I have mentioned resemble Adams courting the heaps of chiseled stone?

Two strategies are available to us in answering these questions. One would be to follow recent philosophers who have provided detailed arguments about the pervasiveness of intentional explanation. Readers, the claim would go in miniature, necessarily resemble Adams courting Chartres Cathedral because doing otherwise would be to treat texts as flukes of nature, akin to the existence of stalactites. Stalactites can be curious, captivating, and maybe even, as Kant said of the "free formations" of nature, beautiful. But they are generally not taken, today, to be *about* anything. This makes them conspicuously different from medieval cathedrals expressing the glory of God and even more conspicuously different from sentences. Sentences consist, no doubt, of marks printed on a page or noises traveling through the air, but if I am to understand a speaker who claims they are *nothing but* marks and noises, I must adopt what Daniel Dennett has called "the intentional stance" and undertake what Donald Davidson has called "radical interpretation."[9] I must, that is, make use of our folk psychology, the mentalistic terms—belief, desire, wish, hope, hatred, love, intention, and so forth—that as language-learners we master in order to swiftly characterize an entity's behavior. Which means that I must ascribe to the skeptic what she says can only be self-mystifyingly ascribed: the wish to make language-like noises rather than wordless melodies, the ability to construct new and complex sentence-strings rather than parrot pre-programmed phrases, the ability to distinguish true from false statements (however this truth and falsity is epistemically determined), the capacity to link her utterance to others in a web of beliefs.

To consistently expunge our folk-psychological terms would therefore be (so this argument would continue) not merely to see a text as dissolving "in the narrowing spiral of a linguistic sign that becomes more and more remote from its meaning," or to analyze the subject-speaker "as a variable and complex function of discourse."[10] It would mean not understanding a text as "signs" or "discourse" in any way at all. Just as there would be no reason to

---

[9] Daniel C. Dennett, *The Intentional Stance* (Cambridge: MIT Press, 1987); Donald Davidson, *Inquiries into Truth and Interpretation* (New York: Oxford University Press, 1984).

[10] Paul de Man, *Blindness and Insight: Essays in the Rhetoric of Contemporary Criticism* (Minneapolis: University of Minnesota Press, 1983), 222; Michel Foucault, "What Is an Author?" in *The Foucault Reader,* ed. Paul Rabinow (New York: Pantheon, 1984), 118. One figure who has discussed the topic

treat a speaker's noises (including my own) as speech without also treating it as a purposive action, so there would be no reason to understand a string of marks on a page as sentences, words, or even letters. This isn't to say that the meanings of such strings are fixed by an author's intentions. Intentions are no more self-interpreting than languages, and a writer's writing a certain sentence or book doesn't boil down to one determinate purpose any more than, say, a person's vacationing in Florida.[11] The point is that treating a text as part of a purposive action is a minimal requirement for calling it a "text" at all, and that refusing to do so is ultimately to treat it as one object among others. Not "*mere* object": things usually called "novels" can be outstanding paperweights and passable frisbees. But when treated in these ways, they say few of the fine-grained things (about, for instance, the game-winning home run, the history of Carthage, the nature of Being) that we often attribute to texts. However spectacular some stalactites may be, they aren't generally taken to be cryptic statements, words we could interpret if we just had the right dictionary or hermeneutic method. We have no idea how to assess whatever beliefs and desires a calcium carbonate deposit is expressing; or, better put, we have no idea which beliefs and desires it *isn't* expressing. With verbal utterances the situation is otherwise. Even when refusing to acknowledge the enticements of Chartres Cathedral, we resemble the devoted Adams simply in the act of articulating our refusal. The writers and philosophers I have mentioned are—Q. E. D.—simply illustrations of this general rule.

Chief among the virtues of this philosophical argument is that it makes explicit a fundamental distinction, namely, that to understand the explorer's description of the stalactite, I have to grasp what he intends, desires, and believes; to understand the behavior of the stalactite itself, I don't.[12]

---

of intention extensively is of course Jacques Derrida, but his views are difficult to pin down. In *Limited Inc* (Evanston: Northwestern University Press, 1988), he acknowledges that "the category of intention will not disappear" in his revised account of meaning and language: "It will have its place, but from that place it will no longer be able to govern the entire scene and system of utterance" (18). Derrida doesn't say much, however, about what exactly this "place" is, which is why most readers have taken his work to emphasize the infinitely non-originary aspects of language emphasized, in different ways, by de Man and Foucault.

[11] The argument that recognizing a "text" entails a belief that an author's intentions fix its meanings has been made by Walter Benn Michaels in *The Shape of the Signifier: 1967 to the End of History* (Princeton: Princeton University Press, 2004); see his discussion of de Man, 105–28. Michaels has always taken seriously the natural/intentional distinction that I'm emphasizing here, but tends to treat intentions as if they were themselves a transparent Super-text standing over and above the text itself. For a case against Michaels's view, from the Davidsonian perspective Michaels sometimes wants to claim for himself, see Samuel C. Wheeler III, *Deconstruction as Analytic Philosophy* (Stanford: Stanford University Press, 2000), 73–87.

[12] Implied in this distinction is a somewhat contentious claim about textual and non-textual artifacts. I'll return to this topic in part II, where I'll ask whether things like paperweights and Frisbees—or, as

As Kenneth Burke once wryly put it, thinkers who "make much show of discarding 'purposes' have plenty of words to replace it. They'll even tell you their purpose in throwing out the term."[13] And yet, for all its importance, and despite the fact that I will return to it in the pages that follow, the argument also has its limitations. This is by no means an anti-theoretical book, but it is animated by the belief that well-wrought philosophical arguments often blind us to particulars of our practices and discourage us from examining the paradigms on which our theories are less-than-consciously built. And this is especially dangerous when the question concerns agency. For in investigating the status of intentions, we shouldn't assume ahead of time that we know who or what *counts* as an intender. Adams, recall, wasn't merely "personifying" Chartres Cathedral for effect (if he were, he wouldn't have been so traumatized later by its seeming to be a mere building). And in some cultures, even the dumb stalactite might be regarded as a sentient, deliberative actor—as when, say, it drops itself onto an impious explorer wandering where the cave gods have forbidden mortals to tread.[14] By the same token, to claim that a text expresses an idea of agency is to say nothing about where to locate this agency, and to say that an action has occurred is not yet to say what sort of actor has performed it. Knowing *that* there is speech is not the same as knowing *who* or *what* is speaking. It is not yet to know, to adopt Wittgenstein's famous phrase, which form of life is doing something.

"Form of life" is not the most transparent phrase that Wittgenstein ever employed, and accordingly has been the object of much scrutiny. As I understand it, to say that "to imagine a language is to imagine a form of life" (*PI* §19), or "the phenomena of hope are modes of this complicated form of life" (*PI,* p. 174), is a way of drawing attention to the variety of entities— things, objects, stuff—to which we ascribe not only sentience, but also intentional attitudes. Some of these entities earn a more complex constellation of predicates than others. Wittgenstein's remark about the "phenomena of hope," for example, turns on a distinction between human and non-human

---

in Ellison's *Invisible Man,* subway cars and passing trucks—exhibit the fine-grained meanings often evident in sentences. It should also be clear here that locutions such as "Mother Nature" or "the language of God" evoke intentional systems that I'll be bracketing off here.

[13] "Burke's Reply," in Wayne C. Booth, *Critical Understanding: The Powers and Limits of Pluralism* (Chicago: University of Chicago Press, 1979), 134.

[14] Consider, in this context, the Reuters report of July 1, 2007, about the religious pilgrimage to a stalagmite that Hindus consider to be a (as the news agency puts it) "symbol" of Shiva. Due to global warming and the body heat of its many visitors, the stalagmite has shrunk in recent years, prompting one pilgrim to say: "I heard that Shivalinga is melting fast so I want to reach the cave as soon as possible to have glimpse of Lord Shiva." (My thanks to Anyssa Neumann for this item.)

animals: "A dog believes his master is at the door. But can he also believe his master will come the day after tomorrow?" Dogs, that is, might be said to entertain thoughts in ways that protozoa cannot, but the patterns of behavior and attitude that would justify our attributing complexly structured beliefs (about, in this case, time and possibility) are missing from what we take to be a dog's characteristic "weave of life" (*PI*, p. 174). Other forms of life are conjured throughout the *Investigations:* a tribe whose entire vocabulary consists of "block," "pillar," "slab," and "beam" (*PI* §2 ff.); rocks with consciousness (*PI* §281); cooking pots that see and hear (*PI* §282); lions who talk (*PI*, p. 223). Some commentators take the plural in "forms of life" to describe the variety of human cultures and natural languages, and the communitarian rules or conventions governing them. In turn they have speculated on what form a Wittgensteinian anthropology might take: how we might understand, say, a Westerner's observations about the Azande tribe.[15] For my purposes, however, such claims not only ossify rules and conventions in ways that Wittgenstein wanted to avoid, but more importantly assume too much about the agents in question. The anthropological sense of the term presupposes that these agents are featherless bipeds, members of the species *Homo sapiens*—in short, are human. There is no *a priori* reason to think that humans are the only kinds of things to which we can, or perhaps will, attribute speech and action. Children's stories, ancient myths, and science fiction films are some of the places where other sorts of agents are richly and regularly imagined.

So too, I will be arguing, are some of the major works of twentieth-century American literature. And this is one reason why this book treats literary texts more extensively than it treats philosophical ones. Unlike most philosophical theories, modern and contemporary literary texts, at least in some of the most powerful and compelling cases, do not assume that we know which things count as sentient forms of life, and which forms of life can perform which actions. Does a dog "really" have beliefs and desires? Does it have more beliefs and desires than Chartres Cathedral? Than the murderous stalactite? Than human beings? How do we judge? The texts I will be discussing here don't decide these questions ahead of time. They challenge and complicate our sense of what counts as a meaningful source of language, what counts as capable of new and complex thoughts, and what counts as capable of, as one commentator puts it, "liability and responsibility,

---

[15] On this theme, see Peter Winch's classic essay, "Understanding a Primitive Society," *American Philosophical Quarterly* 1 (1964): 307–24. The idea that Wittgenstein emphasizes the communitarian "rules" of language-use is notably endorsed by Saul Kripke, whom I discuss briefly in chapters 4 and 5.

of praise, blame, and punishment."[16] If agency persists in the twentieth century, these texts suggest that it isn't in any one determinate form. They ask us to consider not just how a French cathedral can be more than a heap of chiseled stone, but how many things are "more than," and what sorts of privileges this status entails.

My discussions trace the interaction of two broad ideas of agency to which twentieth-century texts drift. The first is what I'll be referring to as "persons." "Person" is a term seldom mentioned in recent literary studies, despite its illuminating etymological history and its central role in legal theory, moral philosophy, religious studies, and anthropology.[17] Within these various regions of debate, there is little consensus about how the concept is or should be used; the status of a fetus, to note the most famously fractious example, has never been definitively settled. As I'll be using it here, "person" is best defined in contrast to the term that Descartes made famous (and that *is* much mentioned in literary studies), namely, the "subject." As Vincent Descombes has noted in a critical discussion of the concept, "subject" cannot get off the ground without a transformation of "the ordinary use of the word"—one drawn from grammar lessons—into a "properly philosophical

---

[16] Amélie Oksenberg Rorty, introduction to *The Identities of Persons* (Berkeley: University of California Press, 1976), 4.

[17] In literary studies, "person" appears most commonly in discussions of law and literature. See, for instance, Stephen M. Best, *The Fugitive's Properties: Law and the Poetics of Possession* (Chicago: University of Chicago Press, 2004), chap. 1; Joan Dayan, "Poe, Persons, and Property," in *Romancing the Shadow: Poe and Race,* ed. Gerald J. Kennedy and Lilianne Weissburg (New York: Oxford University Press, 2001), 106–26; Jennifer Gillan, "Plotting Political Personhood: Literary Self-Making and Contract-Breaking," *Mosaic* 35 (2002): 151–65; Robyn Wiegman, "Intimate Publics: Race, Property, and Personhood," *American Literature* 74 (2002): 859–85. For an overview of the evolution of "person"—its derivation from the Latin *persona,* its evolution through Christianity, its post-Cartesian fate—see William Pietz, "Person," in *Critical Terms for the Study of Buddhism,* ed. Donald S. Lopez (Chicago: University of Chicago Press, 2005), 197–207. For some different uses of "person" in legal debate today, see *Law, Anthropology, and Constitution of the Social: Making Persons and Things,* ed. Alain Pottage and Martha Mundy (Cambridge: Cambridge University Press, 2004). On its use in philosophy, see *The Identities of Persons,* ed. Rorty; Catherine McCall, *Concepts of Person: An Analysis of Concepts of Person, Self, and Human Being* (Aldershot: Avebury, 1990); *The Person and the Human Mind: Issues in Ancient and Modern Philosophy,* ed. Christopher Gill (Oxford: Oxford University Press, 1990); Elmer Sprague, *Persons and Their Minds: A Philosophical Investigation* (Boulder, CO: Westview Press, 1999); Hans-Georg Gadamer, "Subjectivity and Intersubjectivity, Subject and Person," *Continental Philosophy Review* 33 (2000): 275–87. In religious studies, see Stanley Rudman, *Concepts of Person and Christian Ethics* (Cambridge: Cambridge University Press, 1997); *Personhood: Orthodox Christianity and the Connection between Body, Mind, and Soul,* ed. John T. Chirban (London: Bergin and Garvey, 1996). In anthropological research, see *The Category of the Person: Anthropology, Philosophy, History,* ed. Michael Carrithers et al. (Cambridge: Cambridge University Press, 1985); Clifford Geertz, *Interpretation of Cultures,* 2nd ed. (New York: Basic Books, 2000), 360–411; Susan J. Rasmussen, *Spirit Possession and Personhood among the Kel Ewey Tuareg,* 2nd ed. (Cambridge: Cambridge University Press, 2006).

one."[18] When, says Descombes, we learn that the subject of the sentence "Romeo loves Juliet" is "Romeo," we never "have occasion to ask ourselves if the lover is or is not the subject of his amorous desire," since "we do not attribute to him a new property of subjectivity" on top of the property of loving Juliet ("Apropos" 123). But after Descartes, such extra-added attributes proliferate. When Descartes says *I think,* the *I* designates a subject of thinking—not a man of flesh and blood born into a family from Poitiers in 1596, but an *it* that is something within yet distinct from Descartes's body. If "Descartes is a man," summarizes Descombes, then "the true thinking subject (or *that…*which thinks) must therefore be inhuman" ("Apropos" 126). And once we recognize this philosophical inflation, he says, we understand how the critics of the Cartesian subject who dominated so much of French thought in the latter part of the twentieth century—some of whom I noted earlier—recapitulate Cartesian distinctions. For the real motivation of such a critique is not to question the existence of "a subject (*ego* or *id*) distinct from the person"; this is taken for granted ("Apropos" 129). The goal, rather, is to deepen the gulf between the person and the subject by making the latter less anthropological, more "inhuman": e.g., history, language, the unconscious. Escaping Cartesianism once and for all would require questioning this gap between *res cogitans* and *res extensa.* It would mean recognizing how the notion of "subject" depends upon the prior notion of "person," the "subject of a *worldly action*" who "can have a *grasp* on things, so as to modify the source of things in a way that will appear, upon a rational examination, reasonable, inept, or mad" ("Apropos" 132).

Descombes illuminates two related elements that will be crucial in my use of "person" here. One is that the term "person," unlike "subject," refers to material bodies. The "it" that "thinks" in Descartes lacks extension; it cannot be located in space. But a "person," like a pear or porcelain vase, is something that one can point to, push, or pick up. To call something a *person* is to underscore this embodied condition—unlike *human being,* which suggests a generalized membership in a species, or *individual,* which suggests an existence abstracted from a social order and history. It is this embodied condition that is highlighted in many of our everyday and legal expressions: we meet someone "in person," a criminal assault is a "violation of one's person," and genocidal slaughter assails, as the UN Declaration of Human Rights says, "the dignity and worth of the

---

[18] "Apropos of the 'Critique of the Subject' and of the Critique of this Critique," in *Who Comes After the Subject?* ed. Eduardo Cadava et al. (New York: Routledge, 1991), 122. Hereafter cited as "Apropos."

human person."[19] The second thing about "person" that Descombes elucidates is that, in naming perceptible material bodies, it is close to the center of our most basic vocabularies. Implicit in his talk of *res extensa*, grasping things, and "worldly action" is the claim that our earliest terms are those designating middle-sized goods in our immediate environment. A language learner, that is, begins by applying sentences to three-dimensional objects that not only endure more or less over time, but that also, after eons of evolution, our senses are most well-equipped to perceive. As W. V. O. Quine says, words apply first to things that are "public enough to be talked of publicly, common and conspicuous enough to be talked of often, and near enough to sense to be quickly identified and learned by name" (*WO* 1).[20] Such things include Mommy, Daddy, and doggie, but not gravity, quark, or subjectivity. A vocabulary identifying these common and conspicuous objects is one fashioning what Wilfrid Sellars calls, in a term I'll discuss at length in chapter 2, the "manifest image" of the world. And central to this manifest image are those special sorts of material bodies—often human, sometimes not—which are capable of complex speech and action, and which we designate "persons."

As I will be arguing, "person" re-emerges, after three centuries of Cartesian indifference, with particular vigor in the middle decades of the twentieth century. One place it resurfaces is in the Anglophone philosophical tradition which Descombes, not coincidentally, takes as his touchstone, and to which—with the names Quine, Sellars, and Wittgenstein—I have already alluded.[21] Like "person" itself, these thinkers are rarely discussed in literary studies, which for the last several decades has engaged seriously with French and German philosophical traditions but, with the partial exception of speech-act theory and classical Pragmatism, has seldom shown much interest in the themes of English-language thought.[22] I've already indicated why the mutual shunning that characterizes the literary and philosophical segments

---

[19] See the preamble to "Universal Declaration of Human Rights," http://www.unhchr.ch/udhr/lang/eng.htm (accessed June 14, 2007). For a reading of "person" sensitive to the various uses noted here, see Pietz, "Person," 191–92.

[20] Citing this sentence out of context as I've done is misleading, since Quine seems to imply that meanings are built on one-to-one correlations between words and things. Like Wittgenstein, Quine strongly resists this idea, and was one of the first contemporary Anglophone philosophers to pick up the Fregean context principle and defend a strong version of semantic holism—a point that will reappear in several of my later chapters.

[21] As I note in chapter 2, other major figures in this tradition are Winch, Peter Strawson, J. L. Austin, Elizabeth Anscombe, and other mid-century "ordinary language philosophers."

[22] The heyday of literary studies' engagement with speech-act theory, best represented in the early work of Richard Ohmann and Stanley Fish, has passed, but its encounter with classical Pragmatism,

of our intellectual life impoverishes the philosophy, which too often narrows its scope for the sake of argumentative tidiness. But one of my goals in this book is to suggest why this mutual shunning also hampers accounts of modern and contemporary literary texts. Unlike some commentators, I won't be offering extended theoretical arguments to the effect that these philosophers are largely right and literary theorists largely wrong.[23] I do, however, want to suggest why the Anglophone tradition, often caricatured as trivial logic-chopping and scientism, is at its best attuned to the so-called big questions of philosophy, and how Wittgenstein and Sellars, in particular, share an angle of vision—a certain way of thinking about language, interpretation, narrative, science—from which we can see the place of agency in recent literature more sharply than we often do. Working within and often against a tradition that has frequently prized reductionist accounts of behavior, these figures are deeply concerned with investigating the vocabulary of action in its most basic forms.[24]

Recent literary critics writing about agency have at times glimpsed the importance of the tradition these thinkers represent, but they haven't pressed the matter.[25] Nor have they recognized that the return of "person" in mid-century philosophy parallels a similar turn taken in some of the major fiction

---

which began largely with Richard Poirier, continues apace. See Jonathan Levin, *The Poetics of Transition: Emerson, Pragmatism, and American Literary Modernism* (Durham: Duke University Press, 1999); Michael Magee, *Emancipating Pragmatism: Emerson, Jazz, and Experimental Writing* (Tuscaloosa: University of Alabama Press, 2004).

[23] See Reed Way Dasenbrock, *Truth and Consequences: Intentions, Conventions, and the New Thematics* (University Park: Pennsylvania State University Press, 2001); Paisley Livingston, *Literature and Rationality: Ideas of Agency in Theory and Fiction* (Cambridge: Cambridge University Press, 1991); Charles Altieri, *Act and Quality*.

[24] Two addenda. First, as I'll be explaining in chapter 2, the characterization I've given here applies least to Quine, who remains firmly committed to a strict naturalistic ontology. Still, Quine does give us some of the tools to defend the vocabulary of agency, and I'll be putting some of them to use here. Second, the two features of "person" that Descombes highlights—its reference to embodied entities and its conceptual primacy—aren't the only ones that we could attempt to identify. One could also try to define the concept according to psychological criteria (e.g., "the kind of things to which we attribute mathematical and story-telling skills as well as emotions and desires") or according to moral criteria (e.g., "the kind of thing to which we ascribe dignity and rights"). But I'm not confident that there are non-controversial ways to establish either of these criteria, let alone map them cleanly onto one another, and borderline cases such as healthy infants, comatose adults, intelligent aliens, and psychopaths will always frustrate our search for airtight definitions. The use I've stipulated for "person" makes it a minimalist term, which is enough to address the specific literary texts and theories that interest me. On the challenges of defining "person," see Amélie O. Rorty's remarkable essay "Persons and *Personae*," in her *Mind in Action: Essays in the Philosophy of Mind* (Boston: Beacon, 1988), 27–46.

[25] See William Jewett, *Fatal Autonomy: Romantic Drama and the Rhetoric of Agency* (Ithaca: Cornell University Press, 1997) and Katherine Rowe, *Dead Heads: Fictions of Agency, Renaissance to Modern* (Stanford: Stanford University Press, 1999).

of the period. The most compelling expression of this turn comes in the work of Saul Bellow and Ralph Ellison, whom I discuss in chapters 3 and 4. Bellow and Ellison, I'll be arguing, enact extended debates about "person," exploring the various ways that we understand this term and asking how or whether it relates to other concepts such as "human being." They do so in part by taking seriously the ordinary language that Quine sees as our starting point and within which the notion of "person" is initially at home. Nowhere do I argue that Bellow and Ellison were cognizant of what Sellars, Wittgenstein, and Quine were doing in this period, or, conversely, that the philosophers took much interest in their novelist contemporaries. I will, however, be suggesting that certain features of their respective intellectual contexts are less dissimilar than they might appear, and that part of the commonality between these various figures is the difficulty they all present to historians seeking satisfyingly clean classifications. Just as Bellow and Ellison are not easily allocated into stalls such as Modernism or Postmodernism, traditionalism or experimentalism, so the philosophers complicate easy divisions between materialists and intentionalists, anti-humanists and humanists, behaviorists and dualists, historicists and universalists.

If "person" is one pole to which ideas of agency have drifted, the other is what I'll be calling "presence." "Presence" here is not used in the various senses most familiar to literary theory, where it usually implies "immediacy" or "direct contact," but in the more commonplace sense of an immaterial entity—as in a ghost or apparition.[26] It thus resembles a "subject" as Descombes characterizes it: a *res cogitans* rather than a *res extensa,* a being distinct from an embodied person, yet somehow influencing or controlling it. Note immediately that, although "presence" designates no spatial properties and performs no worldly acts, it does designate a sentient thing and purposive being. The *it* that thinks "in" Descartes is a thinking thing, a being capable of reflection and even language, and it is often discussed as confidently as nations, centers of gravity, and other things less readily fixed in space and time than Descartes's body. Unlike the stalactite, it is not merely the dumb upshot

---

[26] "Presence" owes much of its fame to Derrida, who, following Heidegger, associates it with the desire for immediate meaning and eternal forms. The term has been used in a somewhat different sense by Hans Ulrich Gumbrecht, for whom it signifies "things in the world" that have "an immediate impact on human bodies" and implies substance, space, and movement. This presence is diminished or erased, he claims, when we institutionalize "interpretation," and must be recovered through "noninterpretive concepts." Gumbrecht's position is worth noting here because it is in some ways reminiscent of Gertrude Stein's position, which I discuss in chapter 1. See Hans Ulrich Gumbrecht, *The Production of Presence: What Meaning Cannot Convey* (Stanford: Stanford University Press, 2004).

of blind causal forces. Despite this status as a minded entity, however, such agents are not persons in my sense of the term. We may ascribe them beliefs and desires, and thus liability, praise, and blame, but these ascriptions are not made of any particular material bodies. They are more akin to forces or spirits than to pears, porcelain vases, and other—to cite Quine again—"middle-sized, middle-distanced objects" known "through impacts at our nerve endings" (*WO* 4–5, 2). To discuss them is thus to take a first step away from the most basic terms of our most basic vocabularies.[27]

"Presences" come in radically different forms, and a focus on different types makes for radically different sorts of aesthetic projects. One kind, I'll claim, locates agency below the level of the person, a monad generating action from the inside. Describing this type of presence will lead me to Gertrude Stein, whose work arises from what she often refers to as "the inside." A second type of presence locates agency not within the person, but without: not below the level of the perceptible body, but above it. My case study for this idea will be Don DeLillo, whose 1997 novel *Underworld* features a protagonist called "the culture and its loaded words." It should be clear even from these cursory remarks that the idea of a "presence" is hardly unique to the last hundred years or to its literature. Certainly much writing before December 1910 featured descriptions of monadic "inner worlds." Think here of Isabel Archer's famous retort to Madame Merle about the difference between her self and her clothes, or, decades earlier, the "power" residing "within" that Wordsworth calls an "image of right reason" beyond the corruptions of books and social mores.[28] And, to stretch back still further in time, many of our earliest tales tell of spirits housed temporarily in terrestrial bodies. Similarly, writers have long foregrounded what they see as the overarching systems enveloping multiple individual lives. Recall Whitman's references to "essentially the greatest poem," or what Carlyle calls the social "wasp-nest or beehive," "that Tissue of History, which intervenes all Being."[29] And,

---

[27] A terminological question may arise here, since "presences" as I've described them are obviously "persons" on some reckonings—as with, say, a corporation, which counts as a person in many legal systems. Whether presences are necessarily persons, whether they are modeled on persons, whether they are merely "metaphorical" persons or vice versa—these are all questions I address in one way or another throughout my discussions. But anyone arguing that a corporation is a person would have to acknowledge *some* difference (in origins, configuration, dispositions, range of capacities, appearance) between a publicly traded business operation and the human persons who may make up its shareholders.

[28] Henry James, *Portrait of a Lady* (Boston: Houghton Mifflin, 1956), 173; William Wordsworth, *The Prelude,* in *English Romantic Poets,* ed. David Perkins (San Diego: Harcourt Brace, 1995), 416.

[29] Walt Whitman, *Poetry and Prose,* ed. Justin Kaplan (New York: Library of America, 1996), 5; Thomas Carlyle, *Sartor Resartus,* ed. Kerry McSweeney and Peter Sabor (New York: Oxford University Press, 1987), 16–17.

of course, supra-personal presences play the leading role in most ancient religious narratives.

"Presences" may be no more exclusive to the last century than "persons," but at least two things distinguish their more recent versions. First, the sentient forms of life appearing in Stein and DeLillo are sometimes said to be identifiable only under certain strictly scientific descriptions. This may seem an unusual claim. Readers as temperamentally diverse as the New Critics and the Frankfurt School made commonplace the belief that much early twentieth-century literature was a reaction against scientific rationalization and disenchantment, and the experiments of the postwar period have similarly been described as undertaking a "post-secular project of resacralization."[30] There is a lot to be said for these claims, of course, but the same period that has seen repeated literary attacks on positivism and reductionism has also seen a deep fascination with scientific methods, concepts, and achievements.[31] Part of my reason for focusing on Stein and DeLillo here is that they and many of their critical interpreters bring this fascination especially close to the surface. Their texts express a drive for *objectivity*, as Thomas Nagel has used the term: they discount "for the features of our pre-reflective outlook that makes things appear as they do, and thereby to reach an understanding of things as they really are."[32] Often the scientific idioms favored by Stein and DeLillo lead them to describe their work in ways that practicing scientists would find suspect, and at several points I'll pause to ask whether such scientific ideals actually cohere with the vocabulary of agency. But the point for now is that what has looked to many observers like obscurantist "ultraindividualism" in the arts of the last century has often been defended by writers themselves as part of an "objectivist" project of portraying what is really real.[33] Long after

---

[30] The convergence between the Frankfurt School and the New Critics on this score was not accidental, given their shared Kantian inheritance. The claim about "resacralization" in late twentieth-century literature is from John A. McClure, "Postmodern/Post-Secular: Contemporary Fiction and Spirituality," *Modern Fiction Studies* 41 (1995): 144.

[31] The attraction to science among artists is a theme that commentators have increasingly come to take seriously. See Luc Ferry, *Homo Aestheticus: The Invention of Taste in the Democratic Age,* trans. Robert de Loaiza (Chicago: University of Chicago Press, 1994), chap. 6; Daniel Albright, *Quantum Poetics: Yeats, Pound, Eliot, and the Science of Modernism* (Cambridge: Cambridge University Press, 1997); *The Mind of Modernism: Medicine, Psychology, and the Cultural Arts in Europe and America, 1880–1940,* ed. Mark S. Micale (Stanford: Stanford University Press, 2004). Albright's work offers a balanced assessment when he notes that the "theft of the elementary particles of physics" is a "deceptive metaphor" on the part of Pound and Lawrence et al., but that such *"pseudomorphisms"* (Adorno's word) shouldn't bar us from appreciating the "tremendous imaginative energy" such thefts engendered (2).

[32] Thomas Nagel, *Mortal Questions* (Cambridge: Cambridge University Press, 1979), 224.

[33] "Objectivist" and "ultraindividualistic" are Ferry's terms in *Homo Aestheticus,* chap. 6.

Blake mocked Newton's particles of light, Stein and DeLillo do not treat science as irrelevant or empty. By and large they try to accommodate themselves to science, or even justify their work through its vocabulary.

A second important way that writers such as Stein and DeLillo distinguish themselves from predecessors is the extent to which their scientific ambitions determine the aesthetics of their work. Literary aspirations toward science date at least to the Naturalists (sometimes earlier), but while many readers both before and after Georg Lukács have argued that writers like Zola and Dreiser were up to something quite different than Tolstoy and George Eliot, it's no accident that debates have always raged about where precisely to locate the distinction. Not so with Stein and DeLillo, whose works are far more aesthetically innovative and provocative than anything the Naturalists ever tried. What makes their works striking is not only *that* they help us locate the forms of life they do, but *how*. Their efforts to challenge, in Nagel's term, our "pre-reflective outlook" lead them to challenge our pre-reflective ways with words. Just as science is often said to show that, despite our naïve perceptual reports, objects are not "really" colored, Stein and DeLillo ask whether the verbal practices we find intuitively intelligible really capture human experience or adequately represent the ways of the world. Presence-models of agency are not, or not regularly, debated in discussion between characters, as they are when James, working in his early realist mode, conducts debates between Isabel and Madame Merle. Nor are they presented in the course of extended authorial commentary, as when Dreiser editorializes in *Sister Carrie*. They instead begin, in more tangible ways than earlier literature, to penetrate the actual shape of the sentences and stories themselves. Stein and DeLillo do present persons to varying degrees, and to one extent or another these persons take part in dramatic narratives. But unlike the persons *within* the texts, the dominant voices *of* the texts distance us considerably from the ordinary language of middle-sized, middle-distanced objects. They are texts that imagine alternative languages in order to imagine alterative forms of life.

A few last prefatory remarks about the terrain mapped out in this study. The first concerns the term "agency." For all the overlooked commonalities between contemporary philosophy and literary theory that I noted earlier, "agency" is indeed a word that can quickly make these fields seem to talk past one another. In literary studies, the term is generally used as a descendent of *praxis,* the complex Greek word (adopted by Marxists and others) designating behavior associated with life in the *polis.* Thus commentators seek, for example, "resistant political agency that isn't immediately undercut by any of the various infrastructural mechanisms through which it is registered and disseminated," and attempt to locate "the often parodic difference between the communal ideal of free human agency and the actual degraded forms of our alienation."[34] Contemporary philosophical discussion of agency typically begins further upstream; what matters is the line between the actor and the mover, the sapient and the non-sapient. Many of the chapters that follow concern literary texts, but my point of entry is largely philosophical. Why begin here? For one thing, if the minimal senses of agency explored by philosophers seem too cut-and-dry to warrant discussion, then we haven't kept up with the news. In fact intentional behavior has never been so regularly described as reducible to the non-intentional: neural configurations, brain chemistry, genes, and so forth. The problems raised by modern biology and brain science are of course far too large to "solve" here definitively, but they are also too large to pretend they don't exist, and without some attempt to respond adequately, the study of literature may come to seem even less relevant to understanding human history and behavior than it already sometimes does, at least compared to economics, evolutionary biology, probability, and statistics.[35] Taking these minimalist uses of "agency" as the starting point doesn't mean that moral and political uses will never be addressed. Indeed, the literary texts I'll be discussing are themselves concerned with analogies between different notions or levels of agency, and will force us to ask where and how such analogies might be credible. As I'll suggest, however, when the moral and political uses of "agency" are placed close to the center of these texts, they are usually built upon more conceptually primitive ones. Such basic notions of agency are often the province of science fiction, and my readings may at times make Stein, Bellow, Ellison, and DeLillo seem more like Isaac Asimov than they are usually taken to be. But the complex purposive feat of casting a vote, the kind of thing that Hegel associated with "concrete freedom," can only be performed by a creature capable of what he called "abstract freedom," the no-less-purposive feats of judgment, deliberation, and self-reflection.[36] And here at the start of the twenty-first century, neither kind of feat or freedom can be taken for granted.

[34] Brian Michael Harper, *Private Affairs: Critical Ventures in the Culture of Social Relations* (New York: New York University Press, 2000), 36; Daniel O'Hara, *Radical Parody* (New York: Columbia University Press, 1992), 225–26. In addition to the ethical and political inflected uses of "agency" foregrounded in the remarks I have been citing, one scholarly area that has taken the concept of agency seriously is, unsurprisingly, the field of rhetoric. See, for example, the recent exchange in *Rhetoric Society Quarterly* about Ouija boards, initiated by Cheryl Geisler's "How Ought We to Understand the Concept of Rhetorical Agency?" *Rhetoric Society Quarterly* 34.3 (Summer 2004): 9–17.

[35] See Steven Pinker's proposals for educational policy in light of contemporary science in *The Blank Slate: The Modern Denial of Human Nature* (New York: Penguin, 2002), 235–36.

[36] For Hegel's famous discussion of the slave's "re-discovery of himself by himself," see *The Phenomenology of Spirit,* trans. A. V. Miller (New York: Oxford University Press, 1977), 118–19.

A second point concerns an important difference between what I have been saying over the last few pages and what I will be saying from here on. Up to now I have given the impression that Stein and DeLillo, on the one hand, envision forms of agency entirely foreign to Bellow and Ellison, on the other. The trajectory of the book, however, is meant to suggest how the basic thread introduced so far is in fact composed of several tangled strands. Part I, "Agents Within," explores how both Stein and Bellow navigate between inner presences and the social and linguistic world of persons, while in part II, "Agents Without," Ellison and DeLillo will each lead us to examine the relation between embodied persons and certain cultural or historical forms of presence. The relatively wide historical period encompassed by this quartet is intended to suggest how persistent the problems of agency have been over the last century. All the figures described, from Stein between the wars to DeLillo in the 1990s, are working within the context of questions identified by Adams at the start of the century and extended in more complex ways today across various disciplines. It goes without saying that a great many other general conditions—economic, political, geographical, sociological— also shaped the texts discussed here. I lack, however, a comprehensive account of how all these conditions might hold together (I'm not alone in this regard), and the scientific and philosophical questions framing my discussion have allowed me to take a somewhat wider swath of literary history than is perhaps customary in many literary studies today. These questions have also shaped my selection of writers. The four figures here are obviously to some degree representative of different literary moments, and thus provide a usefully eclectic sample of different modes and manners. More importantly, they are all unusually attuned to the problems of agency, to the historical and scientific conditions from which these problems emerge, and to the epistemological and practical questions they engender. This shared attunement derives in part from the fact that questions of mind, meaning, and modern science are at the heart of the particular *Bildung* that each of them received: Stein's medical studies and tutelage under William James; Bellow's early study of Marx, anthropology, and sociology; Ellison's absorption with Kenneth Burke's Aristotelian writings on art and rhetoric; DeLillo's early Catholicism, his ongoing interest in contemporary technology, and his manifest familiarity with postmodern theories of language and knowledge. Given these various backgrounds, it is perhaps unsurprising that the texts this group writes are more intellectually ambitious, more alert to the philosophical debates surrounding the themes they address, than the majority of their literary counterparts. In different idioms and registers, each can be understood as asking about the relation of the intentional to the non-intentional, and this common-thread question allows me to trace the internal relations among them more concretely than with other texts and other writers.

This brings me to a final prefatory point. The hinges on which both parts I and II turn are chapters exploring a range of non-literary figures: Wittgenstein, Sellars, and Quine, as well as others who have received more attention in recent literary studies, such as William James, Steven Pinker, John Dewey, Stanley Cavell, Friedrich Nietzsche, and Niklas Luhmann. Some readers may find this structure unusual, but two things have made it necessary. First, as Socrates said long ago to Ion, literary texts don't deal in neatly circumscribed topics. Given that agency is a far less circumscribed topic than horsemanship or carpentry, and given the tremendous conflicts between philosophical accounts of agency, and given that competing philosophical accounts often underlie competing critical interpretations of literary texts, and given that sketching these different philosophical accounts in a paragraph or two would be to trivialize them beyond recognition, any adequate discussion of the topic demands a room of its own, where different theories can debate one another openly before roaming more widely. Second, the location of these philosophical interludes reflects something important about the literary commentaries undertaken elsewhere. To echo my remark about science fiction a moment ago, I understand the works of Stein, Bellow, Ellison, and DeLillo as extended thought experiments, testing intuitions in much the way that Rousseau does with the natural man at the first brook or Derek Parfit does with his Teleprompter and Branch-Line Case.[37] Each says: *imagine that these words describe us.* But unlike the stories of Rousseau or Parfit (and here one could substitute any number of philosophical tall tales), the literary experiments discussed here are conducted in rich detail for more than a handful of pages and are not positioned within the frame of a larger independent argument. This means that it is up to us as readers to identify what precisely is at stake in the literary texts, what precisely their point is and isn't. It also means that, even when we think we have grasped such stakes and points, unambiguous conclusions are hard to draw. Fictions are simply too anomalous, too full of linguistic distortions and ruptures, too much in need of interpretation, to prove very much in and of themselves (hence the impulse to redescribe and interpret them in the first place).[38] My theoretical

---

[37] Jean-Jacques Rousseau, "Discourse on the Origins and Foundations of Inequality Among Men or Second Discourse," in *"The Discourses" and Other Early Political Writings,* ed. Victor Gourevitch (Cambridge: Cambridge University Press, 1997), part I; Derek Parfit, *Reasons and Persons* (Oxford: Oxford University Press, 1984), part III.

[38] On this large point, see Brett Bourbon, *Finding a Replacement for the Soul: Mind and Meaning in Literature and Philosophy* (Cambridge: Harvard University Press, 2004), especially chaps. 2–3.

interludes are therefore designed not to draw us away from the literary texts, but deeper into them. They force us to recognize both the ideas of agency that these texts juxtapose as well as the particular kinds of ambiguities, ruptures, and interpretive quandaries that these juxtapositions engender. I will return to this literature-and-philosophy theme in my conclusion. But it is important to note here at the start how the alternating literary and philosophical chapters act as motivations for and constraints upon one another. The confusing clash of opinions and mixed affective identifications evident in specific literary cases initiate reflection on general principles and theories, which in turn must be re-tested against, in Wittgenstein's phrase, "the rough ground" (*PI* §107) of actual linguistic and literary practice. My hope in all these crisscrossing discussions is to suggest how contentious the issue of agency has been in recent literature and theory. Asking readers to shift between such radically different texts and contexts is meant to evoke some of the perplexity to which these models have given rise.

❧ PART I

Agents Within

🐌 CHAPTER 1

Sense, Science, and Slight Contacts with Other People's Minds

Pablo Picasso made an impression on virtually everyone he encountered, and Gertrude Stein was no exception. Included in Stein's 1934 collection *Portraits and Prayers* is "If I Told Him: A Completed Portrait of Picasso," which was written eleven years earlier and opens as follows:

> If I told him would he like it. Would he like it if I told him.
>
> Would he like it would Napoleon would Napoleon would would he like it.
>
> If Napoleon if I told him if I told him if Napoleon. Would he like it if I told him if I told him if Napoleon. Would he like it if Napoleon if Napoleon if I told him. If I told him if Napoleon if Napoleon if I told him. If I told him would like it would he like it if I told him.
>
> Now.
>
> Not now.
>
> And now.
>
> Exactly as as kings.
>
> Feeling full for it.[1]

---

[1] Gertrude Stein, *Portraits and Prayers* (New York: Random House, 1934), 21. A recording of Stein reading this text has been made available on UbuWeb at http://www.ubu.com/sound/stein.html (accessed July 6, 2006).

If Stein was not unique in having a reaction to Picasso, the shape of her reaction—this text—is no doubt singular. We can assume that these words in this order are unlike any news reports about Picasso, tributes to Picasso, personal anecdotes about Picasso, reviews of his exhibitions, scholarly analyses of his work, diatribes, eulogies, or anything else. Researching the records might prove otherwise, but if we are looking for the most idiosyncratic written account of the painter, this one would have to be near the top.

Saying that the text is "opaque" is true but uninformative. So can we say, in a relatively precise way, where and how the opacity arises? As the subtitle suggests, the text is ostensibly a description of a person rather than of, say, Stein's drawing room sofa, her pet dogs, Haussmann boulevards, and other things the author would have encountered on a daily basis. How this obvious observation helps us with the rest of the text, however, becomes unclear as soon as we come to the first line: "If I told him would he like it. Would he like it if I told him." Given the title, we likely assume that "him" refers to Picasso, but the antecedent of "it," the thing that he may or may not "like," is more mysterious. Why, too, given that the inverted subject-verb structure of the main clause typically indicates a question in English, is the sentence completed by a period rather than a question mark? And why is this set of clauses rearranged and repeated in the next sentence? Patient but eager for answers, we try to ignore the unclear pronouns and syntax, and proceed to line two: "Would he like it would Napoleon would Napoleon would would he like it." If "he" is the person named in the title, what is Napoleon suddenly doing here? Is *he,* not Picasso, the one who may or may not "like it"? Or is there a relevant resemblance being proposed between Napoleon and the artist? And why, furthermore, are the words so oddly strung together, without the commas and other marks that usually indicate the structure of a writer's thoughts?

Few answers seem forthcoming from the third paragraph, which consists of five sentences asking, again and again, and through various syntactical combinations, if "he" or "Napoleon" would "like it" if the speaker "told him." By this point we might have started wondering about the speaker's stance toward this indefinite "he." Is it supplicant? Or is it speculative, less anxious than curious about "his" possible reaction to something? After the third paragraph, however, the whole issue of Napoleon and his liking anything seems to be promptly dropped with a curt adverb: "Now." Now? Is this meant as a spontaneous cry, or perhaps akin to "Go!" shouted at the start of a race? Or is it more generalized, meaning something like "today" or "this week" or, more broadly still, "in our time"? Or perhaps "now" is modifying a verb, as in "if I told him *now*" or "would he like it *now*"? Venturing

into the next two lines—"Not now. / And now."—only seems to prolong
the uncertainty, an uncertainty that is amplified when a whole new cluster
of terms and troubles is introduced in the following two lines: "Exactly as
as kings./Feeling full for it." What do kings have to do with Picasso? Why
"as as"? What is "exactly" as kings, and how? How is the alliterative phrase,
"Feeling full for it," whatever it means, related to these kings, or for that
matter to anything else in the passage?

I begin with this catalogue of questions about "If I Told Him" not
because a resourceful reader could never answer them, but in order to highlight how many wrinkles such a reader would need to iron out. Moving
in slow motion over the passage is the only way to prevent us from prema-
turely losing sight of the most decisive feature of Stein's writing, namely, its
intractability. Stein was hardly the first to talk or write in puzzling ways.
Prophets, for instance, have often been associated with her kind of odd
linguistic behavior. Few readers, however, have ever felt compelled to treat
Stein as a prophet—which may say less about the power of Stein's work than
about the moral framework within which her readers have encountered
her writing. On a less superhuman plane, strange talk is also characteristic of children, Miss Malaprop, and others who haven't fully mastered the
language. But this comparison, too, falters when we consider the particular
challenges facing Stein's readers. In the case of Miss Malaprop, we usually find we have cultivated enough of the wit, luck, and wisdom that, as
Donald Davidson has said, allows us to cope with strange talk and peculiar
behavior. Stein, however, far outdoes Miss Malaprop, whose mistakes are at
least regular and discrete enough that we can identify and translate them
into more familiar expressions. We could learn to replace "derangement"
with "arrangement" and "epitaphs" with "epigraphs," and go on as usual. In
the case of "If I Told Him," however, the diction is familiar, as critics often
note when praising Stein's "American" attention to ordinary things,[2] but
it is difficult to say why Picasso, rather than another of her famous friends,
or anything else in the universe, has initiated this stream of words. It isn't
clear what would change if the title referred to, say, Matisse—or to her pet
dogs, her sofa, or Haussmann's boulevards. The unity of the proposition
puzzled philosophers in Stein's day; many asked how to explain the difference between the sentence *Socrates is wise* and the string of terms *Socrates,
being,* and *wisdom*. But Stein's text seems intent on pushing such questions

---

[2] On Stein's diction, see Richard Kostalenetz, introduction to *The Yale Gertrude Stein: Selections* (New Haven: Yale University Press, 1980), xiii.

to their limit, undermining even the intuition that any difference at all exists between sentential patterns and simple randomness.[3]

Given these challenges, then, what do we do with the questions posed above? My goal in this first chapter is not to answer them, but to sketch the grounds upon which Stein and many of her readers have recommended for answering them—not, that is, to interpret as much as to identify some of the assumptions and strategies that would make any interpretation plausible at all. And to do this, both the intractability of the text as well as the proposed resolutions need to be kept in full view, the way a dual-language dictionary might occupy the same desk as the text being translated. For reasons that will become clear along the way, "If I Told Him" is a fruitful text to begin a discussion of agency not only because its degree of opacity distinguishes it from news reports, scholarly analyses, and other well-established verbal genres. And it is fruitful not only because it stands in for much of the middle and most radical period of Stein's career, her work between the early prose of *Three Lives* and such later, popularizing works as *The Autobiography of Alice B. Toklas.* It is useful, most importantly, for the claims it makes to describe a particular kind of animate entity. Unlike, say, the texts of *Tender Buttons,* its primary concern seems to be not food, rooms, or objects, but a human being. The expectations that usually attend this sort of description—the grammatical structures that ordinarily characterize descriptions of a human being—are brought sharply to light even as Stein dismantles them. What matters is how the non-sense that results from this dismantling arises not from mere whimsy but from strong beliefs about cognition, perception, time, and ontology. Getting clear about (not clearing up, but getting clear about) "If I Told Him" will involve tracing a winding path of claims that Stein and others have made about her work, and one endpoint of my discussion will be a keener sense of the *presence* model of agency that was sketched in the introduction. Our destination, however, will actually be more like a busy intersection, for as I'll also eventually be suggesting, the seeds of the second model of agency that concerns me here, *persons,* are embedded in Stein's text as well. As an account of Pablo Picasso, "If I Told Him" may present a reader with an unusually

---

[3] For Davidson's discussion of Miss Malaprop, see "A Nice Derangement of Epitaphs," in *Truth, Language, and History* (New York: Oxford University Press, 2005), 89–107. The difference between Stein and Miss Malaprop was first brought to my attention by Brett Bourbon, "A Parable about Syntax" (unpublished manuscript). On the problem of the proposition at the turn of the twentieth century, especially in the work of Bertrand Russell, see Peter Hylton, "The Nature of the Proposition and the Revolt Against Idealism," in *Philosophy in History: Essays on the Historiography of Philosophy,* ed. Richard Rorty et al. (Cambridge: Cambridge University Press, 1984), 375–97.

thorny array of interpretive quandaries. But grappling with these quandaries will make manifest some salient aspects of Stein's writing, and in the process will prepare the way for a number of problems that will recur throughout the chapters to follow.

THE STRANGE TALK OF SCIENCE

Talking to the *Mercure de France* in 1904 (in an interview first published in 1921), Cézanne set out the principles orienting his work: "One must make an optic, one must see nature as no one has seen it before you...I mean by optic a logical vision, that is, with nothing of the absurd...I conceive [art] as a personal apperception. I situate this apperception in sensation, and I ask that the intelligence organize it into a work."[4] Noticeable immediately in these remarks is the technical flavor of the vocabulary: "make an optic," "logical vision," "apperception." It is not entirely clear what Cézanne actually means by any of these terms. A reasonable interpretation would emphasize the Kantian overtones of the remarks and say that painting is a series of spontaneous synthetic acts of the mind uniting the sensible manifold. But however we gloss the sentences, one thing seems certain: the technical vocabulary is designed in part to preserve the legitimacy of artworks by associating them with empirical science. Taking these terms as our guides, Cézanne implies, will allow us to overcome the sloppy sentimentality of nineteenth-century painting and introduce a hardness and objectivity befitting our modern age. The genesis of a painting is not the sublime vision or raw anguish of the artist, but "the intelligence," which is imagined as a quasi-distinct faculty that must be deployed in order to "organize" the work. In short, the goal is to cast off the subjectivistic and the "absurd" in favor of the analytic and the rational, grounded somehow in "sensation" and "logic."

Stein revered Cézanne, of course, and his remark points us in the direction we need for confronting the challenges presented by "If I Told Him." For she, too, often conceived of her work on the model of science and mathematics. In a frequently cited passage from *The Autobiography of Alice B. Toklas,* she describes herself (using, as she does throughout the text, the third person) as having been "possessed by the intellectual passion for exactitude":

> She has produced a simplification by this concentration, and as a result
> the destruction of associational emotion in poetry and prose....[Poetry

---

[4] "Une Conversation avec Cézanne," in *Theories of Modern Art: A Sourcebook by Artists and Critics,* ed. Herschel B. Chipp (Berkeley: University of California Press, 1968), 12.

and prose] should consist of an exact reproduction of either an outer or an inner reality....

Juan Gris conceived exactitude but in him exactitude had a mystical basis. As a mystic it was necessary for him to be exact. In Gertrude Stein the necessity was intellectual, a pure passion for exactitude. It is because of this that her work has often been compared to that of mathematicians and by a certain french critic to the work of Bach.[5]

The scientific drive that Stein attributes to herself here emerged early in her career in a commitment to a form of determinism, whereby the characters of *Three Lives* and *The Making of Americans* are portrayed as strict "types." These texts have often invited comparison to Dreiser, Crane, and Norris, male contemporaries whom Stein respected for their stylistic simplicity and willingness to explore working-class experience.[6] One should be careful not to push these comparisons too hard, since Stein's texts lack anything like the meticulous descriptions of social environments that in much Naturalist fiction dictates a character's fate. But Stein's early characters are indeed defined by the same lack of autonomy that is characteristic of the Naturalists, and, like them, she believed that this concept of character rested on scientific grounds. Even after Stein drifted away from these early conceptions of character, however, she continued to maintain that her writing constituted an important scientific project. This self-understanding manifests itself in various ways, two of which deserve particular attention.

The first is what she often refers to as her resistance to "remembering" and "resembling." Stein associates the act of memory with the perception of resemblances because classifying any given object requires that the observer "remember" a range of other objects that he or she may not immediately perceive. To place a particular object under a description, to see a particular *that* as (say) a "table" or "chair," is to "remember" and to see "resemblances" between this *that* and other *thats* (other tables, other chairs) which we have perceived elsewhere at other times. To do so, suggests Stein, is to misperceive the object standing before us and misunderstand how reality confronts us in immediate experience. Even if two entities are usually categorized together as "chairs," and even if these entities are exact replicas, with the same sort

---

[5] *The Autobiography of Alice B. Toklas,* in *The Selected Writings of Gertrude Stein,* ed. Carl van Vechten (New York: Random House, 1946), 198–99. Henceforth cited parenthetically as *ABT*.

[6] See, for example, the Bedford Cultural Edition of *Three Lives,* ed. Linda Wagner-Martin (New York: Palgrave Macmillan, 2000), where section four of the "Cultural Contexts" appendix includes selections from Garland, Crane, and Norris.

of style, varnish, grain patterns, and so on, they are nevertheless two and not one. Thus it is, she claims, that

> the making of a portrait of any one is as they are existing and as they are existing has nothing to do with remembering any one or anything.... You do see that there are two things and not one and if one wants to make one portrait of some one and not two you can see that one can be bothered completely bothered by this thing.[7]

Stein's friend Donald Sutherland once explained the idea this way:

> When she writes of unique immediacies and suppresses the generic element, one is always or nearly always tempted to puzzle it out, to induce or to restore a generic element which will make the composition "comprehensible." But immediate experience in its real immediacy is not comprehensible, has no meaning, and when you do induce a meaning you falsify the essential immediacy. Gertrude Stein once remarked, "What is strange is this"—meaning that this thing as this thing is new and unfamiliar, as this thing exceeds or comes loose from the class to which it belongs, from identification and identity so to say.[8]

Sutherland's reference here to "the real immediacy" of "immediate experience," and his remark about suppressing "the generic element," implies a radical form of nominalism, casting doubt on all "universals" and "abstractions" ("chairs," "tables") in the face of "concrete" particulars. So when Stein speaks, as she often does, of finding the "essence" of a thing, the essence in question is far from what the Aristotelian tradition had in mind. It is not, for her, what qualifies a thing for membership in a certain class, the property or properties without which it would not be the kind of thing that it is. It is instead what makes it a token rather than a type: its immediate *that*ness, as it "comes loose from" comparisons to—thinking about, remembrance of—other entities. "Essence" is the name for what makes a thing unlike any generic kind, how it is that "each one is that one" (*LA* 119).

The second important way in which Stein thought of her work as scientific follows from this resistance to "remembering," and this is her commitment to what she calls the "continuous present," or, as *Lectures in America* puts

---

[7] Gertrude Stein, *Lectures in America* (1935; Boston: Beacon Press, 1985), 174–75. Henceforth cited parenthetically as *LA*.

[8] "Gertrude Stein and the Twentieth Century," in *A Primer for the Gradual Understanding of Gertrude Stein,* ed. Robert Bartlett Hass (Los Angeles: Black Sparrow Press, 1971), 150. Henceforth cited as *PGU*.

it, "living as we are now living as we have it and now do live in it" (*LA* 104).
Stein is claiming that the present moment is more "real" than the past or
future, more concrete, more "alive" than our habitual conceptualizations.
One cannot step into the same river twice, and any description is betrayed
the moment it gets written down: "Each time that I said the somebody whose
portrait I was writing was something that something was just that much different from what I had just said that somebody was and little by little in this
way a whole portrait came into being" (*LA* 177). One consequence of this
Heraclitean claim, and one which will resurface in the next few chapters,
is that any ontological commitments we might make to the narratives we tell
are always unwarranted. If "reality" lies in the "immediate" moments of the
"continuous present" rather than either the past (previous events, previous
classifications, etc.) or the future (where present phenomena run the danger,
she implies, of becoming hypostatized), any story will be an abstraction away
from our "actual" unmediated existence, which forever lacks any definitive
form. Plots, the kind of verbal constructions that link past events to present
ones and present ones to the future, obscure the essential indefiniteness of
reality and betray a naïve—and, for Stein, patriarchal—conception of experience. In Sutherland's terms, coherent narratives can only "falsify" the essential "immediacy," which "is not comprehensible, has no meaning."

How these interrelated "scientific" aspirations—a resistance to "resemblance" or "remembrance" and a commitment to the "continuous present"—
manifest themselves in "If I Told Him" shouldn't be hard to see. Beyond
being a concatenation of English words, the text, as I've said, "resembles"
no written description ever given elsewhere of Picasso, including Stein's
own earlier portrait, "Picasso," written fourteen years earlier.[9] If, as Stein is
reported to have said, "what is strange is this," then the text certainly can
be understood as enacting some of this strangeness. And it would likewise
be hard to locate any unequivocal reference to actions or events that would be
the seed of a narrative. Indeed, the text is an exemplary expression of what
has been called Stein's "anti-memorialist stance." For Stein, "the knowing
mind has no habit," and among the habits most to be shunned are the perceptual and linguistic routines that obscure the vivid and immediate *thatness*
of the things before us.[10] One sees, as Stein says, "what one sees, the rest is
a reconstruction from memory," and what needs recovery is "things seen

---

[9] This early text was originally published in the August 1912 issue of *Camera Work,* reprinted in
Portraits and Prayers, and again in *Selected Writings,* ed. van Vechten, 333–35.

[10] Claudia Franken, *Gertrude Stein, Writer and Thinker* (Munich: Lit Verlag, 2000), 74, 60.

without association but simply as things seen."[11] Only this kind of anti-memorialist *seeing,* Stein implies, provides us with genuine *knowledge;* any other kind of knowledge is merely second-hand and inauthentic. Hence the "scientific" significance of modern art, the best of which, as she writes in her study of Picasso, expresses "not things felt, not things remembered, not established in relations but things which are there, really everything a human being can know at each moment of his existence and not an assembling of all his experiences."[12]

TWO SCIENCES?

Recent criticism has begun to re-evaluate the active interest that many writers of the early twentieth century took in the revolutionary science of their day, and the literature of the period has come to seem something more complicated than a flat rejection of the disenchanting, rationalizing effects of empirical science. Modernist poetry, for example, has been read as echoing debates in early twentieth-century physics over wave- and particle-models, the former initiating an undifferentiated and jumbled mode (e.g., stream of consciousness) and the latter inspiring the spare, atomistic gem (e.g., Imagism).[13] Among the benefits of this historical revision is that critics have grown increasingly sensitive to the "scientism" pursued in a great deal of the experimental writing of the time. When we read Eliot crediting Joyce's "mythical method" with "the importance of a scientific discovery," or Pound's comparison between the "serious artist" and a medical doctor schooled in "the art of diagnosis" and "the art of cure," we are nowadays prepared to see how such phrases may have been used for more than rhetorical effect.[14]

Given Stein's background in experimental psychology and medicine, it is unsurprising that reference to science has played a more prominent role in critical accounts of her work than in that of most of her contemporaries. Readers have spoken, for instance, of "the intensely theoretical, 'scientific'

[11] Qtd. in Franken, *Gertrude Stein,* 72–73.

[12] Gertrude Stein, *Picasso,* trans. Alice B. Toklas (London: B. T. Batsford, 1948), 35.

[13] See Daniel Albright, *Quantum Poetics: Yeats, Pound, Eliot, and the Science of Modernism* (Cambridge: Cambridge University Press, 1997).

[14] On the "scientism" of the avant-garde, see Luc Ferry, *Homo Aestheticus: The Invention of Taste in the Democratic Age,* trans. Robert de Loaiza (Chicago: University of Chicago Press, 1994), chap. 6. Eliot's remark can be found in *Selected Prose of T. S. Eliot,* ed. Frank Kermode (London: Faber and Faber, 1975), 177. Pound's remark is in *Literary Essays of Ezra Pound* (New York: New Directions, 1968), 43, 45.

approach to phenomena which characterizes all of her work," the desire in her portraits "to come to know people, and to know them as a scientist,"[15] and have claimed that her "fabled obscurity" is in fact "an extreme form of *literalism,*" a "function of what might be called her hyperrealism."[16] And yet an emphasis on Stein's "scientific" dimension brings us to an obvious impasse. For it is not immediately clear how to reconcile this commitment to scientific "exactitude" with the dumfounding linguistic distortions that initiated my opening string of interpretative questions. Put bluntly, "If I Told Him" doesn't look or sound much like the studies found in *Nature* or any other scientific periodical. To be sure, scientists don't always address the "general reader," and to the layman, advanced scientific papers may seem as unforgivingly opaque as some of Stein's most obdurate experiments. But the nature of Stein's intransigence is different from that of research reports in biochemistry or particle physics. The obstacles confronting us in "If I Told Him" don't arise from its author having received a highly specialized training, and our confusion won't be relieved by entering graduate school and studying the latest theorems. How, then, do we understand Stein's claim that she participates in some sort of scientific project?

A lot rides on what we mean by "science" and what it means to seek, as Stein says in distinguishing herself from the mystical Juan Gris, "exactitude." This is the topic of a recent book by Steven Meyer that examines, as his subtitle puts it, "the correlations of writing and science" in Stein's work. Meyer's book is exceptionally thorough, and a brief synopsis of his major points will get some important terms on the table. For Meyer, Stein's work is part of an enterprise that he calls "Romantic" or "poetic" science, an alternative tradition of scientific "experimentalism" arising chiefly from dissatisfaction with Baconian empiricism.[17] Other practitioners of this science, he claims, were Emerson, William James, and Alfred North Whitehead, all of whom Stein admired deeply, and all of whom believed that the conventional explanations of empirical science were unable to account for certain central features of human experience. Specifically, in its commitment to a third-person perspective, modern science forgets that our understanding of the non-human world is always shaped by our distinctly human perceptions of it. The

---

[15] Wendy Steiner, *Exact Resemblance to Exact Resemblance: The Literary Portraiture of Gertrude Stein* (New Haven: Yale University Press, 1978), 38–39.

[16] Marjorie Perloff, *Wittgenstein's Ladder: Poetic Language and the Strangeness of the Ordinary* (Chicago: University of Chicago Press, 1996), 92, 105.

[17] Steven Meyer, *Irresistible Dictation: Gertrude Stein and the Correlations of Writing and Science* (Stanford: Stanford University Press, 2001). Henceforth cited parenthetically as *ID.*

activity of human perception and understanding is a "more" that is always overlooked in physicalism, which ignores the ways in which "experience" is always "experienced" by "experiencing" subjects. In Meyer's account, ordinary empiricism requires "that one divorce the pursuit of knowledge from one's emotional investment in the procedures one has come to follow" (*ID* 11). Poetic science, by contrast, "emerges historically as a corrective to what the poet-scientist perceives as the inadequacies of ordinary science." It is "vigorously nonmechanistic" and "non-Newtonian," and focused upon the traces of human experience "already present in scientific knowledge, although scientists have chosen to ignore it" (*ID* 21).

As with Stein's own self-descriptions, Meyer's account of "poetic" science raises a number of questions. But it is worth glancing first at his discussion of Whitehead, whom he rightly cites as being among Stein's most formative influences.[18] Meyer's discussion of Whitehead focuses on the difference between two kinds of "mechanisms," a distinction that Whitehead had begun to develop around the time of Stein's unexpectedly prolonged visit at the outbreak of World War I. What Whitehead called "materialist mechanism" is the foundation of modern science and is uncompromisingly reductive. The world and all its entities, including humans, are composed of molecules; since molecules run blindly, human beings run blindly, without individual responsibility for their minds and bodies. The study of "organic mechanism," by contrast, admits the existence of molecules, but examines them—Whitehead's words—"according to the general organic plans of the situations in which they find themselves." The principles of nature, in other words, cannot be reduced to mere causality. They also include "the concepts of life, organism, function, instantaneous reality, interaction," and the "order of nature," concepts that, as Whitehead believed, are manifest in "the things which lie around us," the simple immediate facts "that are the topic of interest" of poetry. Investigating these sorts of concepts and orders, he said, would allow us to locate a domain falling outside the purview of "reductive" science. It would give us a way to keep our mental and moral lives sounding legitimate, and preserve some space that causal description could not soil.

This Whiteheadian idea of "organic mechanism" is in part what allowed Stein to understand her work as "scientific." She did not, it should be clear, have much interest in the kind of science practiced in real-life laboratories: "Naturally science is not interesting," she punningly remarked in

---

[18] The following discussion is based especially on Meyer, *Irresistible Dictation,* chap. 4. Quotes from Whitehead here are from *Science and the Modern World,* and are drawn from Meyer's discussion on 174ff.

Everybody's Autobiography.[19] What *was* "interesting" for Stein, and for Whitehead before her, was the term that Meyer emphasizes and which a moment ago I encased in scare-quotes: "experience." "Experience" is a notoriously knotty term. On the one hand, it usually refers to something immediate and incorrigible rather than "second-hand" or "reported." It is something on which one cannot cast epistemic doubt, the ineffable *what it's like* that makes me know that I'm smelling coffee and unable to describe it to someone who has never had a similar experience. On the other hand, "experience" also implies something meaningful, with content. It refers not merely to stimuli hitting one's sensory receptors (the bathing of an olfactory system, flashing lights on a retina, vibrations on an eardrum), but to an intentional relation, an identifiable unity persisting in the memory as a moment of "significance."[20] To the degree that all of us occupy different slices of time-space, to the degree that our bodily structures differ here and there, to the degree that our individual mental associations arise from a vast, idiosyncratic, and unrecoverable personal history—to these varying degrees, we shall inevitably all "experience" the world in different ways. From here it can seem a short leap to the view that a "subjective" standpoint is in some sense as "objective" as the one emphasized in traditional empiricism. Science need not draw the line at investigating phenomena of the physical universe. My mental phenomena are, after all, as undeniable and immediate to me as any of the rocks and trees that I see in the ostensibly "external" world.

Something like this position was implicit in the remarks from Cézanne that I quoted earlier. When he spoke of "apperception," "logical vision," and "sensation," he was using a technical-sounding rhetoric designed to place art on an equal footing with science, but he was also celebrating the allegedly singular vision characteristic of an authentic painter: "One must see nature as no one has before you." One consequence of such mixed claims is that the first-person perspective can come to occupy the same distinguished place in explanation that science usually accords the third-person perspective. For it is here, the suggestion goes, that I can introspectively observe the raw data of my own experience. Looking within provides the indubitable mixture of concepts, perceptions, and emotions that makes up what are—to me—the objective contents of my mental life.

---

[19] Gertrude Stein, *Everybody's Autobiography* (New York: Random House, 1937), 251.

[20] On the ambiguity of "experience" (*Erlebnis*) as it developed in the decades leading up to Stein's work, see Hans-Georg Gadamer, *Truth and Method,* trans. Donald G. Marshall (New York: Continuum, 2000), 60–70.

The privileges that Stein accords the first-person perspective are expressed vividly in a passage from *The Autobiography of Alice B. Toklas,* in which she describes the reception of "Composition as Explanation," the lecture she delivered at Cambridge in the mid-1920s:

> Then up jumped one man, it turned out afterwards that he was a dean, and he said that in the Saints in Seven he had been very interested in the sentence about the ring around the moon, about the ring following the moon. He admitted that the sentence was one of the most beautifully balanced sentences he had ever heard, but still did the ring follow the moon. Gertrude Stein said, when you look at the moon and there is a ring around the moon and the moon moves does not the ring follow the moon. Perhaps it seems to, he replied. Well, in that case how, she said, do you know that it does not; he sat down. (*ABT* 221)

There is no evidence here that the dean was some kind of scientistic ideologue, or even that he had any training whatsoever in the physical sciences. Indeed, far from dismissing Stein as foolish, he admits afterward that her lecture "had been his greatest experience since he had read Kant's Critique of Pure Reason" (*ABT* 222). But the dean does ask something important about the role of verification in Stein's thinking—what role, that is, the intersubjective domain of publicly perceptible events plays, and how we should deal with novel claims of the sort she regularly makes. At issue is a question about the relation between knowing and being. Does the *appearance* to me of a ring around the moon entail the *existence* of such a ring? In responding to him, Stein commits herself to the reality of mental objects, whether they are precise memories, misperceptions, drug-induced hallucinations, or wayward fantasies. Among other things, this emphasis on the first-person perspective immediately muddies distinctions between *seems*-talk and *is*-talk: a ring can truthfully be said to "follow the moon," for that is how it appears to me as I reflect upon the nighttime sky. Faced with the sorts of questions the dean asks, some thinkers—American Pragmatists are the most important example—would temper their radical perspectivism with a practical and post-Darwinian emphasis on adaptive behavior and the utility of coordinating activities with others.[21] But in radicalizing

---

[21] That Pragmatists temper themselves this way is a weakness in the connection sometimes drawn between them and Stein. Drawing this connection requires treating Pragmatism as a version of linguistic skepticism, which is far too flat-footed. As I'll suggest in the next chapter, there are indeed connections between Stein and William James, but they seem to me to arise less from James's pragmatism than from his "radical empiricism."

Whitehead's process philosophy, Stein makes it clear that the dean's practical problems are not the kind that interest her. Reports of rings following the moon, like reports of sticks bending in a river, may be descriptions that normal science will simply pass off as the product of visual illusions. The truth of such reports becomes apparent, however, when we recognize something like "organic mechanism," which allows us to accept phenomena that fall outside conventionally empirical boundaries. Moreover, literary texts, from this perspective, constitute an important new ontological record. They document individual perceptions and weave these introspective reports into the fabric of the world. Whether every reader would find such arguments persuasive is debatable, but Stein apparently convinced not only herself of their cogency. Even by the relatively conventional stylistic standards of the *Autobiography,* the final sentence of the passage quoted has a bluntness that suggests the extent to which the Cambridge dean, for one, found Stein's position unassailable: "he sat down."

 REASONS AND CAUSES

What should we make of Stein's scientific aspirations? The Whiteheadian idea of a science that is "vigorously nonmechanistic" actually involves two sorts of claims, one about introspection and another about the nature of science. These are closely linked in Steven Meyer's account, and for good reason: what is "scientifically" reported in Stein are the inner workings of a mind. But we should be careful not to run these claims together. And it is the nature of science that I want to pause to consider first. My remarks here may sound critical, so I should say immediately that my intention is in no way to attack Stein as a writer. As Coleridge said, we shouldn't wish for an Act of Uniformity against the poets, and the simple fact that I'm discussing Stein's work in detail here is enough to suggest that I consider her central to the literature of the last hundred years. But I do want to explain why appeals to science cannot do the critical work that commentators, including Stein herself as self-commentator, often want it to do. Making this point explicit is critical for my overall discussion, since it will further clarify how "agency" is primarily being used throughout this book. Literary texts, I will argue, are hard to describe in scientific terms because they are both the product of an intentional action and essentially concerned with intentional action. This doesn't mean that agency is a supernatural phenomenon, but it does mean that the language of action and the language of science are like oil and water. That they don't mix will be a theme heard well beyond my discussion of

Stein, indeed in every chapter to follow, so it is important to move slowly here and not get ahead of ourselves.

Let us begin by returning to Meyer's claim that Steinian "poetic" science concentrates on parts of human experience that are "already present in scientific knowledge, although scientists have chosen to ignore it." The problem with this statement is that it implies scientific practices after Bacon and Galileo were founded upon a more or less arbitrary decision to neglect large parts of the universe, as if scientific analyses were pursued merely for the cheap thrill of reduction. When, for instance, Meyer claims that modern scientists typically "divorce the pursuit of knowledge from one's emotional investment in the procedures one has come to follow" (*ID* 11), questions quickly arise. For one thing, he does little to say what he means by the phrase "emotional investments." Are these investments like being in love? Watching an exciting film? Fighting for one's country? Moreover, and more seriously, he says almost nothing about *why* scientists adopt the particular "procedures" they do.

This oversight becomes conspicuous when we consider how little interest "Romantic" science apparently takes in what is one of modern (i.e., non-poetic) science's most important tasks: prediction. In Meyer's account, "poetic science" is presented as a purely descriptive endeavor. The poet-scientist seeks to show how "scientific description becomes poetic and poetic description scientific" (*ID* 48), and makes use "of the resources of poetic description in order to extend the domain of science" (*ID* 22). In this, Meyer is following Stein's own understanding of science, which she claims to have garnered from her Harvard mentor: "When I was working with William James I completely learned one thing, that science is continuously busy with the complete description of something, with ultimately the complete description of anything, with ultimately the complete description of everything" (*LA* 156). But wherever the idea originates, it is not the most adequate conception of scientific inquiry. After all, any educated Mesopotamian could give a detailed "description" of stars, planets, the weather, anatomy, or animals. And as I'll be arguing, we continue to find a pre-scientific idiom indispensable in our descriptions of many phenomena, especially human ones. What distinguishes modern science is that, more regularly and precisely than these older idioms, its descriptions allow us to trace certain effects to certain efficient causes, and hence anticipate future phenomena.

Science is "scientific" on account of what is sometimes called its "nomological" character: where there is causality, there is causal law, i.e., a hypothetically assumed general statement under which individual cases can be subsumed. Despite the complications introduced by the explosion of biological sciences in the nineteenth century, and despite the instabilities that quantum mechanics later introduced, an interest in nomological patterns encompasses the whole of the natural sciences, even beyond the paradigmatic case of physics.[22] As Bjorn Ramberg has written, the special sciences are all characterized by "a certain homogeneity of interest," a "purely predictive aspect." So we are not changing the subject, he says, when we switch from one level of description to another—say, from the level of molecules to the level of tectonic plates—"as long as the switch is motivated by an attempt to better serve prediction in some domain, even a very loosely and tentatively characterized domain, where we change even our conception of the phenomena to be explained."[23] Geology, in other words, may never be as exacting and precise as chemistry, but the fundamental aim of each is identical: to give an account of what is going to happen in a certain portion of the physical world. The Laplacian aspirations occasionally voiced among scientists arise not merely from the powers of "description" that empirical science gives us, but from the future events that these descriptions allow us to forecast.

A question to ask, then, when we read about the scientific status of Stein's work is whether texts such as "If I Told Him" could actually help us predict anything—whether they could be used in the formation of general predictive hypotheses. Putting the matter in these stark terms, we would be hard-pressed to say how they could. In comparison to "This liquid boils at one hundred degrees Celsius," it is not clear what "Would he like it would Napoleon would Napoleon would would he like it" is *about* (a point I noted

---

[22] On the rise of nineteenth-century biology and the challenge it presented to seventeenth-century physics, see Ernst Meyer, *The Rise of Biological Thinking: Diversity, Evolution, and Inheritance* (Cambridge: Harvard University Press, 1982). As for quantum mechanics, it certainly makes the ideas of "causes" and "causal laws" even more perplexing than they were for Hume and others writing in Newton's wake. After Heisenberg and others, we can no longer doubt that, as Albert Einstein and Leopold Infeld said, "physical conceptions are recreations of the human mind and not however it may seem uniquely determined by the external world" (*The Evolution of Physics* [New York: Simon and Schuster, 1938], 33). Yet the goal of quantum "conceptions" was not, of course, to announce the unknowable chaos of the physical world. The goal was instead to make better predictions within a nondeterministic universe and thus explain phenomena that Newtonian physics had trouble handling. Its laws are probabilistic and produced from an eminently human standpoint, with all the interests and habits that constitute our language and theoretical reasoning, but laws all the same. On the nature of nomological theories in a quantum universe, see Peter Railton, "A Deductive-Nomological Model of Probabilistic Explanation," *Philosophy of Science* 45 (1978): 206–26; Davidson, "Laws and Cause," in *Truth, Language, and History*, 201–19.

[23] Ramberg, "Post-Ontological Philosophy of Mind: Rorty Versus Davidson," in *Rorty and His Critics*, ed. Robert B. Brandom (Oxford: Blackwell's, 2000), 366.

at the beginning of my discussion and to which I'll return soon), let alone whether it could count either as evidence or as a hypothetical general statement. Otherwise put: if we understand Stein's text as an "experiment" akin to those in laboratories, what precisely are the states or changes that it identifies? What would ever count as the same result? Just as important, what would count as a *different* result?

Again, to say this isn't to denigrate Stein, and to question the scientific status of "If I Told Him" is hardly to imply that we should jettison all her writing. For it should be clear, even from these preliminary remarks about nomological explanation and prediction, that no literature is "scientific" in the sense I've just outlined. One way of formulating the issue is to recall the case of the dumb stalactite and consider the distinction sometimes drawn between *reasons* and *causes*. Both reasons and causes are offered to explain the behavior of an entity, but unlike causal explanation, justification by reasons involves attributing the mental states of our folk psychology: beliefs, desires, wishes, hopes, hatreds, and so on. Both reasons and causes can be invoked when someone asks "Why?" But a good account of, say, why a stalactite forms or, to take a different example, why a sugar cube dissolves in water requires no reference to what the calcium carbonate deposit "wants" or what the cube "thinks." Though the limestone cave and the water-soluble sugar occupy, in Ramberg's phrase, practically different domains (examined by different kinds of scientists looking at different kinds of phenomena), their behaviors are equally well-captured by causal explanations. But a useful explanation of why Pablo Picasso opens the refrigerator door (something Stein does not seem to describe) will make heavy use of folk-psychological terms: he "wants" some orange juice and "thinks" there is some on the second shelf. Unlike a physical explanation, this account of Picasso's actions requires that we ascribe motivations, attribute purposes, and understand how these motivations and purposes fit with the rest of his beliefs and desires. If he is being rational—"rationality" here being just a generalized term for the rough coherence of one's beliefs and desires—Picasso opens the fridge when thirsty because he believes that doing so will allow him access to the juice, that the juice will slake his thirst, that he wants juice rather than water (or milk or lemonade), that the juice is there rather than under his bed, that it isn't poisoned, that he can't summon the juice into his hand through telepathy, and so on and so on, indefinitely.[24] We might even resort

---

[24] On rationality as internal coherence, see Daniel C. Dennett, *The Intentional Stance* (Cambridge: MIT Press, 1987), chap. 4; Donald Davidson, *Problems of Rationality* (New York: Oxford University Press, 2004). It should be clear here and elsewhere that I am using "belief" in a very low-level way

to psychoanalytic accounts of Picasso's action, for example, "because open-ing the fridge allows him, unconsciously, to repress traumatic childhood experiences." This would be to stretch the range of possible rationalizations, but nevertheless would still be reason-giving descriptions, in the sense of providing justification rather than identifying causation. (A point Freud himself sometimes obscured.)[25]

One way of defining an "agent" is to say that it is the sort of entity whose behavior is efficiently and effectively captured in such reason-giving terms. Hydrogen molecules, tectonic plates, and planetary bodies are all effectively and efficiently described by nomological theories; they move. Agents, by contrast, act. And this is why we should not expect literary texts, which characteristically describe particular actions undertaken in particular places, to be as sharply predictive as scientific accounts of other phenomena. Nor should we be disappointed when they fail to live up to such demands. Reason-giving accounts resemble cause-giving accounts to the extent that they explain what Picasso did and anticipate what he will do next. But unlike scientific accounts, they do so by referring to final causes more than to efficient causes. They predict not nomologically, but "roughly," in light of a specifiable train of prior actions and a specifiable goal or end. There is no way to reduce even the bland action of retrieving orange juice to a formula under which one could subsume other individual actions. Our only hope for an "exact" prediction would be to give a comprehensive catalogue of Picasso's relevant beliefs at a specific moment—which would not only be practically impossible, since everyone's web of beliefs is fantas-tically large and changes in some small measure every second in response

---

that includes the multitude of beliefs about which one is usually barely conscious, but that one would obviously endorse when challenged: e.g., what one's name is, the date of one's birth, what country one lives in, whether one owns a pet iguana, whether one is currently sitting in a Finnish sauna, etc. Such a usage is what permits Davidson and Dennett, among others, to say that most of our beliefs must be true and that most people's beliefs—even people from cultures with vastly different cosmological, moral, political, and religious views—must be shared. For some reflection on this use of "belief" (versus the high-level sort of belief that he calls "opinion"), see Dennett, *Intentional Stance*, 19.

[25] On Freud's blurring of reasons and causes, see Marcia Cavell, *The Psychoanalytic Mind: From Freud to Philosophy* (Cambridge: Harvard University Press, 1993). Contemporary debate about the distinc-tion between "reasons" and "causes" is somewhat more complicated than I'm implying here. In his 1963 paper "Actions, Reasons, and Causes" (reprinted in *Essays on Actions and Events* [New York: Oxford University Press, 1980]), Davidson famously argued, against Elizabeth Anscombe and other Wittgensteinians, that reasons are often causes of action. Yet Davidson never denies that the causes of action are described and understood differently from lawlike physical causes; indeed, he defends such a distinction throughout his work. For my purposes, then, I can treat this complication as a debate among friends.

to new causal stimuli, but would also hardly constitute a simplified general hypothesis. In practice, of course, such rationalizations are routine and such catalogues superfluous. As products of thousands and thousands of years of wondrously complicated evolution, we usually need no step-by-step deliberation. Indeed, the shock we experience when rationalization *is* a struggle—the Monty Python tobacconist coping with an unwittingly lewd Hungarian visitor, the spouse struggling with a mumbling partner drifting into Alzheimer's, the reader encountering a Gertrude Stein text—is testimony to the efficiency and power of our everyday interpretations. But we should not confuse the regularity of habitual action with the regularity of lawlike physical motion, nor overlook the vastly different interpretational strategies used for describing each.

You Cannot Enter into Them

The next few chapters will return to this distinction between reasons and causes and flesh out some of its consequences. Even this initial sketch, however, is enough to understand why "If I Told Him" is not, in practice, grouped with biologists' accounts of plant photosynthesis or the latest medical research into mammalian digestive systems. To put it simply, "non-materialist" mechanisms are not mechanisms, and it adds little to our understanding of either Stein's work or of science to level the differences between them. Exposing this kind of bewitchment, however, gets us only so far. In particular, it doesn't help us much with my original questions about why "If I Told Him" takes the shape that it does. For if, like literary texts generally, it cannot be discussed apart from the vocabulary of agency, it is also not clear what specific sort of agent or action the text captures or displays. As I have said, it would certainly be badly out of place in *Nature* or any other scientific journal. Yet it also doesn't sound much like the tidy tale I've told of Picasso at the fridge.

Here we can return to what I identified earlier as the second strand of Stein's romantic science, namely, her strong commitment to introspection and the first-person perspective. As we saw in her response to the Cambridge dean, her writing is concerned not with being but with perceiving; or better put, it is concerned to obviate the distinction between the two. Like the ring following the moon, "If I Told Him" is to be seen as a report not so much about Picasso as much as about Stein's perceptions of Picasso. The text is an example of what Wendy Steiner has called the most innovative aspect of Stein's portraits, what Steiner calls her "inclusion of the portraitist as one of the 'characters' of the portrait."[26] As Stein herself once put it in a discussion of "Melanctha," her interest is less in "the realism of the characters" than "the realism of the composition of [her own] thoughts" (*PGU* 16).

What should we make of this second pillar of romantic science? Unfortunately the claim that Stein's work is committed to first-person introspection, to the realism of the composition of her own thoughts, runs into as many problems as the claim that it represents a serious scientific endeavor. For in fact it is not at all clear how closely we are supposed to identify Gertrude Stein with the words of "If I Told Him." After all, no native twentieth-century English-speaker sounded—in speech or writing—anything like this text, and presumably even Stein didn't talk this way when she made dinner plans with Alice or chatted with American soldiers. Saying that these words are the outcome of introspection, then, does little to account for the syntactical slippages and obscure indexicals that I've noted, and will not help us say how these words exhibit the "composition" of anyone's "thoughts." They will have no explanatory power, that is, *unless* we make two weighty further proposals. First we have to claim that the "I" accessed by introspection is fundamentally unrelated to the "I" that is ascribed responsibility for ordinary worldly acts (making dinner plans, chatting with GIs). Second, we must believe that this "I" is wholly unexpressed by the previous uses to which our words have been put: its speech is radically unlike our own. And such proposals, unsurprisingly, are precisely what Stein makes in many of the explanations she gives of her work. "Nothing," she said once in an interview, "can be the same to the other person. Nobody can enter into anybody else's mind; so why try? One can only enter into it in a superficial way. You have slight contacts with other people's minds, but you cannot enter into them" (*PGU* 30). Similarly, in "Portraits and Repetition," she describes her portraits as finding out "what was inside any one, and by any one I mean every one I had to find out inside every one what was in them that was intrinsically exciting" (*LA* 183). A noun, she says in "Poetry and Grammar," "is a name of a thing, and therefore slowly if you feel what is inside that thing you do not call it by the name by which it is known" (*LA* 210). And *Three Lives*, she says in the *Autobiography of Alice B. Toklas,* was "concerned with seriousness and the inside of things," a description of "the inside as seen from the outside" (*ABT* 147).

Minds that one cannot enter, what was inside, an inside different from its common name, the inside of things: these formulations suggest that Wendy

---

[26] Steiner, *Exact Resemblance to Exact Resemblance,* 22.

Steiner is somewhat off the mark when she says Stein includes the portraitist as one of the characters in the portrait. Identifying a particular portraitist, after all, usually means identifying a particular body—typically a human one, with a particular human face, a set of limbs, and a torso moving in a physical environment, doing frequently messy work with paints, canvas, brushes, and so forth. This is not, of course, *all* we mean when we identify someone either as a particular person or type of person; other aspects of persons will come to the fore in later chapters. But without at least some degree of physical embodiment, it would have been difficult for even the most clever portrait-ist ever to hit upon the idea of making a *self-portrait*. By contrast, the nouns that Stein uses to pinpoint responsibility for the words of her texts do not designate objects in any spatiotemporal sense. They are, she implies, a kind of nugget housed *within* material bodies, bodies that by definition are the sorts of things one could have "contact with" and "enter into." Yet this "inside" is not itself to be identified with such bodies or among the constituents of the material world. The "thoughts" whose "composition" concerns her in "Melanctha" have no direct or necessary relation to the "characters" they ostensibly describe. In a word, what Stein calls "the inside" plays the role that the cathedral does for Henry Adams: it is a thing that thinks, a locus of meanings and intentions, a *res cogitans* that can be "intrinsically exciting." But it is not, for all that, a *res extensa*.

It was this feature of Stein's work that led Kenneth Burke, reviewing *Lectures in America,* to summarize the Steinian formula this way: "You will talk much about getting 'inside' things. . . . And since you, as an *outsider,* are busied with the literary task of describing things until you get *inside* them, there will necessarily hover about your theories some hint of mystic communion."[27] It was this, too, that provoked Michael Gold around the same time to say that Stein's work represented "the most extreme subjectivism of the contemporary artist," and that led Wyndham Lewis, a thinker whose political sympathies were notoriously far from both Burke's and Gold's, to excoriate Stein for exchanging "our public material paradise" for "the dark-feverish confusion of 'mental truth.'"[28] All these remarks are, of course, meant as censure, but they nevertheless draw attention to a crucial feature of Stein's project and self-understanding. Indeed, shorn of their caricatural edge, they may even

---

[27] Kenneth Burke, "The Impartial Essence," in *Critical Essays on Gertrude Stein,* ed. Michael J. Hoffmann (Boston: G. K. Hall, 1986), 74.

[28] Michael Gold, "Gertrude Stein: A Literary Idiot," in *Critical Essays on Gertrude Stein,* ed. Hoffmann, 76–78; Wyndham Lewis, *Time and Western Man* (1927; Los Angeles: Black Sparrow Books, 1993), 181.

have earned Stein's endorsement. For the conclusion we draw from the sharp distinctions she offers—"the inside as seen from the outside," as she puts it, the "outsider" needing to "get inside," in Burke's terms—is that "If I Told Him" is not only not about Picasso. It is also, and just as startlingly, not an expression of Stein. It is not an expression of Stein, that is, insofar as Stein's identity is connected to a Stein who exists as a body in a physical, social, linguistic, and generally public environment. The model tacitly at work in her self-descriptions is of a physical entity, a human person, propelled into speech and action by a second entity, "the inside," whose behaviors a person can watch or perceive through introspection, and which has a distinctive (if not downright eccentric) mental make-up and way of talking. We grasp a person's intention to retrieve orange juice from the refrigerator (rather than, say, get exercise or go to the public library) not when we understand a certain set of motions as part of an arc of deliberate action, but rather when we access the disembodied presence, the willful but invisible interior agent, that initiates this outer action. On offer in Stein, in other words, is not a first-person account of thought and meaning. On offer is a *no-person* account.

What forces us to draw these curious conclusions is the difficulty we face when trying to apply Stein's language to anything in the world. In claiming, as she does, that "Nobody can enter into anybody else's mind," she implicitly describes beliefs—her belief, for example, that *a ring follows the moon*—as something utterly private that she but nobody else can "have" or "possess." The meanings of these terms are endowed not publicly, but inside, privately, by the sentient thing residing in the human thing. They are not learned within a particular social setting and thus not open to the scrutiny of third-person observers. The speaker understands their meaning immediately and incorrigibly, upon introspection, regardless of the physical, social, and historical environment in which she learned them and in which her body is situated. Given this conception of language, it is no surprise that Stein's writing has the free-floating, unattached quality that it does. A language so deeply estranged from the world could only be spoken by an agent who is deeply estranged from what Quine, as I noted in the introduction, identifies as the starting point of our thought and speech—things public enough to be talked of publicly, common and conspicuous enough to be talked of often, and near enough to sense to be quickly identified and learned by name. "A language tires," says Stein in the 1920 play *Photograph,* "A language tries to be. / A language tries to be free."[29] The "freeing" of the words of "If I

---

[29] *A Stein Reader,* ed. Ulla E. Dydo (Evanston: Northwestern University Press, 1993), 345.

Told Him" from everyday syntax and sense expresses the distance between the presence operating "inside" Stein and the world "outside." The interpretive questions with which I began—about the obscure pronouns, indexicals, syntax, and so on—could therefore only be answered by the author of the passage. And indeed perhaps not even her, since attributing the text to "the inside" means there is no guarantee that even Stein herself properly grasps the words that this entity utters.

In a discussion of the philosophical implications of modern art, Robert B. Pippin has claimed that early twentieth-century art was driven by a sense that "artistic activity alone demonstrates a kind of integrity and autonomy foreclosed in bourgeois life." When modern ideals of "individual autonomy and collective rationality" had shipwrecked, the *sui generis* work of art represented the last hope for any kind of self-determination.[30] Pippin's remarks nicely capture the autotelic ideals that Stein celebrated in the art of her contemporaries. Of Courbet she complained that his colors "were the colors anybody could see," and she contrasted this traditionalism with more contemporary paintings that make no reference to anything beyond themselves: "Whether it is intended to look like something and looks like it or whether it is intended to look like something and does not look like it it really makes no difference, the fact remains that for me it has achieved an existence in and for itself, it exists on as being an oil painting as a flat surface and it has its own life and like it or not there it is" (*LA* 61). This ideal of an art that "has its own life" shapes her literary ideals as well. The characters of nineteenth-century novelists, she said, "were more real to the average human being than the people they knew," but in the twentieth century—and what she says about her younger admirers applies even more ostentatiously to her own work—such conventional expectations are dispelled: "Take Sherwood Anderson, Hemingway, Fitzgerald, in all these cases it is the title and the form of the book that you remember rather than the characters of the book" (*PGU* 21). As I will argue over the next several chapters, this ideal of "independence" (to use Pippin's Hegelian-inflected term) isn't the only one that has arisen in the last century. But Stein's work hardly represents only a passing mood between the wars. Beckett's mid-century trilogy, for example, has been described by Hugh Kenner as a "reduction," beginning "with a bodily *je suis* in *Molloy* and ending with a bare *cogito*" in *The Unnamable,* a text in which "there is no verifiable body."[31] Similarly, the

---

[30] Robert B. Pippin, *Modernism as a Philosophical Problem,* 2nd ed. (Oxford: Blackwell's, 1999), 32, 35.

[31] Hugh Kenner, "The Cartesian Centaur," in *Critical Essays on Samuel Beckett,* ed. Patrick A. McCarthy (Boston: G. K. Hall, 1986), 62.

obstinate emphasis on "syntacticality" in the Language Poets at the end of the century has been described as an effort to find a "pure" form of agency, one that "belongs to no situation," as if the poets were chiefly interested in evoking the inner linguistic "faculty" or "competence" that Chomsky says precedes any worldly uses.[32] To be sure, Stein registers little of the "panic-stricken" mood that (rightly or wrongly) critics have often seen in Beckett, her Irish-French counterpart, and she exhibits somewhat less of the collaborative imperative that one sees in Ron Silliman and Lyn Hejinian.[33] But the radical disruptions that Beckett and the Language Poets introduce in their various ways—the startling shifts in narrative that cloud past and future, the unusual leaps in logic that confute premise and conclusion, the relentless repetition of words and phrases, the resistance to identifiable narrators, characters, and plots—can be understood as descendents of Stein's fractured sentences, words without persons.

 ## STEINIAN PATTERNS, STEINIAN PERSONS

We began this chapter by considering Stein's claim to undertake some kind of scientific project. I then cast doubt on this idea by distinguishing reasons from causes and by suggesting that some notion of agency necessarily underlies Stein's texts. And I've just now argued that we should identify this agency with the so-called "inside": this is the entity responsible for the words

---

[32] Oren Izenberg, "Language Poetry and Collective Life," *Critical Inquiry* 30 (2003), 144, 145, 157. Izenberg is aware that, as he puts it, a "rejection of Chomskyan linguistics is something like an obligatory opening gambit in any work of Language poetry theory" (151). But he argues persuasively that Chomsky's theories provide the best model for the "fantasy of no situation" that underlies many of the Language Poets' claims (148) as well as the sense that, in reading their work, we are encountering "*not* a speaker but a competence to speak" (158). Izenberg is also well attuned to the Romantic and Idealist impulses of Language Poetry, as when he compares them in passing to Wordsworth (145) and Shelley (157). As a way of reinforcing these connections, we might note that Susan Howe's *The Birth-mark: Unsettling the Wilderness in American Literary History* (Hanover: Wesleyan University Press, 1993) describes Emily Dickinson as having been committed, like Anne Hutchison, to a "covenant of grace," rather than a more worldly "covenant of works" (1–2). In my next chapter I touch upon these complex connections between post-Romantic experimental writing and cognitive science when I discuss one well-known Chomskyan, Steven Pinker. The critic who has most carefully delineated analogies between Stein and the Language Poets is Marjorie Perloff, as in her *21st-Century Modernism: The "New Poetics"* (Oxford: Blackwell's, 2002).

[33] "Panic-stricken" is Paul Davies's term for Beckett in "Three Novels and Four *Nouvelles:* Giving Up the Ghost to Be Born at Last," in *The Cambridge Companion to Beckett,* ed. John Pilling (Cambridge: Cambridge University Press, 1994), 47. The "collaborative imperative" of Language Poetry is addressed by Izenberg in his discussion of *Leningrad,* a poem written by Silliman, Hejinian, Michael Davidson, and Barrett Warren; see "Language Poetry and Collective Life," 136–49.

on the page, the thing without which Stein's text would not be. Questions still linger, however. Perhaps the leading one is this: given that "the inside" is the thing accountable for the text, what exactly is this thing saying? We may have determined who, or what, is speaking, but we have not yet said with any precision what precisely is being said. The grammatical and interpretive questions I posed at the beginning haven't vanished, and the contrast between "If I Told Him" and my pedestrian description of Picasso opening the refrigerator could hardly be starker. Identifying what my description is about (*Imagine someone opening a refrigerator*) is as effortless as my own ascription of beliefs to Picasso (*He wants something in the refrigerator*). But in Stein's case, it is still not clear what would change if "If I Told Him" were about Matisse, Hausmann boulevards, or her pet dogs.

If we assume that Stein is not herself the "confused, stammering, rather 'soft' (bloated, acromegalic, squinting and spectacled, one can figure it as) child" that Wyndham Lewis accused her of being—and even Michael Gold confessed that she has a "strong, clear, shrewd mind," "was an excellent medical student, a brilliant psychologist"[34]—we can safely conclude that she is up to something special in allowing "the inside" to utter what seems a non-sensical string of words. The practice of seeking patterns beyond the ordinary sense of a sentence is familiar to readers of early twentieth-century literature, who are accustomed to facing texts that challenge settled notions of linguistic and narrative coherence. For some early readers, a good strategy involved identifying "spatial form." This tactic characteristically pictured a text as a montage of repeated "images," recurrent descriptions of some state of affairs from which some kind of "meaning" is inferable.[35] In the case of Stein's portraits, however, searching for "spatial form" at the level of imagery is bound to be disappointing, for the confusion initiated by her texts arises at a different, and more basic, level than in the texts of her contemporaries. The *Cantos* or *The Waste Land,* for example, are famously "fragmented," but the fragments they present typically come in line-sized or stanza-sized pieces, and the challenge taken up by many readers has been to determine whether and how these textual bits are interconnected. It is relatively clear, for example, what is described in the lines, "I sat on the Dogana's steps / For the gondolas cost too much, that year" or "Summer surprised us, coming

---

[34] Lewis, *Time and Western Man,* 49; Gold, "Gertrude Stein: A Literary Idiot," 76.

[35] The landmark account of this interpretive strategy is Joseph Frank's 1945 essay "Spatial Form in Modern Literature," reprinted in his *The Widening Gyre: Crisis and Mastery in Modern Literature* (New Brunswick: Rutgers University Press, 1963), 3–62.

over the Starnbergersee."[36] But, again, it is considerably less clear what state of affairs is described in the line, "If Napoleon if I told him if I told him if Napoleon." Whereas in Eliot or Pound the text typically loses sense *between* sentences, the sense in Stein's work is lost *within* sentences—to the point that "sentence" is no longer even the appropriate term to apply to her chains of words. Coming away from Pound and Eliot, we recall vivid scenes—the Browningesque speaker looking over Venetian canals, the German countess recalling her youth—which we may or may not be able to relate to other, equally vivid scenes in the text. In Stein, we find plenty of nouns and verbs, but their arrangements are so non-syntactical that it is impossible know what is predicated of what. No scenes, images, or states of affairs materialize for us to link "spatially," even if we wanted to.

With conventional images and scenes unavailable, many readers have accordingly sought other sorts of patterns. One strategy has been to locate what is sometimes referred to as "sound patterning." This is the procedure of, for example, Marjorie Perloff, one of Stein's most astute readers, when she compares Stein's work to that of Wittgenstein. For Perloff, the arrangements of sound in *Tender Buttons* result in the breakdown of conventional syntax, yet this breakdown arises "not out of a refusal to 'make sense' or a predilection for pure nonsense, but because she wants to draw out specific semantic implications not normally present" in ordinary discourse about food, rooms, and objects. Thus in the sixteen-letter phrase "Roast potatoes for," Stein uses only seven phonemes, and the "simplicity" of this arrangement suggests the "simplicity" of the roast potatoes themselves, which, Perloff asserts, is "everybody's food." Stein's experiments, in other words, are not a stage for eccentricity, but, more profoundly, "a way of testing the limits of language." Perloff doesn't discuss "If I Told Him," but if she did, she could similarly point to the music of the text and identify "semantic implications" not immediately noticeable. The chiasmatic structure of line one, the near-rhyme of "told him" and "Napoleon," the round o's of "would" and "told" and "Napoleon," the conclusive "d" chiming between "would" and "told": read in Perloff's resourceful way, these and other features might be said to evoke the geometrical idiom of Picasso's Cubist phase, with its interlocking planes pieced together into portraits of friends and lovers. When, that is, we think of Stein as taking part in what Perloff, adapting Wittgenstein, calls a "poetry game," we can confidently

---

[36] Ezra Pound, *The Cantos of Ezra Pound* (New York: New Directions, 1996), 11; T. S. Eliot, *Collected Poems, 1909–1962* (Orlando: Harcourt, Brace, 1991), 53.

say with her that the curious locutions of "If I Told Him" make "rather good sense."[37]

Three important points should be made, however. One is that, despite Perloff's remarks, identifying the "music" of Stein's work in fact adds little that is "specifically semantic" to it. Perloff's description of the aural effects of "Roast potatoes for" are sharp: the "o–r" is indeed repeated and inverted, and assonance is indeed heard in the places she notes. But when critics try to move from there to saying what the text is about more generally, questions begin to proliferate. Why should the acoustics of "Roast potatoes for" evoke *the simplicity of roast potatoes, which is everybody's food* rather than anything else—say, *the unhealthiness of a starch-heavy diet* or even *the Spanish control over Cuba in the seventeenth century*? If we are appealing to associations, then my preference for these ways of reading "Roast potatoes for" is as impervious to criticism as my preference for chocolate over vanilla ice cream. Why? Because identifying sound patterning is not the same as identifying semantic patterning, and what a sentence suggests is not the same as what it means. As with my occasional references to "ordinary" and "non-ordinary" language here, a distinction between "meaning" and "suggestion" need not be meta-physical, as if any of these concepts had some independent pseudo-Platonic existence. "Meaning" simply refers to habitual ways of coping with noises by ascribing propositional content. But even when meanings are demytholo-gized this way, we should keep in mind how little fine-grained semantic content music and other sound patterns have in and of themselves. The uses of words are regular and stable enough most of the time that we can teach them to children, laugh at puns, play crosswords, and compile dictionaries. But it is hard to imagine how we could ever similarly stabilize the meanings of notes whistled in the shower or heard at the symphony. Certain trains of notes may, of course, carry associations—a melody may remind us of some-thing from childhood or recall a political regime—but these associations in and of themselves are seldom shared enough to act as norms on a par with linguistic ones. By comparison with words and sentences, sound patterns are content-poor. Once again we recall a remark by Kenneth Burke, himself both a music and a literary critic, who in a 1923 review of Stein's *Geography and Plays* complained that Stein is blind to her own medium: "If the musician plays G-sharp he has prescribed no definitions; but if the literary man writes

---

[37] On "Roast potatoes for," see Perloff, *Wittgenstein's Ladder*, 84–86. Analogous discussions of Steinian sound patterning can be found in Perloff's *The Poetics of Indeterminacy: Rimbaud to Cage,* 2nd ed. (Evanston: Northwestern University Press, 1999); Kostelanetz, introduction to *Yale Gertrude Stein,* xxi; Meyer, *Irresistible Dictation,* 310ff.

'boy' he has already laid down certain demarcations."[38] Sounds alone do not semantics make.

The second problem with Perloff's account is that the weakening of semantic patterns in Stein's portraits drastically undercuts the connection Perloff proposes between Stein and Wittgenstein. To emphasize the priority of music over conventional semantics in Stein, Perloff discusses a passage from the *Investigations* in which Wittgenstein compares the phrases "Bring me sugar" and "Milk me sugar," and she rightly notes that the non-sense of the latter phrase, as in Stein, is not metaphysical but practical. It has been "withdrawn from circulation" for specific reasons, and can still manage (like the musician playing G-sharp) to have an "effect." But in discussing Wittgenstein's examples of non-sense—examples that do indeed seem reminiscent of Stein—Perloff overlooks one of Wittgenstein's reasons for identifying them in the first place: to shed light on the various ways in which we often *are* able to make sense of utterances in the most ordinary of cases. Wittgenstein certainly guarded against "subliming" our logic and language, and was anxious to point out the historical character of our sense-making practices. But he was just as concerned to emphasize the normative role that these practices continue to play for us, even after they have been drained of any transhistorical, metaphysical status. As I have argued, the apparent non-sense of Stein's text is supposed to express the flux of human mental life more accurately than anything that a well-formed sentence could provide. Wittgenstein, however, spent much of his life interrogating the idea that language is a "veil" covering our "immediate" mental world, as well as the attendant Cartesian idea that, as Stein says, "Nobody can enter into anybody else's mind." For Wittgenstein, non-sense is simply not "closer" to our "real" thought process. Indeed, given the difficulty we would have in placing the phrase "Roast potatoes for" within a web of beliefs (what would *entail* or *follow from* "Roast potatoes for"?), it would probably not deserve to be called a "thought" at all. He would likely see Stein's work as a collection of personal associations—interesting perhaps to a clinical psychologist, but not much in the way of a full-blooded language. Of interest is not the self-enclosed "games" we can play with non-sense, but what it says about our ways of making sense elsewhere, the *Lebensform* made manifest through and within such phenomena.

And this leads immediately to the third and most important point about "sound patterning." Recall the crucial assumption made at the start of this

---

[38] Kenneth Burke, "Engineering with Words," in *Critical Essays on Gertrude Stein,* ed. Hoffmann, 42.

section when I began to describe how, despite appearances, Stein's texts could be made intelligible. What allowed us to seek the sound patterning in Stein's work was the assumption that Stein is not as "confused, stammering, rather 'soft'," irrational, childish, or deranged as her work sometimes seems. We were applying what is referred to, somewhat misleadingly, as the Principle of Charity: we assumed that the speaker is rational and would hold most of the sentences that we hold to be true, and then began looking for other kinds of significant patterns.[39] But how do we know that this is warranted in the case of Stein? After all, Michael Gold is probably not the only one to have thought that her work resembles "the monotonous gibberings of paranoiacs in the private wards of asylums," and Wyndham Lewis is probably not the only person to compare her to a squinting and spectacled child. To know that Gold and Lewis were wrong, and to know that our own assumption of sense is warranted, we can only do one thing: appeal to Stein's biography and set her individual texts within the course of her development generally. This development would include not only her individual psychology and experiences, but also the culture in which she learned the linguistic norms against which she so often reacted in her work.

Doing so would hardly be a startlingly original interpretive move, of course. However many journal articles have been written about Eliot's conversion or Woolf's sexuality or Pound's politics, critics find refuge in biography as habitually when discussing Stein as they do with any other prominent twentieth-century writer. Her early studies with William James, her emigration, her famous friends, her relationship with Alice, her salon, her work in the war, and so on, are not merely the province of eager biographers, but are an indispensable component of virtually all Steinian criticism. This is true even of Stein's most sensitive and intelligent readers: Donald Sutherland, whose anecdotal explication of Stein's "continuous present" I have noted; Richard Bridgman, who says in his classic study of Stein that the ground of her texts' allusions "lay in Gertrude Stein's head"; Wendy Steiner, who describes Stein's portraits as a radicalization of James's psychology; William Gass, who admits when explicating the "etymological narrative" of *Tender Buttons* that knowledge of "Gertrude Stein's daily life and obsessive concerns is essential"; Richard Poirier, whose explication of Steinian puns is buttressed

---

[39] "Somewhat misleadingly": as commentators have sometimes noted, the term "charity," associated most strongly with Davidson, implies a greater degree of choice than is actually involved in understanding, from a Davidsonian perspective. On the difficulties of this concept, see Bjorn Ramberg, *Donald Davidson's Philosophy of Language: An Introduction* (Oxford: Blackwell's, 1989), 69ff.

by extensive reference to her sexual life with Alice; Lisa Ruddick, who grafts the "drama" of Stein's "private emotional crises" onto the "drama of Stein's self-situation within twentieth-century thought"; and, of course, Perloff, whose descriptions of sound patterns in Stein is reinforced by quiet forays into biography whenever some detail (the identity of René Crevel, Stein's dislike of Marinetti) seems relevant.[40]

This is by no means meant as a criticism of these critics. It hardly could be, since my own discussion in this chapter would have been unthinkable without frequent excursions into biographical details and theoretical statements that fall well outside the confines of "If I Told Him." The point here is that we should be fully aware of just what this critical reflex suggests and entails. In particular, we should recognize how far these references to Stein's biography remove us from the concerns and themes that Stein and many of her readers want us to take as primary. When, that is, we move away from the question of how we are supposed to understand her texts in theory to the question of how readers have actually grappled with them in practice, we find that introspection, inner presences, and the "inside" quickly recede into the background. In her extensive study of Stein's manuscripts, Ulla E. Dydo has described the creative tension between the "centripetal" elements of Stein's writing, which "point inward, to the composition," and the "centrifugal" elements that point out "from the composed text to the world," which she calls "the context of the text."[41] Another way of putting this is to say that, in the shift between the "inside" that is introspected and the "outer" doings of Stein's daily life, we encounter our first case of how presence-models of agency are shadowed by person-models of agency. The reasons for this will emerge more fully over the next couple chapters. But the example of Stein provides an initial clue. If inner disembodied agents can in fact be said to exist at all, and if they can be said to learn norms and ascribe beliefs and desires, then there is strong reason to believe that it is only in the public world of physical bodies that these capacities can actually be recognized. It is only at the level of persons, in our ordinary habits of sense-making, in our experience as language-users within particular environments,

---

[40] Sutherland, *PGU*, 139–54; Richard Bridgman, *Gertrude Stein in Pieces* (New York: Oxford University Press, 1970), xvi; Steiner, *Exact Resemblance*, chap. 2; William Gass, *The World within the Word* (New York: Knopf, 1978), 90; Richard Poirier, *Trying It Out in America* (New York: Farrar, Straus and Giroux, 1999), 183–202; Lisa Ruddick, *Reading Gertrude Stein: Body, Text, Gnosis* (Ithaca: Cornell University Press, 1990), 4; Perloff, *Wittgenstein's Ladder*, chap. 3.

[41] Ulla E. Dydo, *Gertrude Stein: The Language That Rises, 1923–1934* (Evanston: Northwestern University Press, 2003), 19, 23.

that we see whatever effects such inner phenomena are supposed to generate. Alternative modes of making sense—be they "spatial form" or "sound patterning"—are intelligible only if we have already mastered the norms that allow us to make sense of sentences generally, as we interpret the behavior of embodied agents within the context of a specific situation. Stein's work is so drastically unattached to such norms and conspicuous contexts that, as long as we want to defend her against critics such as Gold and Lewis, we necessarily need to track down some supplementary resources and wider frames of reference.

Searching for supplementary resources and wider frames is, of course, not unique to our experience with literary texts. The person riding the unicycle on the sidewalk may seem peculiar until we notice the clown suit he is wearing and the tip jar nearby. Reading is in this sense simply a subclass of a wider phenomenon. But texts like "If I Told Him" push the challenge of making sense to unusual and therefore fruitful levels. It is perhaps no coincidence that the early twentieth century saw not only a great flowering of experimental literature, but also a great flowering of artistic manifestos—documents which set out to clarify the point of what seemed to many readers quite pointless. Making sense of a text through recourse to other things a person has said and done, however, is only the initial step toward locating it within a still wider domain of norms, environments, and situations. This is not to say that recourse to biographical and cultural details will always determine the content of what Stein writes. Such details are themselves not self-interpreting, and understanding always entails the possibility of misunderstanding. But herein lies the great interest of Stein's writing. The obscurities of her work throw our range of ordinary practices—our descriptions and comprehension of the world and of each other—into far sharper relief than they are normally allowed. This process has nothing to do with anything scientific, but this is hardly to Stein's detriment. It is because her words are so in need of interpretation that we are forced, eventually, to make ourselves explicit, to reflect upon that wide, indefinite *Lebensform* of which, at most times and with most texts, we remain only dimly aware.

✖ CHAPTER 2

Embodiment and the Inside

The end of chapter 1 approached a conceptual crossroads. Through most of the chapter we traced a path that led to a model of agency as an internal disembodied presence, "the inside," which according to Gertrude Stein and many of her readers generates the words of her works. As I suggested there, this (in Ulla Dydo's term) "centripetal" aspect of Stein's writing could be seen as shaping not only her works but also, to one extent or another, those of later figures like Beckett and the Language Poets. Inscribed above the gate to this path is a sentence quoted earlier from Stein: "You have slight contacts with other people's minds, but you cannot enter into them." At the end of the chapter, however, a second route came into view, leading us to consider how regularly Stein's readers take recourse to her romantic life, her circle of friends, and other fine points of her biography. This critical habit, I argued, forces an investigation of agency in a different, "centrifugal" direction, one that ties Stein's words closely to the embodied objects and persons that are identified in our most elementary, ordinary language.

In this chapter I want to explore in more detail the intersection to which Stein leads by considering a few theoretical figures who commit themselves to one avenue or the other. Of interest in the first section are two thinkers working at opposite ends of the twentieth century: William James, who was Stein's mentor, and Steven Pinker, who has recently done as much as anyone to popularize certain versions of contemporary cognitive science.

James and Pinker may seem an odd couple, and in many respects they are. But in their different ways they have each been deeply influential on recent literary studies—James in the recovery of American Pragmatism, Pinker in the rise of cognitivist models of reading and writing—and the distances separating them should obscure neither the structural analogies between their arguments nor the way they ground, clarify, and develop many of Stein's intuitions about language and agency. Indeed, the fact that they are so dissimilar only reinforces my suggestion that, though Stein is in some ways representative of her time, the aesthetic and philosophical impulses expressed in her work cannot be identified exclusively with one particular period of the twentieth century, or even with one particular genre.

In the second and third parts of the chapter, I'll move in a quite different direction and try to chart the person-model of agency that began, faintly, to emerge at the end of the last chapter. Doing so will lead me to a series of arguments that rose to prominence in the middle third of the century, and which take pains to show why talk about "the inside" implies the inside *of* something. Here the work of Quine and, still more importantly, Wittgenstein and Sellars will act as our main signposts. As my introduction noted, these figures have been more or less ignored in literary studies, and for this reason some of my discussion will consist of straightforward exposition; I'll be assuming relatively little familiarity with any of them. But tracking their claims about science, folk psychology, and what Sellars called the "manifest image" will also fill in some of the intellectual-historical background for part I, and should crystallize the debates about agency running through the literary work of Stein and, as I'll argue in the next chapter, Saul Bellow.

 TWO VIEWS FROM THE INSIDE

When Descartes famously doubts the existence of anything beyond his own thinking, he escapes his solipsism in part through an ontological proof for the existence of God: existence is surely a characteristic of perfection; God is by definition perfect; therefore, God exists. This argument, he implies, allows us to understand why doubts about the external world are no more justifiable than stories about an "evil genius" who (as the first *Meditation* imagines him) tricks us into believing in the idea of heaven and earth. When, two and a half centuries later, William James ponders divine existence, he by contrast finds that the idea of God provides not an escape from privacy, but a validation of it. As he says in the conclusion of *Varieties of Religious Experience* (1902), the experiences of religious conversion, saintliness, and mysticism can only be grasped from "the personal point of view," which science has "ended by utterly repudiating." As long as "we deal with the cosmic and general," he claims, "we deal only with the symbols of reality, but *as soon as we deal with private and personal phenomena as such, we deal with realities in the completest sense of the term.*"[1]

Varieties is a useful point of entry because it exemplifies how James's work begins and ends with the first-person point of view. James was remarkably given to self-revision, but through all the zigs and zags of his thinking—his psychology, pragmatism, radical empiricism, panpsychism, research into the paranormal—he never has misgivings about the methodological primacy of "*private and personal phenomena.*" Such an assumption is obvious in *Principles of Psychology* (1890), and has garnered much commentary. James was writing at a moment when the behaviorist revolution loomed, yet he never wavered in his belief that the "way of analysis," a phenomenological description of how mental states are experienced, takes precedence over "the way of history," a causal account of the events and environments that produce mental states.[2] A first-person stance likewise inflects James's pragmatism; indeed, it is usually cited as the trait that distinguishes him from his fellow founding pragmatists Peirce and Dewey. The former lamented James's "unexamined incapacity for mathematical thought," which had led him to take pragmatism "to such extremes as must give us pause,"[3] and the latter, whose studiously impersonal writings were concerned chiefly with the nature of modern social institutions, began his career as a student of Hegel, the very philosopher whom James often rebuked as the arch-rationalist bent on justifying a closed and deterministic universe.[4]

While the privileges accorded to the first-person standpoint in James's psychology and pragmatism are no secret, less frequently discussed is how this presumption also seeps into the late essays in radical empiricism. Like traditional empiricism, radical empiricism, as James characterizes it, casts off

---

[1] William James, *Writings, 1902–1910,* ed. Bruce Kuklick (New York: Library of America, 1987), 440, 446. Henceforth cited parenthetically as *Writings.* For a reading both critical and appreciative of James's religious interiority, see Charles Taylor, *Varieties of Religion Today: William James Revisited* (Cambridge: Harvard University Press, 2003).

[2] On this distinction, see William James, *Principles of Psychology,* vol. 2 (Cambridge: Harvard University Press, 1981), 913. On James and later anti-introspective philosophers and psychologists, see William Lyons, *The Disappearance of Introspection* (Cambridge: MIT Press, 1986).

[3] *Collected Papers of Charles Sanders Peirce,* vol. 6 (Cambridge: Harvard University Press, 1935), 182; *Collected Papers of Charles Sanders Peirce,* vol. 5 (Cambridge: Harvard University Press, 1935), 2. For an overview of Peirce and James, see Christopher Hookway, "Logical Principles and Philosophical Attitudes: Peirce's Response to James's Pragmatism," in *The Cambridge Companion to William James,* ed. Ruth Anna Putnam (Cambridge: Cambridge University Press, 1997), 145–65.

[4] For James on Hegel, see "Hegel and His Method," in *A Pluralistic Universe* (*Writings,* 668–89).

aprioristic reasoning and lends no credence to "abstractions." The conception of experience with which James works, however, is less parsimonious than the traditional empiricist's focus on sense-data, the stimuli and impressions from which (they claim, contra the rationalist) all our ideas originate. As Steven Meyer puts it in his discussion of Stein and "romantic science," James stresses "the decisive role of processes and procedures, of conjunctive as well as disjunctive relations, in the composition of experience."[5] For James, that is, sense-data of the Humean sort might be adequate for ordinary science, but human experience—"pure experience," as he calls it—exhibits a range of other phenomena for which a reductivist can find no place. Swimming in the flow of consciousness are not only perceptions of colors and sounds and smells, but also the fantasies, emotions, mental associations, and other distinctively human phenomena that inevitably accompany the raw and unmediated percepts of the human mind. Whereas Humean empiricists saw objects perceived by the mind as "'loose and separate' as if they had 'no manner of connection,'" a genuinely radical empiricism "*does full justice to conjunctive relations*" (*Writings* 1161).

One reason readers have often missed the first-person prejudice in these accounts of radical empiricism is that James sometimes denies having one. In emphasizing "conjunctive relations" between things as much as the things themselves, he presents himself as rejecting distinctions between "subject" and "object." "Consciousness," he claims, designates not a substance distinct from the material world, but a function within it: "There is, I mean, no aboriginal stuff or quality of being, contrasted with that of which material objects are made, out of which our thoughts of them are made" (*Writings* 1142).[6] But James's anti-Cartesian protestations cannot carry the weight he wishes. For although he firmly rejects substance dualism of the kind Descartes favored, the opening gambit for his essays in radical empiricism is the same as that of the *Meditations,* namely, that one's self-knowledge is always immediate, intrinsic, and certain. Even in the later stages of his career, he is as loyal to the idea of private experience as he was in the *Principles,* and his goal accordingly remains, as Richard M. Gale has put it, "to penetrate to the inner life of everything."[7]

---

[5] Steven Meyer, *Irresistible Dictation: Gertrude Stein and the Correlations of Writing and Science* (Stanford: Stanford University Press, 2001), 13. For Meyer's wider discussion of James's radical empiricism, see especially chap. 5.

[6] Cf. "A World of Pure Experience," on "the artificial conception of the *relations between knower and known*" (*Writings,* 1165). Such ideas led to James's occasional willingness to see radical empiricism as a form of post-Kantian *Identitätsphilosophie;* see *Writings,* 1191.

[7] Richard M. Gale, "John Dewey's Naturalization of William James," in *Cambridge Companion to William James,* ed. Ruth Anna Putnam, 65.

Take, for instance, James's description of "continuity," a paradigm of the sort of "conjunctive relation" that radical empiricism wishes to salute:

> What I do feel simply when a later moment of my experience succeeds an earlier one is that though they are two moments, the transition from one to another is *continuous*. Continuity here is a definite sort of experience; just as definite as is the *discontinuity-experience* which I find it impossible to avoid when I seek to make the transition from an experience of my own to one of yours. In this latter case I have to get on and off again, to pass from a thing lived to another thing only conceived, and the break is positively experienced and noted. (*Writings* 1163)

When I perceive, say, a mug and the desk on which it sits, my grasping of these items is "experienced" as a unity. For practical purposes my mug-perception and my desk-perception are distinguishable as "loose and separate"; I can isolate them when my Humean friends demand. But when we give a sincere introspective report, we have to admit that the continuity between them is as strongly felt, as "impossible to avoid," as any discontinuity posited after the fact.

Three features of this passage stand out. The first is something that came up in the last chapter: James's use of *experience* is fraught with troubling ambiguities. As in Stein and her commentators, it is hazily perched between the intentional and non-intentional, the semantic and the physical, and this slippage is the kind of thing that gives rise to belief in non-mechanistic mechanisms and other dubious phenomena. The second feature is that judgments about the "continuity" of such "experiences" are based on what James claims to "feel." "Feel" exhibits as many ambiguities as Steven Meyer's term "emotional investments," the thing that Meyer claims is ignored in normal science. Presumably, James doesn't think we feel continuities in the way that we feel powerful affection for a child or mild disappointment with one's tennis game. So the best synonym may be something like "sense," which tempers at least some (though certainly not all) of James's vagueness. But however we gloss the phrase, the point is that such feelings are described as wholly independent of how *others* feel things. My perceptions of the desk and mug are direct and incorrigible, an instance of what James calls—anticipating the two-knowledge theory that we saw in Whitehead—"knowledge by acquaintance" rather than mere "knowledge about." (Whitehead, we might note, praised James for "the inauguration of a new stage of philosophy.")[8]

---

[8] On "knowledge-about" versus "knowledge by acquaintance," see *Writings,* 1165ff. Whitehead's remark is in *Science and the Modern World* (1925; New York: Free Press, 1997), 143.

The "experience" of the mug on the desk could be expressed by the sentence *I perceive a mug and I perceive the desk on which it sits.* James wouldn't deny that such a sentence exhibits certain conceptual and logical relationships: singular objects such as a *mug* and *desk,* the spatial relations designated by *on,* the unity expressed by the conjunction *and.* But he would question whether these relationships are acquired by our mastering anything *taught* to us. The "continuity" between distinct perceptions of two different objects in space is known without the aid of any languages and judgments. The intrinsicality of the relation is grasped without any of the filters that learned meanings seem to involve.

The third thing to note about the passage is James's account of the "break" entailed in the transition from myself to another. The discontinuity of the transition, like the continuity of the mug- and desk-experiences, is "felt," and earns one of James's characteristically homey metaphors: "I have to get on and off again." By this he means that the immediacy of my own self-understanding contrasts sharply with what happens in trying to understand another person, a process that involves hurling oneself, as it were, from something "lived" toward something merely "conceived," "known-about." As James says later in the same paragraph, "the sameness of object and interest is unbroken" when I pass "from one of my own moments to another," and both moments are "directly lived." But the moments of another person are accessed with a great deal of "difficulty and uncertainty," and can be "ascertained expressly" only "after the break has been felt" (*Writings* 1163). Knowing how *you* experience the mug on the desk necessarily remains a mystery to *me,* an outside party, and can never be as undeniably concrete as my own experience of them. If James is, as Gale says, seeking always to "penetrate to the inner life of everything," then he clearly feels that some inner life—the one taking place within the confines of his own skin and his alone—is more penetrable than others.

These various claims about "experience," the "feeling" of continuity, and the "break" between persons do not in themselves entail any and all forms of skepticism. Responding in 1905 to a critic challenging the "solipsism" of radical empiricism, James insists that his refusal "to substitute static concepts of the understanding for transitions in our moving life" (*Writings* 1205) makes external-world skepticism implausible: we are always bathed in the environment around us. Yet if James's radical empiricism resists external-world skepticism, it takes for granted skepticism about other minds. I may be able to cognize the mug and the desk, but the basis of this cognition is my own present perceptions and beliefs. Those of other perceivers and believers, both today and in the past—*including those who taught me how to apply the terms "mug" and "desk" in the first place*—play no role whatsoever. Accordingly, in his view, we know other minds only by virtue of an analogy to our own. I "feel," he claims, a "connection" between two things by observing myself immediately, but the "break" between us makes knowledge of your mind indeterminable. The best I can do is to infer that mental states are happening in you as I am certain they are happening in me: "I see your body acting in a certain way. Its gestures, facial movements, words and conduct generally, are 'expressive,' so I deem it actuated as my own is, by an inner life like mine" (*Writings* 1176). I know my own inner life is endowed with expressiveness and meanings, but my best bet for deciding what *your* inner life and expressions mean is projection—casting my own private meanings onto what you seem to be doing.

What allows James to maintain that "realities in the completest sense of the term" are "private and personal," and what forces him into this argument from analogy, is his basic distrust of language. Precisely like Stein, he sees language as falsifying our immediate experience of the world. Indeed, not only is he one of the last major introspective psychologists before behaviorism, but he is one of the last major Anglophone philosophers before the linguistic turn.[9] James's perspectivism may often be tempered by his pragmatism, as some commentators have emphasized, but whatever faith he has had in shared social enterprises is largely missing in his late epistemological writings. Language is regarded as a prison-like system, an imposing logical and semantic institution that incarcerates our anarchically immediate "much-at-once" experience of the world, and he views this experience as so singular and subjective that he was reportedly frustrated even by the expectation that different people should use the same alphabet.[10] Concepts, he says, "are only man-made extracts from the temporal flux"—not, as Socrates assumed, "a superior type of being, bright, changeless, true, divine" (*Writings* 728). "Life is confused and superabundant," he writes elsewhere, "and what the younger generation appears to crave is more of the temperament of life in its philosophy, even though it were at some cost of logical vigor and of formal purity" (*Writings* 1159). Or, as he says in praise of Bergson, the member of the younger generation whom he found most inviting (and who was of course a

---

[9] Clearly not every Anglophone philosopher after James has endorsed the linguistic turn initiated by Frege and Russell. But unlike James, later philosophers who rejected it did so with a full awareness of what they were rejecting.

[10] On the tempering influence of James's pragmatism, see Owen Flanagan, *The Science of the Mind*, 2nd ed. (Cambridge: MIT Press, 1991), 31. One could reinforce this claim by pointing to James's consistent commitment to practical questions of democratic politics. James's ideas about the alphabet is noted by Louis Menand in *The Metaphysical Club: A Story of Ideas in America* (New York: Farrar Straus Giroux, 2001), 88.

great influence on Whitehead as well): "Concepts . . . are static, and can never be adequate substitutes for a perceptual flux of which activity and change are inalienable features. [They] make things less, not more, intelligible, when we use them seriously and radically" (*Writings* 1266).

From statements such as these arose Wittgenstein's criticism of James in the *Investigations* and elsewhere. To James's claim that "Our vocabulary is inadequate," Wittgenstein drolly rejoins: "Then why don't we introduce a new one?" (*PI* §610).[11] Before turning to such criticisms, however, I want to look briefly at Pinker in order to suggest how the idea of an internal presence, given early-century literary incarnation by Stein and philosophical incarnation by James, has evolved in the decades since. It would, of course, be misleading to say that language isn't taken seriously by Pinker, who is, after all, a linguist by training and who would balk at the claim that the logical relations of sentences are grounded on "feeling" (however understood). It would also be a mistake to say that, like James, Pinker puts much stock in introspection and the privileged access it allegedly gives to the mind's doings. The modules and mechanisms that Pinker sees as underlying cognition are largely unknowable even for the subject, and any mental phenomenon will be, in his view, fully explicable in third-person terms.[12] Moreover, the fact that Pinker sees these modules and mechanisms as species-wide makes him far less skeptical about other minds than James. Our human nature shows genetic and other variability, but on the whole our perceptual and mental capacities are defined by enough common structure and implementation to assume that other people generally perceive things the way we do. Whereas, too, James was often wary of scientific systematizing—science, recall, had "ended by utterly repudiating" the "personal point of view"—Pinker doesn't shy away from a tough-minded stance and embraces a frankly naturalistic ontology.

Pinker, however, has lauded what he calls James's "rich psychology" and "theory of mental life,"[13] and for all their obvious differences of temperament and context, the two bear more than a passing family resemblance. Consider,

---

[11] One shouldn't overemphasize Wittgenstein's resistance to James. Wittgenstein considered James one of the few philosophers worth re-reading, and he would've considered his criticism a mark of respect, not disdain. On the relation between the two, see Russell B. Goodman, *Wittgenstein and William James* (Cambridge: Cambridge University Press, 2002).

[12] An exception to this rule is consciousness, a topic on which Pinker seems agnostic. For an introduction to his thinking on this problem, see his "The Mystery of Consciousness," *Time,* January 29, 2007, 58–70, as well as the attendant sidebars of philosophico-scientific commentary from Dennett, Antonio Damasio, and others.

[13] Steven Pinker, *The Blank Slate: The Modern Denial of Human Nature* (New York: Viking, 2002), 19. Henceforth cited as *BS.*

for example, Pinker's *The Language Instinct,* a book whose title would seem to rebuff James's Bergsonian fight against the iron cage of concepts. In it Pinker gives a streamlined, non-technical survey of post-Chomskyan linguistics, which has served as the basis for his own version of cognitive science. The book sets out from a familiar Chomskyan observation: "No mute tribe has ever been discovered."[14] Not only has a mute tribe never been discovered, but, when analyzed methodically, the languages of particular tribes prove to have comparable richness and complexity. "There are," as Pinker says, "Stone Age societies, but there is no such thing as a Stone Age language" (*LI* 14). The presence of complex languages across cultures implies that language is to some non-trivial extent "innate." It reflects not merely the exigencies of human experience, a resourceful thing invented to cope with, say, our biological need for water, but is something we're born with, what Pinker calls a "distinct piece of the biological make-up of our brains" (*LI* 4). Our knowing how to speak is comparable to the spider knowing how to spin webs—"no more a cultural invention than is upright posture" (*LI* 5).

Critics of this position have targeted various elements, in particular its insistence on Darwinian explanations and its claims about innateness.[15] But we can grant Pinker his observations about word order, sounds, hearing, and other features that he claims are built into the brain by natural selection. What warrants comparison to the presence-models of agency at work in Stein and James is Pinker's theorizing about a "language of thought" or "Mentalese." "Mentalese" is the title of chapter 3 of *The Language Instinct,* which Pinker begins by citing a passage from George Orwell's appendix to *1984.* Orwell suggests that, "at least in so far as thought is dependent on words," the language of Newspeak might eventually make us unable to conceive of the word *free* outside of mundane contexts such as "This dog is free from lice" or "This field is free of weeds." Newspeak would introduce (Pinker's phrase) "thought control" by eliminating all but the most inconsequential senses of "free," since, as Orwell says, "political and intellectual freedom no longer

---

[14] Steven Pinker, *The Language Instinct* (New York: Perennial, 1995), 13. Henceforth cited as *LI.*

[15] Theoretical questions about Darwinian explanation have been raised, most interestingly, by Chomsky himself. For a review of Chomsky's skepticism about evolutionary accounts of language, see Pinker and Paul Bloom, "Natural Language and Natural Selection," *Behavioral and Brain Sciences* 13 (4): 707–84. For an analogous response to Pinker on this score, see Fodor, "The Trouble with Psychological Darwinism," <http://www.lrb.co.uk/v20/n02/fodo01_.html> (accessed January 12, 2007). For an early philosophical criticism of language as innate, see Hilary Putnam, "The 'Innateness Hypothesis' and Explanatory Models in Linguistics," in Stephen P. Stich, *Innate Ideas* (Berkeley: University of California Press, 1975), 133–44. For a more recent and more thorough scientific criticism, see Michael Tomasello, *The Cultural Origins of Human Cognition* (Cambridge: Harvard University Press, 2001).

existed even as concepts, and therefore were of necessity nameless" (*LI* 45). Pinker uses Orwell's disturbing thought experiment about "freedom" to ask how dependent upon words our thoughts really are. Do people literally think in English, Apache, or Chinese, natural languages in which the term "free" could, after some political or natural calamity, become a quaint residue from days gone by? Or, alternatively, "are our thoughts couched in some silent medium of the brain" and "merely clothed in words whenever we need to communicate them to a listener?" (*LI* 45).

Pinker opts—and in this his work chimes with Chomsky as well as Jerry Fodor, the originator of the term "language of thought"—for the latter: words may be publicly traded, but thoughts are articulated in a silent medium in the brain. They are, as he puts it, the "representations underlying thinking" (*LI* 72), which are his version of Adams's Chartres Cathedral, a locus of meanings and intentions. Lodged in our heads, that is, are particular tokens that intrinsically represent the state of, say, wanting to visit Paris, and the spoken or written sentence *I want to visit Paris* is the external garb making this inner, pre-verbal semantic item visible. The language of this inner thought, he says, "probably looks a bit like" natural languages such as English and Chinese, insofar as such thoughts must have "symbols for concepts, and arrangements of symbols that correspond to who did what to whom" (*LI* 72). But Mentalese need not be identical to any particular natural language. The model of a Turing Machine shows how a non-natural language can reproduce the discrete combinatorial system that forms a generative grammar (*LI* 64–69). Knowing a language, Pinker says, is thus really knowing "how to translate mentalese" of the Turing Machine variety "into strings of words and vice versa" (*LI* 73), much as a computer "translates" its internal ones and zeroes into an expert word-processing program.

This position is sometimes called an "internalist" picture of meaning, and its core idea is captured in the title of one of Chomsky's early books, *Cartesian Linguistics,* which was an effort to trace the concept of generative grammar to Descartes, Humboldt, and the Port Royal School. The basic claim is that our spoken and written sentences refer not to things in the world, but, in Pinker's phrase, to the "representations underlying thinking." To support his internalist theory, Pinker points to a variety of riddles it apparently solves. Ambiguity, for instance: *Our mothers bore us* (an example from Quine) can only be cleared up when we posit that "there can be two thoughts corresponding to one word" (*LI* 70). Or co-reference: we can only understand that *the former governor, him, the man at the teleprompter,* and *the President* all target the same person, provided we postulate that "something in the brain must treat them as the same thing" (*LI* 70). Such thoughts, Pinker suggests, are "trapped inside the head of the thinker" (*LI* 57), but it is they, not "palpable" words (*LI* 48), that define us as intelligent creatures. Only when we posit such thoughts can we be sure that languages like Newspeak will never vanquish us completely. The concept "freedom" will remain buried deep in the fortress of our heads, whatever the fate of our more visible vocabulary on the shifting battlefield of culture and history. Since "mental life goes on independent of particular languages," he concludes, "concepts of freedom and equality will be thinkable even if they are nameless" (*LI* 73).

Not all of these claims would sit well with a radical empiricist. From James's perspective, Pinker's rationalist talk of innateness may seem to imply that we are somewhat less than infinitely revisable. But Pinker's claims about an active mental life beneath our public languages, the difference between our words and the inner workings of our experience, would clearly have been applauded by James, who, like Stein, can be seen as a kind of proto-internalist. We should recognize, however, just what Pinker's specific arguments imply. After all, even a cursory glance at the course of human history suggests that *freedom* has never been identified in any single determinate way. Isaiah Berlin's distinction between positive and negative freedom gives us one way of thinking about this historical variability, but even within this rubric, we can distinguish a number of activities, practices, social institutions, and forms of power. *Freedom* means one thing to Locke and another to Kant, one thing to Hegel and another to Nietzsche, one thing to Jerry Fallwell and still quite another to Hugh Hefner. And this is to say nothing of "free from lice," "free from weeds," or any of the other humdrum uses of the concept that Orwell cites. Pinker's argument is that, for all these variable uses of the term, there is in fact one distinct notion of *freedom* underlying them all, buried deep in our internal wiring. Believing otherwise means accepting the "conventional absurdity" of "linguistic determinism" proffered by contemporary relativists, who would make the notion of "freedom" into a mere cultural construct. And if *freedom* stands clear of the social practices of a given historical community, the same must be true of other linguistic expressions that, for Pinker, reflect innate components of our mental make-up: the entrenched gulf between *he* and *she,* the idea of *consciousness,* the unambiguous notion of *the same person* (*LI* 47–48).

Discussing the internalism of Pinker and others, Davidson has argued that although evolution may constrain the syntax of our language, it cannot determine its semantics. We may be programmed, that is, to combine sounds and words in certain ways, but nature cannot tell us much about the meanings of these sounds and words—i.e., what these sounds and words are *about.* In Davidson's view—and in this he forecasts the position to which I'll turn in a moment—we learn how to use words and sentences only in a public environment, where we "triangulate" between ourselves, another speaker, and the shared social setting. Without another embodied agent in a common slice of space and time, we would have no way of knowing whether our own utterances refer to mugs and tables or to hallucinations of mugs and tables.[16] But like James, Pinker has only an attenuated sense of the way such shared physical and social environments shape our thoughts. And as a result, he exhibits a phobia that on the face of it would seem to hinder a linguist from doing his job: the sort of skepticism about language that James praises in Bergson, a sense that "our vocabulary is inadequate." Attacking the "conspiracy theorists" of postmodernism, Pinker has said that "the idea that language is a prisonhouse denigrates its subject by overestimating its power" (*BS* 208). Stein and James criticize such overestimations on the grounds that conventional words and sentences dim our perception of the authentic flux of experience. Pinker similarly warns us against ignoring the "mental life" underlying our "palpable" expressions. To be sure, Pinker's idea of pre-verbal mental life is not of an unstructured, non-conceptual chaos; the infant's instinctual desire for Mommy is taken for evidence that his or her mental life consists of "thoughts" and "representations" rather than the "one great blooming buzz confusion" that James commemorates in the *Principles*.[17] We'll return at the end of the chapter to this distinction between James's primitive anarchy and Pinker's primitive order. But the point for now is that if Pinker's commitments are more mechanistic than vitalistic, he shares with Stein and her mentor a belief that the behavior of a given body, including its verbal behavior, cannot make sense until we grasp the events going on within it. Pinker may represent a rationalist enterprise that is at odds with James's empiricism, but we should not be surprised to hear him praising the "numerous mechanisms" James posits in his theory of mind, or to hear him lamenting how the ideas of Stein's teacher "all joined the index of forbidden concepts" during the dark age of behaviorism (*BS* 19).

 ## MAKING OURSELVES MANIFEST

Some comments by Richard Bernstein will allow me to backtrack to the end of chapter one and turn away from the internalist presences evoked, in

---

[16] See Donald Davidson, *Truth, Language, and History* (Oxford: Oxford University Press, 2005), 127–41. More than many other internalists, Chomsky has recognized the challenges Davidson presents. See, for instance, his *New Horizons in the Study of Language and Mind* (Cambridge: Cambridge University Press, 2000), 46–74.

[17] James, *Principles,* 462.

various ways, by Stein, James, and Pinker. Writing in the early 1970s, Bernstein observed that there had been a sea change occurring in contemporary Anglophone philosophy during the previous two decades.[18] Early analytic philosophy, as it developed from Frege to the Vienna School, pursued the ideal of scientific precision and explanation, devoting itself to questions about the foundations of knowledge and the logical grammar of propositions. It demanded that philosophy achieve the clarity of structure and form characteristic of *Bauhaus* architecture, to which it occasionally compared itself.[19] But around 1950, says Bernstein, philosophers began to develop more careful accounts of how human purposes fit into the physical universe. The most significant figures in this "revolution" (*PA* 254) were Wittgenstein and, Bernstein implies, Sellars. The first generation of analytic philosophers showed "scarcely any direct concern with the nature of human action" (*PA* 234), but the second led the charge to bring this topic—raising a hand, going to the fridge for juice—back to the center of discussion.

Looking back from a later point in time, Richard Rorty has spoken of the middle decades of the century in similar terms. Contextualizing a field he often criticized as unwilling to contextualize itself, Rorty singles out three texts that mark a watershed in Anglo-American philosophy: Quine's "Two Dogmas of Empiricism" (1951), Wittgenstein's *Philosophical Investigations* (1953), and Sellars's "Empiricism and the Philosophy of Mind" (1956). With the appearance of these texts, says Rorty, analytic philosophy began to grow out of its positivist infancy into what he calls its "post-positivist" phase, one that was, as he puts it, "beyond" both empiricism and rationalism. These texts point for Rorty to a future from which—a vision Bernstein also entertained—the "tiresome 'analytic-Continental split' is looked back upon as an unfortunate, temporary breakdown of communication," and from which Davidson and Gadamer, Putnam and Derrida, will seem fellow travelers on the same journey rather than mutually uncomprehending antagonists.[20]

Rorty's and Bernstein's historical claims about the post-positivist turn of Anglophone philosophy are decidedly upbeat. The rise of cognitive science, including Pinker's mélange of Darwin and Chomsky, is evidence enough that philosophy's scientific aspirations didn't end in the 1950s, and readers of Putnam and Derrida do not seem a great deal closer nowadays to any final

---

[18] Richard J. Bernstein, *Praxis and Action: Contemporary Philosophies of Action* (Philadelphia: University of Pennsylvania Press, 1971), xvi. Henceforth cited as *PA*.

[19] Comparisons to *Bauhaus* were made by Rudolph Carnap in *The Logical Structure of the World,* and are discussed by Bernstein, *PA* 238–39.

[20] Rorty, introduction to the re-edition of Sellars's *Empiricism and the Philosophy of Mind* (Cambridge: Harvard University Press, 1997), 12.

rapprochement. Indeed, one could argue that the middle decades of the century saw the hardening and institutionalization of methods developed by the first generation of analytic thinkers, and that the figures Bernstein and Rorty cite were, with the partial exception of Quine, atypical of the period.[21] If, however, Bernstein and Rorty are distinctly Whiggish, they are right to say that the middle third of the twentieth century witnessed the rise of a distinctive strain of thought, and that much of what sets this movement apart is the way it returns to the question of what distinguishes human activity from the countless other goings-on of the universe. The answers given have little to do with "the inside," "pure experience," or "Mentalese," and point toward a quite different idea of how to interpret agents and tell stories about them.

Let's begin with Sellars, who has been hailed as "the greatest American philosopher since Charles Sanders Peirce,"[22] but who, in part because of a style that has seemed monumentally dense even to his most well-versed admirers, is the least widely known of the figures Bernstein and Rorty cite. Of particular importance to us is a phrase mentioned earlier, namely, the idea of the "manifest image," which Sellars sees as central to accounts of how the behavior of humans differs from that of plants and planets. The term may seem unusual, so a good way to start is to ask a simple question: manifest as opposed to what? An answer comes most clearly in Sellars's 1962 essay "Philosophy and the Scientific Image of Man," and it is this latter term— "scientific image"—that we need to see as the initial contrast class. Sellars describes the "scientific image" in various ways, but we can distill the idea by citing the following formulation: "the postulation of imperceptible entities, and principles pertaining to them, to explain the behavior of perceptible things" (*SPR* 7). Two features of this definition stand out.

---

[21] See John McCumber's *Time in the Ditch: American Philosophy and the McCarthy Era* (Evanston: Northwestern University Press, 2001) for an interpretation of the disciplinary evolution (or devolution) of Anglophone philosophy in the face of mid-century McCarthyism and the Cold War. I cite Quine as a partial exception here because, more than Sellars and far more so than Wittgenstein, he maintains a belief that philosophy of science, as he once said, "is philosophy enough." *The Ways of Paradox and Other Essays,* rev. ed. (Cambridge: Harvard University Press, 2006), 151. Accordingly, he is one of McCumber's chief examples of analytic philosophy's neglect of culture and history. But while McCumber's account complicates the historical narrative, it is notable that the figures he praises for recognizing the deserts of analytic philosophy—Bernstein, Rorty, Putnam, Cavell—turn to Sellars and Wittgenstein as oases. We should bear in mind, too, that even Quine was skeptical about many positivist forms of foundationalism, and defended what he termed "a more thorough pragmatism." *From a Logical Point of View,* 2nd ed. (Cambridge: Harvard University Press, 1961), 46.

[22] See "Editor's Introduction," in *The Space of Reasons: Selected Essays of Wilfrid Sellars*, ed. Kevin Scharp and Robert B. Brandom (Cambridge: Harvard University Press, 2007), vii. Compare Dennett's assessment of contemporary philosophy of mind: "Almost no one cites Sellars, while reinventing his wheels with gratifying regularity." *The Intentional Stance* (Cambridge: MIT Press, 1987), 349.

One is the term "postulation." Modern science is of course often credited with a revolutionary new respect for observation over scholastic theory-building. This was Bacon's point in the preface of *The New Organon* when he honored the "evidence of the sense" over "the mental operation which follows from the act of sense."[23] But as Sellars sees it, this hardly means that empirical inquiry is free of "mental operation." Laboratory researchers do not simply stare harder and longer than lay people do at stars moving across the sky or stones falling from a tower. What scientists are skilled at doing is taking these observations about stars and stones and developing theories designed to explain why they have behaved as they have in the past and to predict how they will behave in the future. And in the course of fashioning such theories, scientists are often led to postulate entities that are not evident to the senses endowed to us by evolution. We can't lay eyes on a half-inch of gravity, and before astronomers had ever perceived Pluto, the planet was posited theoretically in order to account for the perturbations in the orbit of Neptune.[24] Moreover, such a postulational strategy can be used to tackle any and all "perceptible things." To a theoretical physicist, as Sellars notes, bodies are "a swirl of physical particles, forces, and fields" (*SPR* 20), regardless of whether these bodies are planetary, human, or anything else.[25] And unlike tables and chairs, which any three-year-old child could successfully identify and talk about, our theoretical posits are intelligible only as part of a sophisticated vocabulary that even many well-educated adults never fully master. Understanding concepts like *invisible gravity* and *imperceptible Pluto* requires, in Bacon's terms, a complex "mental operation which follows from the act of sense" as much as the "evidence of the sense" itself.

Empirical science, however, is more than simple postulation. It uses the entities it postulates—and this is the second aspect of Sellars's synopsis that we should highlight—to "explain the behavior" of observable phenomena. "Explanation" is a term that appeared in chapter 1, where I was associating it with nomological (lawlike) descriptions. But Sellars adds something important to this basic idea. Scientific theorizing, he says in "Empiricism and the Philosophy of Mind," amounts "to erecting temporary bridges which permit the passage from sentences in observational discourse to sentences in

---

[23] *Francis Bacon: A Selection of His Works*, ed. Sidney Warhaft (Toronto: Macmillan, 1965), 327.

[24] The case of Pluto is from Brandom's "Study Guide" to the 1997 Harvard re-edition of Sellars's *Empiricism and the Philosophy of Mind*, 164.

[25] Sellars makes this remark while distinguishing "man as he appears to the biochemist, to the physiologist, to the behaviorist, to the social scientist" (*SPR* 21). On the unity underlying these special sciences, see *SPR* 21, which closely parallels Bjorn Ramberg's discussion of "the purely predictive aspect" nature of scientific explanation (see chapter 1, footnote 23).

[a] theory" (*SPR* 181). We can, that is, correlate empirical observations about, say, the temperature, volume, and pressure of a particular gas to theoretical statements specifying certain statistical measures of populations of molecules. Given this-or-that observation about this-or-that gas, we can calculate a certain number of molecules, and this estimate will allow us to anticipate future events. Similarly, to describe the behavior of a human gymnast in terms of particles and forces, we have to move back and forth—build bridges— between these theoretical entities and the gross features of the body as it spins and flies into its triple-back salto dismount.

Note immediately what this contrast between theory and observation *doesn't* rest upon: it doesn't rest upon differences between linguistic and non-linguistic sorts of knowledge or awareness. Indeed, the better part of Sellars's project is directed against what he calls "the Myth of the Given," the idea that observation reports (saying *a red triangle is now in front of me* when a red triangle is in front of me) can be made without the norms that distinguish human thought, knowledge, and discourse. Recognizing a red triangle and positing a quark both require a rich vocabulary; intuitions without concepts are indeed blind.[26] It is not that the language of observation gives us "concrete" things whose reality cannot be doubted, while the language of theory gives us fuzzy "abstractions," let alone "inventions." Rather, what leads us to differentiate the red triangle from the quark is how we come to know these different items. To put the matter bluntly, we never have to infer the existence of red triangles in the way we *initially* infer the exotic entities envisioned by theoretical physics. Unlike the report about the quark, the report about the red triangle requires none of the "bridge-building" and correlations that are the hallmark of a full-fledged scientific vocabulary. The difference between the red triangle and the quark isn't a difference in ontology, or, as Sellars says, "a *substantive* distinction between theoretical and non-theoretical existence." It is rather "a *methodological* distinction between theoretical and non-theoretical discourse" (*SPR* 174). The difference, that is, reflects not The Nature of the Universe, but the fact that Mommy and Daddy first teach us words designating things near enough to sense to be quickly identified and learned by name. The complicated trick of making inferential reports is something we learn only later on down the line.

Sellars's description of the "scientific image," with its distinction between gross material objects and the imperceptible posits used to explain them,

---

[26] See Kant's famous dictum in the *Critique of Pure Reason* (A51/B75), which is the inspiration for much of "Empiricism and the Philosophy of Mind."

should sound familiar to us by now. The explanatory role that an imperceptible "swirl of physical particles, forces, and fields" plays for the theoretical
physicist is essentially the one played by the inner "experience" of James in
perceiving the mug and the desk, and by the generative grammar of "Mentalese" posited by Pinker. These terms all name the imperceptible bustlings
that are supposed to explain the outer bustlings of perceptible bodies. Similarly, one way of re-stating my conclusions in the last chapter would be to
say that readers' forays into Stein's biography are symptomatic of a need, in
reading her, to erect "temporary bridges" between the inner imperceptible
entities she takes herself to be describing—"the inside"—and the publicly
available world. Indeed, this analogy between the Steinian "inner" and the
"posits" of science may be part of what drives commentators to describe
her work in scientific terms in the first place. This is not to deny the differences between the literary author and the empirical scientist. As Sellars
says, "nominal causes, so to speak, have real effects" (SPR 171), and given
what I implied in chapter 1, we may be inclined to say that Stein's postulations resemble those of Ptolemy more than those of Galileo. Nevertheless,
if her nominal causes have few real effects, it is true that the things allegedly
ordering her strings of words are "inner" movements and entities—"inside
every one what was in them that was intrinsically exciting"—rather than the
observable bodies of the perceptible world. Like James and Pinker, she shares
with scientists the basic "experimental" assumption that, whatever exists in
the universe, it isn't exhausted by our ordinary, non-inferential observation
reports.

Given this conception of the "scientific image," the phrase "manifest image"
comes into sharper focus. First, to talk in terms of the manifest image is to take
perceptible bodies, not imperceptible entities, as the starting point for describing worldly phenomena. To use an example that Sellars himself considers,
it is to take a pink ice cube as being pink "through and through, as a pink
continuum, all the regions of which, however small, are pink" (SPR 26). Such
a view is, of course, scientifically unconvincing (the particles of an ice cube
aren't themselves pink or any other color), but the cube looks uncontrovertibly pink, and when someone challenges our judgment on this score, we compare it to cotton candy, baby's cheeks, and other pink things.[27] Accordingly, to

[27] In "On the Radical Incompleteness of the Manifest Image" (PSA 2 [1976]: 335–43), Bas C. van
Fraassen says that Sellars's account of the pink ice cube consists of a "phenomenological description" (339). If this is true, however, we should emphasize the second term here as much as the
first. If, that is, the manifest image entails doing "phenomenology," it is what Austin, describing
his own work, termed "linguistic phenomenology, only that is rather a mouthful." Philosophical

think in terms of the manifest image of a human being is to take embodied persons rather than disembodied forces as the primary objects in descriptions of behavior. When, that is, we explain why so-and-so did such-and-such—why Picasso retrieved juice from the refrigerator—our initial strategy is to give a description of the behavior as an *action* on the part of a particular person, and no special talk about quarks, gravity, or any other imperceptible particles or forces need be added. Second, to amplify an idea first sketched in chapter 1, such descriptions are not "explanations" in the sense of strict causal accounts: they do not evince any lawlike generalizations. In Sellars's terms, they are not made "no holds barred," but "all things considered," in light of a person's previous behavior, current beliefs, and future plans. Telling a story about why Picasso will retrieve orange juice is less a matter of calculation than of understanding a holistic web of beliefs and desires: where the juice is, where it isn't, whether it will poison him, can be retrieved telepathically, and so on, indefinitely.

I'll come back to these terms "action" and "holistic" in a moment, but first a clarification. Sellars's contrast between the scientific and manifest images seems to rely on a sharp rift between modern and pre-modern modes of thought, scientific and pre-scientific culture. Is the "manifest image," then, just a fancy way of saying "traditional"? Or perhaps, in a slightly different locution, "common sense"? Not quite. The problem with terms like "traditional" or "common sense" is that they fail to register the tacit claim in Sellars that the manifest image is an *achievement,* an intellectual and moral accomplishment, something historically earned and for that reason always fragile. More specifically, if the manifest image is distinguished on one flank from the scientific image, with its frequently fantastical theoretical posits, it is distinguished on the other from what Sellars calls the "original image of man-in-the-world." This early conceptual framework, as Sellars describes it, is one in which "*all* the objects are persons." Plants, planets, people—all are seen in this view as animate beings pursuing some end or carrying out a particular function. To conceive of the universe in these terms is not merely to have different ("superstitious") beliefs from those of the modern day. It is,

Papers, ed. J. O. Urmson and G. J. Warnock (Oxford: Oxford University Press, 1961), 182. Sellars's entry point for addressing philosophical questions is the words used to describe actions and events. But he starts here with the implicit understanding that he is looking, as Austin puts it, "not *merely* at words (or 'meanings', whatever they may be) but also at the realities we use the words to talk about: we are using a sharpened awareness of words to sharpen our perception of, though not as the final arbiter of, the phenomena" (182). If, in other words, Sellars is doing phenomenology, he harbors no Husserlian fantasies about gaining a "presuppositionless" understanding, one which, as he says, would "break out of discourse to an *arché* beyond discourse" (*SPR* 196).

more radically, to describe it with a different set of categories. "A primitive man," says Sellars, "did not *believe* that the tree in front of him was a person, in the sense that he thought of it as a tree *and* a person." The truth, rather, "is that *originally* to be a tree was *a way of being a person,* as, to use a close analogy, to be a woman is a way of being a person, or to be a triangle is a way of being a plane figure" (*SPR* 10). As phenomena began to be explained and predicted roughly in the way that Galileo advised, the world was "de-personalized." The river described by one's ancestors as "lazy" or "angry" is regarded now as neither rational nor irrational; the wind blowing down a hut is no longer seeking punishment for the impieties of its owner. "Person," as Sellars says, is a category that begins to be applied "in a pruned or truncated form," while "the sense in which the wind 'did' things" is also circumscribed, used now chiefly for "poetic or expressive purposes" (*SPR* 12–13). From a world in which "*all* the objects are capable of *the full range* of personal activity," nature now "became the locus of 'truncated persons'" (*SPR* 13).

Given Sellars's hostility to the Myth of the Given, the adjective "personal" here should be taken to mean "of or relating to a person" rather than "individual" or "private." But doing so only spawns a further question. If it is true that we have seen a "pruning" of "person," what then is left? When is *person* properly applied? What counts as "the *full range*" of personal activity when this excludes the behaviors of winds, rivers, plants, and planets? As I noted in my introduction, such questions have made for contentious debates in moral and political theory, not to mention courtrooms and legislatures. Henry Adams treats certain French cathedrals as embodied agents, and lawsuits have been filed in defense of the rights of trees.[28] If, however, there are no hard and fast rules about when "person" is "poetic and expressive," and if our legal, moral, and theological uses may not always cohere smoothly, and if ambiguous cases (chimps? fetuses? robots?) are not hard to fathom, a concept is no less a concept for having, in Wittgenstein's phrase, "blurred edges" (*PI* §71). Sellars's account of personhood is designed to identify family characteristics rather than define a common essence. Like Wittgenstein, his goal is description rather than prescription, and he nowhere denies that complications and ambiguities persist. The line he draws between the manifest and scientific images engenders a minimal rather than substantive account of personhood, one that has caused us post-Galilean moderns to give equal weight to two basic properties. Persons are on the one hand a type of entity

---

[28] On trees as rights-bearing intentional beings, see Miguel Tamen, *Friends of Interpretable Objects* (Cambridge: Harvard University Press, 2002), chap. 5, and Walter Benn Michaels, *The Shape of the Signifier: 1967 to the End of History* (Princeton: Princeton University Press, 2004), chap. 2.

ascribed complex qualities of *Geist:* they are "impetuous" or "set in their ways," applying "old policies" or adopting "new ones," "immature" or with "an established character" (*SPR* 11). But on the other hand, and just as important, a person is a type of entity ascribed certain corporeal qualities: a *res extensa,* a thing identifiable, like the pink ice cube, without the aid of sophisticated theoretical vocabularies and inferences. In a moment I will give a somewhat fuller account of how these two basic properties are co-ordinated with one another, but even this preliminary description is enough to suggest how marginal a role the concept of a person plays in Stein and her philosophical cousins James and Pinker. In their different ways, Stein, James, and Pinker each imply that we could understand properties of mind wholly apart from properties of perceptible matter. Sellars picks up the issue from the other handle. Just as the concept of a birth depends upon the concept of animal, and the concept of erosion implies the concept of cliff, we could not understand something as "impetuous" or "immature" without first having the notion of material bodies that could be cubed or colored.[29]

 ## PRECEDENTS, PERFORMANCE, AND AN ESSENTIALLY NARRATIVE IDIOM

More than most of his analytic contemporaries, Sellars has a keen sense of intellectual history, and his echoes of previous philosophers are seldom acci-dental. Perhaps the most crucial early ancestor is Aristotle, who offers a model of how to avoid mind-body dualism without falling for reduction-ism. For Aristotle, the discrete parts of a person are only identifiable *as* such parts when recognized against the background of an entire animate body. "A hand cut off," says Sellars, alluding to the *Metaphysics,* "is a logical subject on its own, but a hand in name only."[30] In saying this he updates the Aristote-lian idea that, while "no bodily part of a person is the 'organ' of conceptual thinking," we should not therefore postulate "an unbodily organ of thought" (*SM* 170). The dualist "thinks of the person as a family or team, a mind that

---

[29] Birth/animal and erosion/cliff are examples from Strawson, *Individuals: An Essay in Descriptive Metaphysics* (London: Methuen, 1959), 42, 47. Strawson is cited sometimes by Sellars as an analogue to his own work, and deserves more discussion than I can give him here. Suffice it to say that he is among the "Oxford Aristotelians" Sellars praises, and that this rich text provides further evidence for the mid-century philosophical shift that I'm sketching here.

[30] Wilfrid Sellars, *Science and Metaphysics: Variations on Kantian Themes* (London: Routledge & Kegan Paul, 1968), 170. Henceforth cited as *SM.* Cf. *Metaphysics* VII: "since it is not any sort of a finger that is a finger of an animal, a dead finger being a finger in name only." Aristotle, *Metaphysics,* trans. Richard Hope (Ann Arbor: University of Michigan Press, 1960), 151.

thinks and a body that runs," but the Aristotelian functionalist recognizes that "it is the same thing," "a *person, which both thinks and runs."*[31]

A chronologically less distant predecessor that Sellars sometimes invokes is one that I have mentioned already, and recalls Rorty's and Bernstein's accounts of "post-positivist" philosophy. This is the later Wittgenstein, who, after publishing the *Tractatus* in 1921 and abandoning philosophy, returned to it around the time that Sellars was a student in the late 1920s and '30s. Wittgenstein, says Sellars, did "increasing justice to the manifest image," "isolating it in something like its pure form" (*SPR* 15), and inspired—in a reference to Gilbert Ryle, J. L. Austin, Peter Strawson, Elizabeth Anscombe, and others—the "Oxford Aristotelianism" of mid-century Britain (MCP 220). This last remark reminds us that, while Wittgenstein was a less systematic and historically informed philosopher than Sellars, many of his most notable followers have championed what has been called "the return of Aristotle" in contemporary philosophy.[32] Though he never introduces handy phrases such as "scientific image" and "manifest image," Wittgenstein repeatedly describes our verbal lives as an amalgam of language games, and warns often against forcing or expecting non-scientific vocabularies to behave like scientific ones—the temptation, that is, to overlook the city's ancient maze of roads in favor of the tidy streets of the new suburbs.[33] And like Sellars, too, his

---

[31] Wilfrid Sellars, "Metaphysics and the Concept of a Person," in *The Logical Way of Doing Things,* ed. Karel Lambert (New Haven: Yale University Press (1969), 220. Henceforth cited as MCP. Another important historical predecessor is Hegel. "Philosophy and the Scientific Image of Man" often plays distinctly Hegelian motifs: the historical shift between different "images of man"; the rejection of the "Robinson Crusoe conception of the world," which overlooks the "mediation of the family and the community" in the constitution of thought (*SPR* 16). In his introduction to the 1997 Harvard University Press re-issue of Sellars's *Empiricism and the Philosophy of Mind,* Rorty draws extended connections between Hegel and Sellars (see especially 8–12), and Bernstein makes a similar comparison (see especially *PA,* 301–4). Sellars himself, however, rarely draws such analogies, and accordingly I've bracketed them off here. Presumably he plays down this precedent because invoking Hegel would have earned him few points among his mid-century analytic colleagues. The history here is complicated, but we should remember that Hegel was often associated with early twentieth-century German nationalism, and that many of the founders of analytic philosophy were German-speaking Jews who left Europe when Hitler rose to power. Several decades later, the political consequences of Hegelianism seem more open to debate and, appropriately, some of Sellars's most ardent disciples—not only Rorty and Bernstein, but also Brandom and John McDowell—have helped initiate a Hegel revival among Anglophone philosophers.

[32] "The Return of Aristotle" is the title of part I of Hilary Putnam's *Words and Life,* ed. James Conant (Cambridge: Harvard University Press, 1994). The Aristotelian-Wittgensteinian synthesis is most obvious in Anscombe, Wittgenstein's literary executor, but other major figures in this line include McDowell, Stephen Toulmin, Anthony Kenny, Alasdair MacIntyre, and Charles Taylor.

[33] See *PI* §18. Whether a scientific vocabulary could someday replace an intentional vocabulary is a question on which Sellars and Wittgenstein seem to disagree. On this difference, see Bernstein's discussion of "the displacement hypothesis," *PA* 281–99.

starting point for exposing these prejudices was a sustained attention to the distinctions embedded in our ordinary speech between actors and movers. "Look at a stone," he proposes, "and imagine it having sensations" (*PI* §284). "Person" is only one of the terms Wittgenstein uses when distinguishing the sapient from the non-sapient; "human being" (*Mensch*) is more common. But the concept of something that "both thinks and runs," a thing that is not merely a "family or team," underlies the whole of his later work.

This refusal to separate the thinker from the runner is what will allow me to tie the loose ends of my discussion of Stein in the last chapter to the discussion of Bellow in the next. But it is worth noting, first, that this refusal is also what makes Sellars and Wittgenstein often sound like the behaviorists whose influence Chomsky and Pinker so often lament. The person described as a "manifest image" by Sellars is identifiable first and foremost as a body, a *res extensa* in a physical environment. Without some prior idea of Picasso's body, we couldn't describe his search for orange juice in terms of particles and molecules, and for similar reasons we would be hard-pressed to describe it folk-psychologically as an expression of what Picasso *wants, hopes,* or *intends*.[34] As Sellars puts it in one of his scrupulous grammatical investigations, the sentence *John has a pain* should not be seen as describing a "relation" between a man (John) and a state (pain), as if these were two free-standing entities (MCP 230–35). Wittgenstein makes the identical point with the identical example: "Pain-behavior can point to a painful place—but the pain is expressed by the suffering person" ["*aber die leidende Person ist die, welche Schmerz äussert*"] (*PI* §302).[35] Many of the most frequently cited dicta from the *Investigations* sound like polemical marginalia that Wittgenstein might have jotted while reading Stein, James, or Pinker: "An 'inner process' stands in need of outward criteria" (*PI* §580); "What we deny is that the picture of the inner process gives us the correct idea of the use of the word 'to remember'" (*PI* §305). Indeed, in uncovering what he calls the

---

[34] Sellars's parallel between his account of mental states and his account of "theoretical entities" in science is made explicit in his most well-known thought experiment, the story of "our Rylean ancestors" and "the myth of Jones." The Ryleans are a tribe whose vocabulary (as in caricatural accounts of Gilbert Ryle's work) lacks terms for inner episodes and whose most basic descriptive vocabulary refers only to public spatiotemporal objects. Jones is a genius who hits upon the idea of attributing beliefs and desires to some of these objects, "inner episodes which are neither overt behavior nor verbal imagery and which are properly referred to in terms of the vocabulary of *intentionality*" (*SPR* 188). For the full argument, see *SPR* 178–96.

[35] Anscombe's translation of this last clause is: "but the subject of pain is the person who gives it expression." I've altered it here (changing, in the process, Wittgenstein's active verb to a passive one) because the misleading term *Subjekt* appears nowhere in the passage, and because the term *Person* is not, I think, used accidentally.

"slight giddiness" of introspection, Wittgenstein can sound as deflationary as B. F. Skinner: "But what can it mean to speak of 'turning my attention on to my own consciousness'?... It was a particular act of gazing that I called doing this. I stared fixedly in front of me—but *not* at any particular point or object" (*PI* §412).

One effect of sounding these behaviorist notes is that some of the key-words of modern philosophy, and in turn much literary-theoretical discussion, simply fall by the wayside. *Consciousness,* for instance, plays hardly any role whatsoever in either Wittgenstein or Sellars. Why? Both before and after Descartes, *consciousness*—or *spirit,* or *mind*—has been seen as the outstanding property granting special status to you and me but not to Mount Everest or the Atlantic Ocean. These properties are add-on features that in theory are detachable from bodies—most vividly, though not exclusively, in religious visions of an immortal soul. For Sellars and Wittgenstein, by contrast, these terms are potentially bewitchments. They bewitch us not because they are unthinkable apart from embodied beings (they obviously are), but because we overlook how they are *modeled upon* embodied beings. As Sellars puts it, "spirit" and "soul" designate a "ghostly *person,* something analogous to flesh and blood persons which 'inhabits' them, or is otherwise intimately connected with them" (*SPR* 11). Wittgenstein voices this idea in one of his most famously enigmatic remarks: "The human body is the best picture of the human soul" (*PI*, p. 152). Elsewhere in the *Investigations* human beings are described as our paradigm for animate life: "It comes to this: only of a living human being and what resembles (behaves like) a living human being can one say: it has sensations; it sees; is blind; hears; is deaf; is conscious or unconscious" (*PI* §281). When we try to understand an entity's worldly acts, the question of whether its "inside" consists of circuits, cells, or spaghetti sauce—what John McDowell calls "the machinery of mindedness"—is secondary.[36]

---

[36] On the machinery of mindedness and what he calls "bald naturalism," see McDowell, *Mind and World* (Cambridge: Harvard University Press, 1994), xx–xxii. My mention of McDowell isn't meant to suggest that he would agree with everything said here. Indeed, *Mind and World* is respectfully directed against something like the reading of Sellars that I have been giving.

Including Wittgenstein next to Sellars also requires some qualification. Wittgenstein's writing is immensely complex, built upon analogies and striking images and brief, densely woven numbered sections. The *Investigations* is, as he says in the preface, "an album," "a number of sketches of land-scapes" (*PI* ix), and resists striving for knock-down arguments in the way of Sellars, who is in this respect a more traditional analytic philosopher. This has led some important commentators, such as Stanley Cavell and Richard Eldridge, to argue that Wittgenstein's relationship to the pictures holding us captive is much more ambivalent than usually assumed. Indeed, in his *Leading a Human Life: Witt-genstein, Intentionality, and Romanticism* (Chicago: University of Chicago Press, 1997), Eldridge even

Persons, in short, precede presences. Yet if Sellars and Wittgenstein endorse a form of behaviorism, their behaviorism does not, in the vein of Skinner, aim to expunge aims or any other intentional attitudes. They resist facile dichotomies implying that any phenomena not captured by naturalistic description are somehow otherworldly. And they refuse the companion idea that, as E. O. Wilson has recently put it, "[e]ither the great branches of learning—natural sciences, social sciences, and humanities—can be connected by a web of verifiable causal explanation or they cannot."[37] For while intentional states make no sense apart from bodies, they are also not reducible to bodily states, whether "state" refers to a gross physical motion, molecular configuration, or anything else. Neither Wittgenstein nor Sellars denies that our descriptions of human behavior, unlike our usual descriptions of stalactite or plant or planet behaviors, are shot through with some form of dualism. They each endorse what Quine refers to as an interpretive "double standard": the thinker who runs is still a thinker, and the material bodies that are cubed or colored can still be impetuous or immature.[38] In the *Investigations,* Wittgenstein's interlocutor raises the specter of behaviorism explicitly: "Are you not really a behaviorist in disguise? Aren't you at bottom really saying that everything except human behavior is a fiction?" To which Wittgenstein replies: "If I do speak of a fiction, it is of a *grammatical* fiction" (*PI* §307).

Calling it a *"grammatical* fiction" is a way of saying that if beliefs and desires and intentions are illusions, they are not illusions in the way that a magician's tricks are. We obviously do often say that someone *wishes* or *hopes* something will happen, and when we do so, we usually know perfectly well what we are doing. Moreover, we often can effectively distinguish between someone who really believes (wishes, hopes, etc.) something and someone who merely pretends to believe (wish, hope, etc.) something. Rejected in Wittgenstein and Sellars instead is the tradition that identifies wishes, hopes, and beliefs with what happens exclusively in the head, as opposed to what happens in the feet, forearms, and rest of the body as it interacts with an environment at a specific time and place. Thinking, says Wittgenstein in the

refers to the main speaker of the *Investigations* as "the protagonist," in order to maintain the ambiguity of the different voices and positions in the text. The point is crucial, but it raises considerations that are impossible to address without my discussion going far afield. I can live with my simplified picture in part because it will be rectified somewhat in my discussion of Cavell in chapter 5.

[37] E. O. Wilson, "Forward from the Scientific Side," in *The Literary Animal: Evolution and the Nature of Narrative,* ed. Jonathan Gottschall and David Sloan Wilson (Evanston: Northwestern University Press, 2005), vii.

[38] W. V. O. Quine, *Word and Object* (Cambridge: MIT Press, 1960), 216. Henceforth cited parenthetically as *WO.*

opening pages of *The Blue Book,* is "essentially the activity of operating with signs," and this activity "is performed by the hand when we think by writing; by the mouth and the larynx, when we think by speaking."[39] No brain surgeon has ever stumbled across a Mentalese Thought Chamber where beliefs, wishes, and hopes are stored for future use. Whatever is literally "in the head" consists, after all, of neural tissue and other messy, thoroughly non-semantic matter—not a promising environment for meanings, beliefs, and intentions. But the absence of such Thought Chambers does not mean that persons do not "think."

Another way of putting this is to recall a distinction I cited earlier and say that the behaviorism of Sellars and Wittgenstein is not metaphysical but methodological—"not a thesis," Sellars says, "about the *analysis* of *existing* psychological concepts, but one which concerns the construction of new concepts" (*SPR* 184). Much as Karl Marx hopes to describe how labor-products are transfigured over time into fetishized commodities, Sellars and Wittgenstein trace the origins of mentalistic terms in order to avoid their reification. Ordinary language isn't the last word on how the world works, but it *is,* as Austin said, the *first* word.[40] Hence the acute interest taken by both of them in the grammar and training of language, and in the ways our words mislead and deceive when removed from the stream of our lives—"when language *goes on holiday,*" in Wittgenstein's well-known metaphor (*PI* §38). It is not an accident that the *Investigations* opens with Augustine's story of how as a child he learned to talk of objects and mental states, or that so many commentators have read it as a book about education.[41]

Asking how we learn our words, where their "homes" are, how they fit into the "weave of our lives," forces us to recognize that even the most seemingly "immediate" experiences (recall here James's "*private and personal phenomena*" or Stein's ring following the moon) can be identified only by creatures already embedded in a language learned in a public environment. This doesn't negate the asymmetries that often distinguish first- and third-person knowledge. My "avowals" of pain don't require observing my own behavior in the way that I must do when "attributing" pain to another, and in most cases, my beliefs and desires are indeed transparent to me in a way they are not for others. The crucial point here, rather, is that terms for pain and other "inner" states do not have different *meanings* for different users,

---

[39] Ludwig Wittgenstein, *Blue and Brown Books* (New York: Harper and Row, 1958), 6.

[40] Austin, *Philosophical Papers,* 185.

[41] Perhaps the most prominent commentator to have seen the *Investigations* as a pedagogical text is Cavell, as we'll see in chapter 5.

and that we come to apply these terms, even to ourselves, only after some training in the language.[42] We presumably felt sensations before we knew how to speak, but we couldn't have identified and known them *as* sensations, let alone any sensations in particular: "You learned the *concept* 'pain'," Wittgenstein puts it starkly, "when you learned language" (*PI* §384). Or, to turn the point around, we may eventually be able to distinguish states from behaviors, genuine pain from feigned writhing, but these discriminations are available only to a creature already arrayed with a rich set of concepts. Which is to say, in effect, that "thinking" is a mode of intelligent performance. "Performance" here includes, in part, the astonishingly complex behavior—bodily activities—characteristic of human beings: writing words, cooking meat, cultivating plants, decorating homes, and other tasks that any ordinary adult could master but that would permanently stupefy even the brightest of Jane Goodall's primates. But "performance" also includes less demonstrably corporeal activities: the ability to make judgments and apply concepts, to place our descriptions within a web of logical relations, to reason coherently from *All men are mortal* to *Socrates is mortal.* "Performance" doesn't mean simply feeling a pain, but knowing that pains are a kind of sensation, that they're unpleasant, that they're not things you wear, that they have duration, that they have degrees of intensity, that they're not colored, and so forth. If we couldn't make enough of these inferences, we would not know that it was a *pain* we were experiencing, and it is the possibility of such failure that makes these activities reason-governed and normative rather than simply causal. Correctly knowing when to say *I feel a migraine coming on* isn't a matter of taking dictation from a vitalistic or Mentalese "inside." *Having* a migraine certainly requires no special skills, but *recognizing* one is part of a practice, one with a place for "migraine" and associated concepts like "headache" and "agony," learned within a social context, much in the vein of playing tennis or holding elections, and with all the possibilities of success and failure that such activities entail.

Doing, talking, performance, learning over time, bodies in an environment, the weave of our lives: we are approaching the deeply literary dimension of these philosophical claims. For to conceive of actions as performances—be

---

[42] Discussion of the distinction between "avowal" and "attribution" has been importantly renewed in recent years by Richard Moran's *Authority and Estrangement: An Essay on Self-Knowledge* (Princeton: Princeton University Press, 2001). Moran takes himself to be challenging Davidson and Dennett (see especially 25–26), whom he claims are incapable of accounting for specifically first-person knowledge. For one potential response, see the first part of Davidson's *Subjective, Intersubjective, Objective* (New York: Oxford University Press, 2001), 1–91. The asymmetries of first- and third-person knowledge will be an important theme running through part II.

they "mental" acts or "physical" acts—is to think of agency in essentially narrative terms. A waltz is not made intelligible by piecing together discrete movements that we can identify ahead of time, one-by-one. Apart from the waltz as a whole, a reverse turn is not only not isolatable; it isn't even a "reverse turn"—as opposed to, say, a curious New Age exercise or two drunks shambling to the left. And the same is true for trains of thought, mathematical calculations, weekend planning, and other typically "mental" activities. To attribute, say, *hope,* we don't unearth the disembodied presence invisibly animating someone's "experience" or the Mentalese representations buried in his or her mental modules. We begin by recognizing a narrative of bodies, environments, and worldly situations: the baseball fan with eager eyes hoping for a strikeout; the anxious student hoping for a good grade; the pregnant woman hoping for a healthy baby; the family hoping to move to a new neighborhood; the nation hoping for the end to war. As Wittgenstein says of *game* (*PI* §65–71) and *reading* (*PI* §156–71), there is no reason to think that all these versions of *hope* share some common essence, and yet they are all equally good cases of it. Moreover—and this is the point here—all these shades of *hope* are recognized only in the context of broader narratives. Within these narratives, the nuances of past and present experiences bleed into one another in innumerable distinct ways, much in the way that, to borrow an image from Garry Hagberg, the studio microphone of one instrument always faintly picks up the sound of other instruments, making no sound in a recording perfectly isolatable from another.[43] Whether expressed in the fan's eager eyes or in the diffuse web of conversations and events constituting "the national mood" (a notion to which we'll return in part II), hope is only identifiable as *hope* when we perceive a narrative trajectory linking a complex constellation of movements, utterances, and environments. There is nothing beneath the surface of any of these phenomena; their surfaces are themselves part of the family of cases of *hope* (*PI* §164). An entire assembly of events is required before we can single out any one of them.

It is for these reasons that Quine calls the vocabulary of intentional attitudes an "essentially dramatic idiom" (*WO* 221). The hopes of the fan, student, mother, family, and nation are each the germ of a good yarn. For some philosophers, the radical holism and narrativity of intentional attitudes makes them ontologically suspect. Indeed, this is Quine's own official view of mental states. The impossibility of matching them up with discrete physical states removes them, he claims, from the "true and ultimate structure of

---

[43] Hagberg, "Davidson, Self-Knowledge, and Autobiographical Writing," *Philosophy and Literature* 26 (2002): 357–59.

reality" (*WO* 221). (Quine was, we should note, a longtime friend of Skinner.) Yet while this stance distinguishes Quine sharply from Wittgenstein and Sellars, he also recognizes (unlike Skinner) that a holistic vocabulary of aims and purposes is "practically indispensable," and that we would never want to "foreswear daily use of intentional idioms" (*WO* 221). Obviously none of these figures would deny that we routinely experience breakdowns in understanding. Conversations go at cross-purposes; we get into muddles; things fall apart. But they would all also argue that the very idea of muddles and things falling apart is intelligible only if we also have some relatively rich notion of something's making sense, be it a conversation, baseball game, or world-historical event. "He who wants to doubt everything would not even get as far as doubting anything," says Wittgenstein, for the "game of doubting itself presupposes certainty."[44] Human understanding, indeed even basic survival, will depend upon the degree to which one can make things add up, cope with local dislocations, and grasp the larger patterns of one's experience as a more or less unified item. Literary texts, from this point of view, specialize in such "essentially dramatic idioms." They display some of the characteristic patterns and circumstances of, say, *hope, anger, wanting, wishing, hating.* Some patterns and circumstances are more widespread than others. Patterns of *mourning a loved one,* for instance, are probably less parochial today than those for *paying tribute to the sun gods.* But in either case, a discursive account focused on inner workings—be they vitalistic celebrations of "experience" or cognitivist arguments about computationalism and genetics—misses the larger dramatic, social, and historical background against which such intentional ascriptions necessarily occur. The story of *mourning a loved one* or of *paying tribute to the sun god* need not describe one and only one physical state. They can tell of many types of behaviors and events. Which is why, to update a thought from Kenneth Burke, who would be very comfortable with the claims I've been outlining here, and whose dissatisfaction with Stein I noted in chapter 1, literary texts are works that name "typical, recurrent situations," that "size up situations in various ways and in keeping with correspondingly various attitudes."[45]

In a moment I'll turn to Saul Bellow to explore how these themes of embodiment, narrative, and agency appear in more complex and vividly

---

[44] Ludwig Wittgenstein, *On Certainty,* trans. and ed. G. E. M. Anscombe and G. H. von Wright (New York: Harper and Row, 1972), 118 (§115). Henceforth cited parenthetically as *OC* according to the number of the remark. Here and elsewhere I am slightly altering the translations.

[45] Kenneth Burke, *The Philosophy of Literary Form: Studies in Symbolic Form,* 3rd ed. (Berkeley: University of California Press, 1973), 293, 304.

dramatic terms than I have been using here. But, by way of transition, a few last points should be made about where the discussion has been and where it is headed, in particular, as it concerns the ontological commitments implied in the various philosophical claims I have been surveying. Here I want to circle back to the distinction I suggested earlier between Stein and James, on the one hand, and Pinker, on the other hand, and describe the different kinds of contrast these figures make with the mid-century views that have just been sketched.

Common to James and Stein and to philosophical holists like Wittgenstein and Sellars (here Quine is a complex case) is a wish to undermine what has been called "metaphysical realism." This is roughly the belief that truth is a matter of transparent correspondence to mind-independent things and that, with the proper physics, we could someday give a God's-Eye view of the universe and a final inventory of the Furniture of the World.[46] In James and Stein the urge to undermine this vision derives from the belief that conventionally shaped sentences and narratives can only be a fraudulent formalization of reality's flux. The "inside" they envision is largely chaos. Whatever occurs in experience, it is falsified by the cut-and-driedness of syntax and stories. This is, of course, a familiar idea in literary theory, which over the last several decades has frequently sought to expose textual moments where such falsifications are misleadingly suggested to be part of nature's plan. Teleology equals ideology, or as Stein less aphoristically puts it, "Nothing should follow something because in this way there will come to be a middle and a beginning and an end and of course that does make identity but not the human mind or not the human mind."[47] The starting point for Sellars and Wittgenstein (and here Quine returns to the fold) is that, in practice, human beings do sometimes effectively describe themselves as acting purposefully and do sometimes tell stories that help them flourish as biological, cognitive, and moral creatures. But this faith in our occasional success doesn't mean that they are any more interested than Stein in ranking tables, quarks, and beliefs into some kind of metaphysical hierarchy. When Sellars distinguishes the manifest from the scientific image, we shouldn't ignore the suggestion of *creating* or *making* that is evoked in these uses of *image*. Frameworks are always the products of human discourse, whether they foreground particles and quarks or beliefs and desires. And when we appreciate

---

[46] The term "metaphysical realism" is Hilary Putnam's; see his *Reason, Truth, and History* (Cambridge: Cambridge University Press, 1981).

[47] Gertrude Stein, *Geographical History of America* (1936; Baltimore: Johns Hopkins University Press, 1995), 117.

this metaphysical neutrality, we feel no need to treat concepts, sentences, and narratives—things fashioning "identity," in Stein's broad term—as inherently suspect impositions betraying what is really real. Accordingly, the sense of "person" in Sellars and Wittgenstein is not the kind informing recent anti-postmodern accounts of literary character. They don't begin with elaborate presuppositions about, say, the deep interiority of human beings.[48] But they do emphasize the kinds of languages, concepts, beliefs, and social practices by which we typically try, sometimes successfully, to make sense of the world, especially ourselves and each other. Whether these strategies provide what is really real is only a secondary concern—indeed, perhaps even question-begging: "real" as opposed to what? What matters is whether interpretive strategies are effective at allowing us to explain actions and events coherently and to survive effectively. To do these things, we need no God's-eye view of the physical world and no account of the ultimate structures of reality. But we also need not dismiss science by saying, with Stein, that "naturally science is not interesting." Nor do we have to deny that reference to mental states grants us an enormous amount of explanatory power.

The ontological tightrope walked by Wittgenstein and Sellars leads them likewise away from Pinker and the models of interpretation engendered by his and related forms of internalism. Pinker's cognitivism assumes, as I said earlier, not blooming buzzes of confusion but a degree of primitive order, and in this it can seem to parallel the Wittgensteinian holist. For both, ascribing beliefs, desires, and intentions is the chief thing distinguishing persons from non-persons, a distinctive part of this complicated *Lebensform.* Indeed, the fact that we often do make sense of the world is more or less obvious for both sides. "In order to make a mistake," says Wittgenstein, "a person must already judge in conformity with humanity" (*OC* §156), and this claim is something that Pinker would accept. Faced with the Steinian who finds such confidence unwarranted, each would point not to complex verbal artifacts but to more pedestrian cases of sense-making, cases whose banality underscores their indisputability: try to see a timid face, with powerful fear alive in the features, as being courageous; try to imagine

---

[48] See, for example, James Wood's *The Irresponsible Self: On Laughter and the Novel* (New York: Farrar Straus Giroux, 2004) or Alex Woloch's *The One vs. The Many: Minor Characters and the Space of the Protagonist in the Novel* (Princeton: Princeton University Press, 2003). Wood speaks often of "the human" (Franzen's *The Corrections,* for instance, is said to be most affecting when it "is cleaving to the human"), but nowhere does he offer any defense of his term. Woloch's account of "human interiority" (evident in, say, Austen's Elizabeth Bennett) depends upon a reading of Schiller and Marx that the author similarly avoids scrutinizing in much detail.

streams of water flowing from someone's eyes without recognizing them as tears.[49]

But the coalition between the cognitivist and the Wittgensteinian splinters when we ask about the sources of such understanding. One way of marking the difference is to note that, as Wittgenstein puts it in the sentence just quoted, a person's judging arises from being "in conformity with humanity," a point he reiterates a little later: "The child learns by believing the adult. . . . I learned an enormous amount and accepted it on human authority" (OC §160–61). Understanding timidity and tears, that is, can indeed be effortless, but only in certain contexts, only to someone who has mastered a particular training, and only in the face of potential misunderstanding. Environments, norms, training, and authorities aren't wholly absent in Pinker's account, but they are decidedly relegated to the background. Our judgments are said to conform instead by virtue of the mental modules generating what he calls "the representations underlying thought." And while Pinker hardly represents the whole of cognitive science, this basic way of thinking about thinking has had an enormous influence. Indeed, Pinker's use of the term "underlying" is common whenever cognitivist commentators—and whatever their particular affiliation or school—turn to literary phenomena: "the very skeletal generic space underlying" banal metaphors like "Death finally won," for example, or our habit of interpreting Peter Walsh's tears in *Mrs. Dalloway* "in terms of underlying mental states," or the "underlying mental world" by which we understand Samuel Richardson's characters, or the "underlying mental reality" that Hemingway's narratives make manifest, or the "embodied simulation which underlies our understanding of" actors on stage.[50] "Underlying" is part of the general imagery of "the inside" that

---

[49] The first of these examples is from Wittgenstein, *PI* §536; the second is from Lisa Zunshine, *Why We Read Fiction: Theory of Mind and the Novel* (Columbus: Ohio State University Press, 2006), 13–14. Not all commentators, we should note, have seen cognitivism as being congenitally opposed to postmodernism; see, for instance, Ellen Spolsky, "Darwin and Derrida: Cognitive Literary Theory as a Species of Post-Structuralism," *Poetics Today* 23 (2002): 43–62. It is important, however, that Spolsky can make such a comparison only by making cognitive theory sound more skeptical about knowledge and meaning, more attuned to unstable "gaps," than thinkers such as Pinker and Chomsky typically are.

[50] Mark Turner, *The Literary Mind: The Origins of Thought and Language* (New York: Oxford University Press, 1996), 92; Zunshine, *Why We Read Fiction*, 7, 84; Alan Palmer, *Fictional Minds* (Lincoln: University of Nebraska Press, 2004), 140; Yanna Popova, "'Little Is Left to Tell': Beckett's Theater of Mind, *Ohio Impromptu*, and the New Cognitive Turn in Analyzing Drama," *Style* 38 (2004): 459. For an excellent overview of the overlapping research programs—Cognitive Rhetoric, Cognitive Poetics, Evolutionary Theory, Narratology, Cognitive Materialism—that have emerged under the umbrella of "Literary Cognitivism," see Alan Richardson, "Studies in Literature and Cognition: A Field Map," in *The Work of Fiction: Cognition, Culture, and Complexity,* ed. Richardson and Ellen Spolsky (London: Ashgate, 2004), 1–29.

runs throughout cognitivist criticism, evident when readers speak of the "deep structure of literary representation," the "nested structure of processing strategies" required for "narrative competence," or "the computational substrate upon which domain-specific capabilities" such as story-understanding are built.[51] To specify the organization of such inner domains, some commentators have moreover identified an array of clever internal gadgets: central meaners, general workspaces, auditory rehearsal loops, visuo-spatial sketchpads, mental lexicons, spaces available for conceptual blending.[52]

The Wittgensteinian holist doesn't deny that *some* kind of machinery must be involved in mindedness, let alone that some parts of the body are imperceptible to the naked eye. But she would resist the idea that unseen machinery is where we properly and practically locate full-fledged meaningful action. As Dennett says, summing up the different levels picked out by causal and intentional description: "*I* feel pain; my brain doesn't. *I* see things; my eye doesn't"—to which one should now add, "*I* imagine things, not my visuo-spatial sketchpad" (assuming such a site could ever be identified at all).[53] Saying this is a way of claiming that, while Wittgenstein and Sellars agree that something counts as a mind only insofar as it is ascribed a basically coherent array of intentional states, they're not *realists* about these intentional states in the way that the Pinkerian internalist is. Obviously physical processes take place whenever we mourn a loved one, hope for a strikeout, or listen to stories about such phenomena; these are not supernatural affairs. But mourning, hope, and understanding are not rocket boosters in the head propelling one's body in various directions. There is no reason to think that any *particular* state of the brain, eye, or any other physical item corresponds

---

[51] Joseph Carroll, "The Deep Structure of Literary Representation," in *Literary Darwinism: Evolution, Human Nature, and Literature* (New York: Routledge, 2004), 103–28; David Herman, "Scripts, Sequences, and Stories: Elements of a Postclassical Narratology," *PMLA* 112 (1997): 1053; Michael I. Jordan and Stuart Russell, "Computational Intelligence," in *MIT Encyclopedia of the Cognitive Sciences,* ed. Robert A. Wilson and Frank C. Keil (Cambridge: MIT Press, 1999), lxxvi.

[52] See Patrick Colm Hogan, *Cognitive Science, Literature, and the Arts: A Guide for Humanists* (New York: Routledge, 2003), chap. 2. Hogan draws his terms from a variety of sources, but relies especially on the work of Joseph LeDoux. "Conceptual blending" is an idea primarily associated with Mark Turner.

[53] Daniel C. Dennett, "Philosophy as Naïve Anthropology: Comment on Bennett and Hacker," in Maxwell Bennett et al., *Neuroscience and Philosophy: Brain, Mind, and Language* (New York: Columbia University Press, 2007). Dennett is self-consciously reiterating his 1980 response to John Searle's Chinese Room thought experiment, where he claimed that *he* understands English, not his brain or any of the parts that might be said to "process" incoming sentences. These claims are actually part of his effort to soften the line between attributes ascribed to the personal level and those ascribed to the sub-personal level, and are directed against Peter Hacker's more stringent compartmentalization and interpretation of Wittgenstein. But my (and Dennett's) point here stands.

always with these *particular* intentional states. There are many circumstances in which these attitude might be attributed, many situations that, to repeat Kenneth Burke's phrase, they might "size up." Interpretation, from this point of view, doesn't involve exposing metaphysical groundlessness, but it doesn't involve identifying the right module, either. It is a matter of finding a good way to describe a text and its attitudes, relative to the particular circumstances and contexts we are investigating. If we should be more confident than the Steinian about our ability to make sense of a character's actions or an author's motivations, we should be less confident than the Pinkerian realist that these actions and motivations are describable apart from the wider story of a life, culture, and history.

It is these kinds of wider stories to which the next chapter turns. Bellow's *Henderson the Rain King,* I will be arguing, can be understood as thematizing and formalizing debates about the manifest image, the scientific image, and what is said to lie both inside and outside the perceptible body. The great benefit of turning to Bellow's novel, however, is that it begins to take these debates into regions typically avoided by the philosophers who have developed the concept most explicitly and extensively. The manifest image is, as I'll suggest, the concept that ties "agency" in the sense of knowing to "agency" in the sense of doing—the sense relevant to judgments or evaluations on a broad scale, the substance of one's practical reasoning and practical identity.[54] What I've been describing thus far are the sorts of things that must be in place for an entity to believe that the orange juice is in the fridge, and to act on this belief in some basic way. But such simple beliefs and simple actions are not the only kind that interest us, either as readers or as human beings. And texts such as *Henderson* display the kind of complicated scenarios that, as I noted at the end of my introduction, outdo even the most imaginative and carefully crafted philosophical thought experiment. This doesn't mean that the text explicitly endorses any particular ethical or political theory (utilitarian, deontological, communitarian, and so on). But in taking seriously both embodied persons and their environments, it does begin to make explicit the conceptual space from which such theories could ever be imagined and within which they could ever seem plausible.

---

[54] This isn't to say that the philosophers I have been discussing in this chapter have been silent on the theme of practical reasoning. See, for example, Sellars, *SM,* 175–229. On Wittgenstein's views, see James C. Edwards, *Ethics without Philosophy: Wittgenstein and the Moral Life* (Gainesville: University Press of Florida, 1983); and, for a somewhat different view, Eldridge, *Leading a Human Life,* who questions Edwards at 113–17.

✹ CHAPTER 3

The Prose of Persons

Living in Paris after the Second World War, Saul Bellow occasionally ran into Richard Wright, who had arrived a couple years earlier to the kind of warm welcome the French pay to persecuted foreign writers and intellectuals. Wright was immersing himself in phenomenology under the tutelage of Sartre and de Beauvoir, an immersion that would eventually shape his 1953 novel *The Outsider.* Bellow's interests lay elsewhere, however. "Seeing Wright in Saint-German-des-Prés," he said, "deep in a thick, difficult book, I asked him why this was necessary, and he told me that it was indispensable reading for all writers and that I had better get a copy of my own. I wasn't quite ready for Husserl. As often as possible I went to music halls and the Cirque d'Hiver."[1]

One inference to draw from this anecdote is that, though Bellow's mature work appeared at the very time that Sellars was conceiving the notion of a manifest image and Wittgenstein was, as Sellars says, "isolating it in something like its purest form," we should not be under the illusion that *The Adventures of Augie March* or *Seize the Day* were deliberate responses to Descartes, let alone to any twentieth-century epistemologists.[2] At the same

---

[1] Saul Bellow, *It All Adds Up* (New York: Penguin, 1994), 106.

[2] Bellow refers to Wittgenstein very rarely in his novels and usually only as an uninformative catchword for "important thinker": a minor character in *Humboldt's Gift* (1975; New York: Penguin,

time, however, we shouldn't assume that Bellow's preference for music halls over the *Meditations* captures all the motivations of his fiction. He was far removed from the world of his philosophical contemporaries, but internalist "presences" of the kind I have been describing, with their emphasis on the distinction between visible behavior and the inner processes generating it, were as unavoidable in his milieu as theirs. As the example of Stein suggests, one prominent strand of early twentieth-century art can be understood as making Cartesian demands for radical autonomy into a set of linguistic and aesthetic ideals. Bellow's career began just as the last monuments of Stein's generation—*Finnegans Wake, Doktor Faustus,* the *Pisan Cantos,* the *Four Quartets*—were being erected, and he never hid his distaste for some of his High Modernist predecessors.[3] Not only that, but Bellow was often deeply skeptical about the particular descriptions of autonomy and self-determination endorsed among his literary and cultural contemporaries. As his anecdote about Wright reminds us, the postwar period was the height of American fascination with French existentialism, a time when Sartre's roster of intensely Cartesian themes—the never-ending conflict of Ego and Other, the rejection of social and psychological determination, *"L'homme est ce qu'il se fait"*—found a remarkably receptive audience. These were the early days of the Beats, who popularized the Sartrean longing, described in Norman Mailer's "The White Negro" (1957), "to divorce oneself from society, to exist without roots, to set out on that uncharted journey into the rebellious imperatives of the self," to "open the limits of the possible for oneself, for oneself alone, because that is one's need."[4] The flowers of the sixties counterculture were planted by fifties bohemia, and while it is misleading to caricature Bellow as a "conservative," it is true that he wasn't always sympathetic to these developments, either.[5] It would, of course, be a mistake to believe that all the figures mentioned here, from Joyce and Eliot

---

1984) is said to "want to make a Major Statement like Albert Schweitzer or Arthur Koestler or Wittgenstein" (269) and another character in *The Dean's December* (1982; New York: Penguin, 1998) is said to have "quoted Verlaine or Wittgenstein—in fact he quoted them too much" (121–22). Unsurprisingly, he shows no awareness of more specialized analytic figures like Sellars or Quine.

[3] See Bellow's remarks on Joyce and Eliot in his *Paris Review* interview of 1966, reprinted in *Writers at Work: The Paris Review Interviews,* ed. George Plimpton, 3rd series (New York: Penguin, 1977).

[4] Norman Mailer, *Advertisements for Myself* (1959; Cambridge: Harvard University Press, 1992), 339, 354. For a sense of Sartre's influence on mid-century American thought, see Ann Fulton, *Apostles of Sartre: Existentialism in America, 1945–1963* (Evanston: Northwestern University Press, 1999).

[5] While a novel such as *Mr. Sammler's Planet* (1970) does give voice to a deep skepticism about postwar counterculture, it will also become clear here that other novels—most notably in the current context, *Henderson the Rain King*—frustrate the impulse to pigeonhole Bellow one way or the other, artistically or morally. Indeed, Bellow was quite receptive to some of '50s bohemian life, as his interest

to Sartre and Mailer, would have accepted and appreciated either Stein's work or her self-descriptions. But to one extent or another, they all share with her the sense that the shared literary and moral languages of the previous century had been exhausted. And in such an environment, the kind of radical texts and theories that Stein presents can often seem representative rather than ridiculous.

So although Bellow, on the one hand, and Wittgenstein, Sellars, and Quine, on the other hand, emerge from quite different environments, they are similarly dissatisfied with what they perceive as the over-inflated inward turn that marks their respective surroundings. Turning to Bellow's fiction, however, will allow me to consider the analogy mentioned at the end of the last chapter—namely, the one linking agency in the sense of knowing to agency in the sense of doing. It is not a coincidence that my brief references here to Bellow's immediate literary-cultural context have shifted the discussion somewhat from mind to morals, from words referring to thought and knowledge to ones referring to action and value. For if Bellow's work takes little open interest in modern epistemological questions, it shows a keen awareness of modern practical ones. At the heart of his work—and this is especially true of *Henderson the Rain King,* the 1959 novel I'll be discussing here—is what Chick, the narrator of *Ravelstein,* identifies as "the challenge of modern freedom, or the combination of freedom and isolation which confronts you."[6] It is the challenge, that is, of leading a meaningful life when a person is regarded not as part of an ordered cosmos or *polis* or spiritual order, but as a fully autonomous thinker and doer. As I've argued, when such a condition is cast in epistemological terms, the result, as in Stein, can be a deep distrust of our ordinary language. *Henderson,* the story of an independently wealthy American who garrulously travels through Africa in search of spiritual peace, does something quite different. This isn't to say that the novel fails to acknowledge the power of a Steinian stance, nor to claim that it presents anything like a fully worked out moral theory or catalogue of political principles. But it can be understood, I will be claiming, as situating agency at the level of the embodied persons whom Stein relegates to the background, and in doing so it gives rise to a different set of questions than we encountered in Bellow's expatriate predecessor.

---

in Wilhelm Reich (a topic I'll be addressing later) suggests, and he shares with the Beats and others a powerful distaste for modern bureaucratic and corporate America. For a discussion questioning the caricature of Bellow as a "neoconservative," see Amy Hungerford, *Holocaust of Texts: Genocide, Literature, and Personification* (Chicago: University of Chicago Press, 2003), 146–48.

[6] Saul Bellow, *Ravelstein* (New York: Viking Penguin, 2000), 132.

PLANTATIONS, PERSONS, AND OTHER MATTER

I begin with a thought experiment. Imagine a young agronomist is given the following instructions by his new boss at the Ministry for Agriculture: "Inspect and survey Jones's banana plantation, and report on the operations of the owners." That afternoon he arrives at Jones's plantation and begins recording what he observes. He takes careful note of the soil composition, calculates the average number of bananas per tree, and assesses their median length and width. The trees are set out in neat rows of eighteen or twenty-six, and these, too, the agronomist enumerates fastidiously. After several hours, he approaches a garden that has a dozen thin young orange trees no bigger than an average-sized person, and once again he painstakingly records the arrangement in his notebook. Adjacent to the garden is a house, and, peering through a window, the agronomist sees two living bodies. One is that of a young-looking dark-skinned boy, who is holding a tray and stepping toward the second body, that of an older, light-skinned female seated on a couch. The agronomist dutifully whispers his instructions to himself, and again inspects, surveys, and records the state of affairs before him, identifying (for short) the woman as "A..." and the servant as "the boy." Notebook after notebook is filled, beginning with this:

> To the left, the office door has remained wide open... But the slats of the blind are too sharply slanted to permit what is outside to be seen from the doorway.
>
> It is at a distance of less than a meter only that, in the successive intervals, in parallel bands separated by the wider slider slats of grey wood, the elements of a discontinuous landscape appear: the turned wood balusters, the empty chair, the low table where a full glass stands beside the tray holding the two bottles, and then the top part of the head of black hair, which at this moment turns toward the right, where above the table shows a bare forearm, dark brown in color, and its paler hand holding the ice bucket. "A...'s voice thanks the boy. The brown hand disappears. The shiny metal bucket, immediately frosted over, remains where it has been set on the tray beside the two bottles....

The meticulous care our agronomist takes in diagramming the details of the scene, moving methodically from the half-drawn window blinds to the various bodies in motion, displays precisely the kind of capacities one looks for in a good scientist. So why, when he finishes his two-thousand-page report on Jones's banana plantation, does the Minister rip up his report and fire him immediately?

The answer, of course, is that when the Minister said to inspect, survey, and record the state of affairs at Jones's plantation, she meant only the *relevant* states of affairs—relevant, that is, to bureaucrats at the Ministry of Agriculture. The description of the plantation's trees and gardens was exemplary, but the account of the "operations of the owners" went badly awry, and not just because information about long-term business—crop rotations, harvesting schedules—is more helpful than knowing the activities of a single afternoon. What went most deeply wrong was that the agronomist didn't adopt the proper *stance* when recording the activities. One could easily imagine cases in which the description given of the woman and servant would be entirely apropos—say, as a script for a puppet show. But how the owners care for the plantation, how they estimate harvests, what they plan for the future: determining *these* kinds of things requires drawing upon the full resources of our folk psychology. As it stands, the passage identifies persons only by the motions of certain body parts, which are themselves marked off not by possessive adjectives but by impersonal articles: "the head of black hair" that turns, "a bare forearm" and "its paler hand" bringing the bucket, "the brown hand" that disappears when the work is done. The physicalist motivations of the passage are perhaps most startling in the succinct sentence that reports the woman's response: "A...'s voice thanks the boy." It isn't difficult to describe body hair or even forearms and hands as things in the world, on a par with balustrades and ice buckets. Dropped on a table and deprived of their functions, they may be, as Sellars says, "hair," "forearms," or "hands" in name only, but the sight of such items is at least familiar from haircuts and horror films. It is more unusual, however, to describe voices as free-floating things, especially when they are successfully performing complicated acts such as expressing thanks. What makes the agronomist's description so jarring is simply the reverse of what makes entities like whispering winds and HAL 9000 seem so spooky.

So the young agronomist fails at the Ministry of Agriculture. If, however, he ever published his study of Jones's plantation as a novel, he might have more success—might even be hailed as ground-breaking. Hailing is precisely what Roland Barthes did in a well-known essay on Alain Robbe-Grillet, the former agronomist and statistician who (truth be told) actually wrote the above passage in *La jalousie,* his 1957 novel about French colonials on a banana plantation.[7] For Barthes, such writing represented a rejection of the

---

[7] Alain Robbe-Grillet, *La jalousie* (Paris: Editions de Minuit, 1957), 51–52. For Robbe-Grillet's background in agronomy and statistics, see Ben Stoltzfus, *Alain Robbe-Grillet: Life, Work, and Criticism* (Fredericton, NB, Canada: York Press, 1987), 9.

"traditional novel," which has been "secularly instituted as an experiment in depth"—"social depth with Balzac and Zola, 'psychological' depth with Flaubert, memorial with Proust"—and so has been concerned always with "the degree of man's or society's *inwardness*."[8] Robbe-Grillet, by contrast, pursues a *"littérature objective"* that records "man's direct experience of what really surrounds him without his being able to shield himself with a psychology, a metaphysic, or a psychoanalytic in his combat with the objective world he discovers" (LO 591). What I described as the meticulous attention of the agronomist, Barthes identifies as the "anthological" character of Robbe-Grillet, his practice of "examining without emphasis, favoring no quality at the expense of another" (LO 581–82). Objects in his work, according to Barthes, are absorbed wholly by their "optical natures," their "sheer existence," rather than their human-imposed "function." Just as the humans in the above passage are picked out by the motion of their bodies rather than the ends of their actions, a plate of food would in Robbe-Grillet's books be described not as "so-and-so's dinner," an object with "an alimentary function," but rather as "three thin slices of ham laid across a white plate" (LO 583).

Barthes's assessment of Robbe-Grillet's project was bolstered when Robbe-Grillet himself, responding to his critics in the late 1950s, wrote a series of polemical essays defending his work. The world, he declared, "is neither significant nor absurd. It *is*, quite simply."[9] Accordingly, whereas Balzac had written in a period "that marked the apogee of the individual" and in an age that still believed in the "interventions" of a God-like narrator, the novelist of today must realize that our world "is less sure of itself," and that the cult of the "human" has given way to something "that is less anthropocentric" (*PNR* 28). One symptom of the "anthropological atmosphere" is metaphor. In arguments Paul de Man would later make famous, Robbe-Grillet described metaphor as a "figure that is never innocent," an "anthropomorphic analogy" betraying a "total metaphysical system," one staked on the belief that "there is only one answer to everything: man" (*PNR* 53). Humans humanize the world with "animistic or protective adjectives," thus falsifying and mystifying what should be recognized as "crude reality," the "clear and smooth" objects that are "neither dubiously glittering, nor transparent" (*PNR* 20).

As with my eager agronomist, then, Robbe-Grillet's account of the world ignores the different descriptions under which we routinely place different kinds of entities, in particular the intentional descriptions paradigmatically

---

[8] Roland Barthes, *"Littérature objective Alain Robbe-Grillett,"* Critique 86–87 (July–August 1954), 590–91. Henceforth cited parenthetically by page number as LO.

[9] Alain Robbe-Grillet, *Pour un Nouveau Roman* (Paris: Editions de Minuit, 1963), 18. Henceforth cited as *PNR*.

(though not exclusively) applied to human bodies. He denies not that, as Wittgenstein says, the notion of an inner process gives us the correct use of terms like *remember* (*PI* §305), but more dramatically that terms like *remember* identify anything in the world at all. Indeed, his phrase "clear and smooth" strikingly echoes a contrast Wittgenstein makes between the difficulty of ascribing sensations to a stone and the ease with which we ascribe them to a wriggling fly: pain "seems able to get a foothold" in the latter case, whereas in the former, everything is "so to speak, too smooth for it" (*PI* §284). It is no surprise that in the late 1960s Barthes, Robbe-Grillet's advocate, became famous for claims about the Death of the Author. But as forward-thinking as Barthes considered Robbe-Grillet to be—and five decades after his writing began to appear, it still throws the uninitiated reader off-balance—my association between *La jalousie* and the agronomist's report is meant to suggest that Robbe-Grillet's work is in fact representative of a long-standing tradition. In stripping away the vocabulary of intentions and "significations," and in the accompanying drive, as Barthes says, to "exhaustively interrogate the object, from which all lyric impulses are excluded" (LO 590), Robbe-Grillet betrays the anti-intentionalist assumptions that in the last chapter I associated with Sellars's scientific image. To be sure, the passage quoted from *La jalousie* identifies gross features of reality (women, servants, ice buckets, hair) rather than the "swirl of physical particles, forces, and fields" that, as Sellars says, would stand out for the theoretical physicist. The passage is closer to B. F. Skinner than to Enrico Fermi. And the fact that Robbe-Grillet maintains an interest in the middling features of ordinary human perception is ultimately very telling, as I'll argue later. But for now it is important simply to note that the jarring effects generated by *La jalousie* arise from many of the same ingredients as the theories originating among philosophical reductionists. What counts as *real* in the passage I have quoted are material bodies and their non-intentional properties: size, shape, weight, density. Indeed, not only is it unsurprising to learn of Robbe-Grillet's background in agronomy and statistics, it is also unsurprising to hear the same deflationary swagger that has often characterized reductionists, from the birth of the Scientific Revolution onward.

La jalousie is not, however, the only work of mid-century fiction to show an interest in a more "basic account" of "crude reality." Two years after Robbe-Grillet's novel appeared, the protagonist of Bellow's *Henderson the Rain King,* Eugene Henderson, concludes a discussion of World War II—"The war meant much to me"—with a story that can be understood as rewriting the passage from *La jalousie* quoted earlier:

> Beside my cellar door last winter I was chopping wood for the fire...and a chunk of wood flew up from the block and hit me in

the nose. Owing to the extreme cold I didn't realize what had happened until I saw the blood on my mackinaw. [I]t wasn't broken. I have a lot of protective flesh over it but I carried a bruise there for some time. However as I felt the blow my only thought was *truth*. Does truth come in blows? There's a military idea if ever there was one. (*HRK* 22–23)

Henderson commits himself here to a particularly harsh form of physicalism: reality not only consists of the causally governed arrangement of intentionless objects, but is so brutish that these objects sometimes smack us ruthlessly in the face. Indeed, here and elsewhere, Henderson pledges himself to the scientific image even more explicitly than Robbe-Grillet's narrator. "The world of facts is real, all right," he claims at one point, "and not to be altered. The physical is all there and it belongs to science" (*HRK* 167). And, to a certain extent, Henderson's materialist sense of "the world of facts" is a source of pride in much the same way it is for Robbe-Grillet. This is most evident when he travels to Africa and is confronted with tribal customs that he considers to be ridiculous superstitions. The Arnewi tribe's dread of the frogs occupying their cistern is "pish-posh" (*HRK* 59), and the sacred duties of the Rain King, the title he earns among the Wariri tribe, are carried out with a boyish smirk. But this skepticism in fact appears long before Henderson sets foot in Africa. He chastises his wife Lily for habitually "moralizing" with naïve "ideas of goodness" (*HRK* 150) and for simple-mindedly hoping they can live by a catalogue of sentimental maxims: "One can't live for this but has to live for that; not evil but good; not death but life; not illusion but reality" (*HRK* 16). Like the narrator of *La jalousie,* Henderson never delves too deeply into the particulars of microbiology. But he is, like Robbe-Grillet, a thoroughgoing modern who equates tradition with mythology and who is keenly aware of the explanatory powers of empirical science. He is aware of the dangers of ascribing a "metaphysical system" to the world of "purely physical data," and wary of proclaiming, in Robbe-Grillet's phrase, that "man is everywhere" (*PNR* 48).

Where Henderson would have picked up such a skeptical sensibility is debatable, but it is helpful to recall that his creator, seven years Robbe-Grillet's senior, was trained in sociology and anthropology as both an undergraduate and graduate student.[10] Social scientists may never be accepted uncontroversially by the entire scientific community, but in principle their work consists in

---

[10] On Bellow's training in the social sciences, see James Atlas, *Bellow: A Biography* (New York: Modern Library, 2000), 48–57.

the analysis of causal determinations yielding lawlike conclusions. So Bellow arguably learned from his formal education something like what Robbe-Grillet learned from agronomy and statistics—that, as the latter put it, the "omnipotence of the person" is a problematic notion, and that "personality" is not, as it was for Balzac, "both the means and the end of all exploration" (*PNR* 28).

But here the comparisons between Robbe-Grillet and Bellow come to an end. For even more telling than their shared sense of the disenchanted universe is the attitude their speakers adopt toward this disenchantment. In Robbe-Grillet, the world that is "without signification, without soul, without values" presents to us "a smooth surface"—an apt phrase for our passage from *La jalousie,* with its icy survey of the plantation and house. To Henderson, by contrast, an attention to the "world of facts" entails a keen awareness not only of smooth surfaces, but also of surfaces that are a great deal less than smooth. Truth, recall, comes for him "in blows," and the physical world is chiefly a realm of death, disintegration, and destruction. Reality is, according to Henderson, "horrible" (*HRK* 105), and only because he is "an adorer of life" does he seek to experience this "real" as fully as possible: "I love the old bitch just the way she is and I like to think I am always prepared for the very worst she has to show me" (*HRK* 150). This attitude explains the novel's absorption with the messiest aspects of creaturely existence. The frogs in their "home medium" of the Arnewi cistern sit "with eyes like ripe gooseberries, submerged in their slums of ooze" (*HRK* 107). Statues from Florence and Salzburg have been toppled by the pigs on his farm, where sows "eat their young because they need the phosphorus" (*HRK* 21). A wild cat abandoned by a tenant on his estate once "fought all the barn toms and gave them septic scratches and tore out their eyes" (*HRK* 91). And, most jarringly, on what Henderson calls the "day of tears and madness"—the day that drives him to travel to Africa in search of solace—his maid drops dead unceremoniously in his kitchen: "The eggs were still boiling; they bumped the sides of the pot as eggs will do when the water is seething... Dead! Her small, toothless face, to which I laid my knuckles, was growing cold" (*HRK* 39). "You, too, will die of this pestilence," he concludes: "Death will annihilate you and nothing will remain, and there will be nothing left but junk" (*HRK* 40).

Ooze, dung, septic scratches, pestilence, junk: it is the incessant attention paid to these aspects of reality that distinguishes Henderson from Robbe-Grillet's narrator. Robbe-Grillet's fiction does not, of course, wholly eschew the horrible and brutal. *La jalousie* is punctuated by the image of Franck, A...'s would-be lover, crushing a caterpillar so mercilessly against a wall that

A... herself seems distraught. But the novel's dispassionate narrative voice suggests that these scenes are not to be regarded as disgusting "in themselves" nor Franck's action oddly barbaric. Such judgments, the text implies, are merely subjective and hence groundless reactions to the facts of the matter. For Henderson, the scientific image is a source of pride, but as in Henry Adams (who, he tells us, was an old friend of his father), it is also a cause of worry. If the world, including ourselves, is ultimately just a swirl of physical particles and forces, it is unclear what happens to our traditional descriptions of a human being, most of which are built upon a Quinean "double standard," with its implicit distinctions between intentional and non-intentional, human and junk. With the arrival of the scientific image, such conventional categories, and the *telei* they imply, are liable to seem flimsy, forever reducible to "factual" states devoid of meaning.

The collapse of an interpretive double standard and the corrosive power of the scientific image are themes that haunt all of Bellow's fiction, but one reason for singling out *Henderson* is that, with the frenzied self-searching of its narrator, it gives a particularly vivid catalogue of such breakdowns. As I've noted, Henderson sees little point in endorsing the religious beliefs of the Africans or, for that matter, any other faith; fashioning himself as a child of God is simply unfeasible. For similar reasons, it is important that Henderson, the only significant non-Jewish protagonist in Bellow's oeuvre, is without the strong ethnic identity and rich sense of communal traditions felt by Augie March, Moses Herzog, Artur Sammler, or Charlie Citrine.[11] Henderson is also left without any stable role in—to recall a quite different ancient tradition—the *polis*. In a family of diplomatic and scholarly distinction, he is clearly the black sheep, and he betrays little interest in the kind of honor accorded other, more philanthropic millionaires. Nor has Henderson, unlike the Romantic poet-questers whom he in many ways resembles, used his youth and education as a purposive time of self-discovery and *Bildung*: a Schillerian unity of human nature is far off indeed. In short, many of the most powerful models of human flourishing have collapsed in *Henderson,* and the result is genuine anguish. Henderson's repeated threats to kill himself— "I'm going to blow my brains out!"—have a vaudevillian air about them, but as Bellow himself said to one admirer of the novel, "monster of despair" could serve as *Henderson*'s subtitle.[12] This is worth observing if only because

---

[11] Cf. Bruce Michelson, "The Idea of *Henderson,*" *Twentieth-Century Literature* 27 (1981): 314.

[12] The admirer was Anne Sexton, who recounts her correspondence with Bellow in her 1968 *Paris Review* interview. See *Writers at Work,* ed. George Plimpton, *4th Series* (New York: Penguin, 1977), 410.

commentators have sometimes described the book as a "parody"—a parody of Hemingway, of stoical existentialists, of the "mythic method" advertised by Eliot, of Freudian personality theory.[13] This description isn't false, but it runs the risk of making Bellow into a satirist lording over his clownish characters. At issue for Bellow is less the problems identified by other writers than the solutions they offer. Whereas Robbe-Grillet celebrates the melting away of the "anthropological atmosphere" as a "revolution," *Henderson* begins from the very real difficulty of knowing what to make of human beings once their "functions" have been stripped away. "What should I concentrate on?" Henderson asks Willatale, the wise "Bittah woman" of the Arnewi tribe. "Marriage and happiness? Children and family? Duty? Death? The voice that says *I want?*... So, in short, what's the best way to live?" (*HRK* 81). If the "objective world" in its "sheer existence" makes up "reality," what is to be done? Can accounts of physical measurements, "optical natures," and nerve endings provide any direction to a life?

 ## More Real Because Imaginary

His jesting comments about Wright aside, Bellow was never unfamiliar with the intellectual debates of postwar Paris, and seventeen years after *Henderson* appeared, he made these questions about the scientific image the centerpiece of his Nobel Prize speech. And to formulate his questions, he singled out Robbe-Grillet. Quoting Robbe-Grillet's recommendation for "entities" over "individuals" in modern fiction, he claimed that his French counterpart had followed certain "serious essayists" who view modern art as a necessary reflection of an industrialized society, and who demand, accordingly, that we "purge ourselves of bourgeois anthropomorphism and do the classy thing that our advanced culture requires."[14] But the fact "that the death notice of character has been signed by the serious essayists," rather than (on the whole) novelists themselves, "means only that another group of mummies—certain respectable leaders of the intellectual community—has laid down the law" (NL 91). A proper response to our situation, Bellow continued, would question whether the avant-garde has not lost touch with the way we actually live our lives, and would scrutinize the "marked contempt for the average reader and the bourgeois mass" (NL 94)—and, one might add, our ordinary

---

[13] See Gloria Cronin, "*Henderson the Rain King:* A Parodic Exposé of the Modern Novel," *Arizona Quarterly* 39.3 (1983): 266–76.

[14] "Nobel Lecture," in *It All Adds Up,* 91. Henceforth page numbers are cited parenthetically as NL.

language—that characterizes so many twentieth-century intellectuals. We are reluctant to discuss the "sense of our real powers," he said, because "there is nothing we can prove," and because "few people are willing to risk the embarrassment. They would have to say, 'There is a spirit,' and that is taboo" (NL 97). As part of the individual's struggle "with dehumanization for the possession of his soul," the writer should abandon the obscurantism of a self-declared vanguard, must "come again into the center" of the culture and explore "the essence of our real condition, the complexity, the confusion, the pain of it" (NL 96–97).

As a response to Robbe-Grillet, the "Nobel Lecture" displays Bellow's characteristic sensitivity to intellectual history, but in itself isn't wholly satisfying. For one thing, with its appeal to "powers" and "spirit," it suggests how the theistic undercurrents of Bellow's work, undercurrents that inspired Iris Murdoch to place him among the "mystics" of postwar fiction, had grown more outspoken by the mid-1970s.[15] But this is a secondary issue in the current context. Whatever its place in his later fiction, a specifically religious stance is as difficult to construe in *Henderson* as it is in Sellars or Wittgenstein.[16] A graver problem with the "Nobel Lecture" is the one-sidedness of Bellow's description of Robbe-Grillet—a one-sidedness to which I've also lent credence up to now. For while Bellow's account of Robbe-Grillet's scientism is accurate, Robbe-Grillet does not in fact always evade questions about how to live after the scientific image has disintegrated most of our ordering self-descriptions. In singling out the reductivist ambitions of Robbe-Grillet's fiction, Bellow ignores the fact that his contemporary betrays a second, quite different strain of thought, one strongly committed to an idea of agency, and that the great interest of Robbe-Grillet's work is the way this idea moves in tandem with his intensely materialist impulses.

We can begin articulating Robbe-Grillet's conception of agency by amplifying a point that popped up earlier: the objects under the most intense scrutiny are, and are identified as, human beings. Our passage from *La jalousie* casts its cold eye as much on the window blinds as on any characters, but the dominant interest throughout the novel is the inter-personal relationships,

---

[15] See the title essay in Iris Murdoch's *Existentialists and Mystics: Writings on Philosophy and Literature,* ed. Peter Conradi (New York: Penguin, 1997), 221–34. On Bellow's growing religious sensibility, see Ellen Pifer's *Saul Bellow against the Grain* (Philadelphia: University of Pennsylvania Press, 1990).

[16] This is certainly not to say that commentators haven't tried to construe a religious position in Wittgenstein. On this large topic, see Wittgenstein's *Lectures and Conversations on Aesthetics, Religion, and Religious Belief,* ed. Cyril Barrett (Oxford: Blackwell's, 1970); *Religion and Wittgenstein's Legacy,* ed. D. Z. Phillips et al. (London: Ashgate, 2005).

most particularly those between A... and her would-be lover, Franck. Robbe-Grillet was not forced to do this. Plenty of stories are told about objects that seem to lack a complex web of intentions. Geologists tell tales of rock-formation, astrophysicists spin yarns about planetary rings, and Robbe-Grillet himself, as we have seen, once wrote reports on soil composition. Like most people called novelists, Robbe-Grillet apparently accepts that there may be little of interest in stories about molecules and gravity, as opposed to things within our ordinary, middling range of perception.

But the prohibition on anthropomorphic atmospheres in *La jalousie* breaks down in more far-reaching ways as well. Consider a simple question: who speaks all the words of the novel? As commentators have observed, the pun that goes missing in English translations of the title—*jalousie* can mean either "jealousy" or "venetian blind"—is a signal to the reader that the scenes recorded so meticulously (the conversations of A... and Franck, the men building the bridges, the caterpillar crushed on the wall, and so on) emerge from a particular point of view: the jealous husband of A... who, gazing from behind the blinds, is the unspecified thing not "to be seen from the doorway" in the opening sentence of the passage I quoted earlier. The words presented in the book, that is, come not from a disengaged and neutral perspective. They come instead from a distinctly human one, indeed a most singular point of view, a man on the verge of madness. And this is a point that Robbe-Grillet's essays are not shy about reiterating. Unlike Balzac's books, with their illicitly omniscient narrators, the *nouveau roman* is always told from the point of view of an actual person, someone who is "*always* engaged... in an emotional adventure of the most obsessive kind, to the point of often distorting his vision and of producing imaginings close to delirium" (*PNR* 118). The *nouveau roman* aims "only at total subjectivity," indeed is "the purest expression of human subjectivity that exists" (*PNR* 117–18).

The particular vocabulary shaping these claims about "total subjectivity" derives in large part from Robbe-Grillet's extensive reading in phenomenology, which, thanks to Sartre, had gained considerable renown in postwar intellectual circles, both in and out of the cafés. When, for instance, one of Robbe-Grillet's essays describes the "absolute reality" of imaginary seagulls, seagulls that are "somehow more real *because* they were now imaginary" (*PNR* 139), we are meant to hear echoes of Husserl's efforts to "bracket off" the "objects of consciousness" from the empirical world. And when he ascribes comparable "absolute reality" to "the things that Kafka describes" (*PNR* 141), we are meant to recall Sartrean distinctions between the "transcendence" of consciousness and the mere "facticity" of bodies and social existence.[17] Whatever Husserl or Sartre would have thought of their younger admirer, Robbe-Grillet's understanding of these phenomenological fathers is what allows him to shift from a radically physicalist vision, on the one hand, to one that is, as Husserl himself puts it, "seriously solipsistic" on the other. It allows him, in other words, to subsume a reductivist description of the world under a drastically different one that—Husserl again—gives the transcendental ego "pure existence and pure capacities," that "eliminates as worldly facts from [one's] field of judgment both the reality of the objective world in general and the sciences of the world."[18] "I do not transcribe," announces Robbe-Grillet, "I construct" (*PNR* 139). Reality is not "already entirely constituted" when "the writer arrives on the scene" (*PNR* 137–38), but something brought into existence by his or her perceptions and words. To adapt the title of one critical study of Robbe-Grillet, his narrators are not merely trying to make sense of and cope with their environments, but are actually "inventing the real world."[19]

So what Robbe-Grillet's mid-century essays take with one hand they give with another, and the Quinean double standard is lost from another direction. Whereas one side of his thinking ignores the intentional vocabulary routinely applied to persons, the second side focuses exclusively on the mind's constitution of the world, discounting the material predicates that are typically thought to name mind-independent properties. An object is no longer a *res extensa* devoid of signification, but is itself a product of signification, a mental construction. The artist thus comes to represent the paradigm of the autonomous mind, and Robbe-Grillet's attacks on anthropomorphizing analogies are followed repeatedly by emphatic celebrations of the maker's spontaneous creativity. The true artist, he says, "renounces the used-up formulas and attempts to create his own way of writing" (*PNR* 26). Rejecting "prefabricated schemes people are used to," with "their ready-made idea of reality," he or she "invents quite freely, without a model" (*PNR* 30). Indeed, not only does the artist invent without a model, but—and the Biblical

---

[17] This is not to suggest that Robbe-Grillet was uncritical of Sartre. But his criticisms are usually targeted at Sartre the artist, not Sartre the philosopher—as in, most notably, "Nature, Humanisme, Tragédie," *PNR,* 58–61.

[18] Husserl, "Paris Lectures," in *Phenomenology and Existentialism,* ed. Robert C. Solomon (New York: Harper and Row, 1972), 50, 52. "Seriously solipsistic" appears at 44.

[19] Marjorie H. Hellerstein, *Inventing the Real World: The Art of Alain Robbe-Grillet* (Selinsgrove, PA: Susquehanna University Press, 1998). On Robbe-Grillet's reading of phenomenology, see Hellerstein, *Inventing the Real World,* 10–12; Stoltzfus, *Alain Robbe-Grillet,* 11; Gerald Prince, "The Nouveau Roman," in *A New History of French Literature,* ed. Denis Hollier (Cambridge: Harvard University Press, 1989), 989.

echo here can hardly be inadvertent—"he must create a world," "starting from nothing, from the dust" (*PNR* 42). True art is "self-sufficient," creating "its own equilibrium and its own meaning," and can thus be described as "*the most important thing in the world*" (*PNR* 36). As Barthes himself eventually had to admit, these kinds of claims generate something like "two Robbe-Grillets": one the "*choseiste*" and naturalistic "destroyer of meanings" that Barthes had praised (and Bellow disparaged), the other a "humanist" continually reworking sources, archetypes, and literary traditions.[20]

The pendulum swinging Robbe-Grillet from reductive physicalism to strong internalism is not something we haven't seen already. A similar set of conceptual moves was evident in my earlier discussion of Stein. Stein's work, I argued, is often described as an outgrowth of her interest in science, but the internalism that marks her texts implies something altogether different. This internalism is haunted, I claimed, by the very bodies and environments that it ostensibly rejects, but at least in theory she is committed to an idea of agency that identifies beliefs and desires with a presence located deep "inside." Robbe-Grillet's work retains the full syntax of sentences, and thus manages to represent states of affairs (characters, actions, events) in ways that Stein's work does not. Readers are less plagued by the question of what his strings of words are *about*. But he breaks drastically from other aspects of our ordinary language, in particular, the assumption that the things and states of affairs described in his sentences are things and states that are part of a public world, common and conspicuous enough for the reader to know from his or her own perceptions. What exactly is described in *La jalousie*? Not a world, but a free-standing "consciousness," an "inner" wholly unlike or incommensurate with any other "inner." Which is to say that, when Robbe-Grillet talks of "total subjectivity," when he insists on the absolute reality of imaginary seagulls and the things that Kafka describes, when he implies that *La jalousie*'s descriptions of balustrades and ice buckets should be seen as the "constructions" of a mind rather than "transcriptions" of the world, he is insisting, along with Stein, that our "contact" with other minds can always be only "slight"—that we cannot, as she says, "enter into them." It is not for nothing that Husserl, Robbe-Grillet's philosophical master, drew early inspiration from the introspective psychology of William James, Stein's most important mentor. And it is not for nothing that one critic, writing a few years after the appearance of *L'Année dernière à Marienbad,* Robbe-Grillet's

---

[20] See Barthes's foreword to Morrissette's *The Novels of Alain Robbe-Grillet* (1963; Ithaca: Cornell University Press, 1971).

1961 screenwriting debut, believed that "the possibilities of Gertrude Stein's theories" had at last been realized.[21]

 ## The Case for Being the Sungo: For and Against

Is the best response to a virulently reductive picture of agency a virulently internalist one? We have seen philosophical arguments in chapter 2 to the effect that it is not. As Rorty puts it, Wittgenstein, Sellars, and Quine help to get us "beyond" both empiricism and rationalism—beyond, that is, the misguided hope that knowledge and certainty will be grounded once and for all either in the world or in our head. A similar view, I'll argue, is suggested in *Henderson*. Bellow's "Nobel Lecture," as I noted earlier, fixes on the anti-intentionalist dimension of Robbe-Grillet's modernity at the expense of his equally modern internalism. But part of the power of *Henderson* is the way it avoids this one-sidedness. If, to use Sellars's Aristotelian terms, the mind that thinks and the body that runs are mutually exclusive in Robbe-Grillet's work, *Henderson* suggests that it is the same thing, a person, that does both.

Now, Bellow is a writer of fiction rather than a philosopher, and these problems are played out most importantly in his work at the level of aesthetics—of, that is, his work's style and manner and action. But to set up a discussion of these matters, I want first to consider a series of dialogues and dramas that take place within the story of *Henderson* itself. The internalist conception of agency is voiced in *Henderson* mainly by Dahfu, the Wariri prince with whom Henderson has extended philosophical conversations in the latter half of the book. Dahfu is not the first royal figure that Henderson meets in Africa. He leaves the U.S. accompanied by an old school friend, but quickly sets off on his own in search of a more authentic experience of the continent. Before long his guide Romilayu has taken him to meet the Arnewi, where he meets Itelo, the prince of the tribe, and Willatale, the wise "Bittah" woman. But Dahfu is more central to the book than these other royal figures, and after Henderson disastrously tries to help the Arnewi with their cistern problem—it is full of frogs, and custom prevents them from

[21] Strother B. Purdy, "Gertrude Stein at Marienbad," *PMLA,* 85 (1970): 1096. We might also note in this context that, when Robbe-Grillet came to prominence in the 1950s, he was often discussed in association with Beckett, who was about a decade and a half older and whose kinship with Stein I mentioned in chapter 1. For Robbe-Grillet's understanding of Beckett, see "Samuel Becket ou la presence sur la scène," in *PNR,* 95–107. On the relation of James to Husserl and phenomenology, see James M. Edie, *William James and Phenomenology* (Bloomington: Indiana University Press, 1987).

drinking from it—the book moves Henderson quickly to the Wariri tribe and its heir to the throne. For one thing, Dahfu is critical for Bellow's plot: Henderson would not believably (and believability is, as we'll see, a crucial question in the text) survive in an African tribe without some kind of guide around the community's practices, at least if the book is going to cover less than a couple decades of time and remain under several thousand pages. Dahfu has lived abroad and studied medicine at a university, which effectively spares us from reading pages and pages of Henderson learning how to translate *gavagai* without a dictionary. But Dahfu's deeper importance becomes clear in his philosophical reflections on human "self-making." As he sees it, the state of one's body can be exactly identified with one's mental states, and what we imagine as possibility can be transformed into actuality:

> "The career of our specie," he said, "is evidence that one imagination after another grows literal. Not dreams. Not mere dreams. I say not mere dreams because they have a way of growing actual.... All human accomplishment has this same origin, identically. Imagination is a force of nature. Is it not enough to fill a person full of ecstasy? Imagination, imagination, imagination! It converts to actual. It sustains, it alters, it redeems!... What homo sapiens imagines, he may slowly convert himself to." (*HRK* 271)

The first thing to note about this passage is how Dahfu's remarks about a "force of nature" that "converts to actual" places him squarely within the two-science tradition I identified with Whitehead in chapter 1 and James in chapter 2. On the one hand, Dahfu counts himself a modern naturalist: he criticizes his tribe for "living in the old universe" and describes himself with pride as a "reader of science and sympathy" (*HRK* 271). And it is partly this familiarity with the Sellarsian scientific image that makes Dahfu seem to Henderson worthy of respect; he doesn't seem to Henderson as blatantly "irrational" as the Arnewi living in fear of the frogs occupying their cistern. On the other hand, Dahfu does not draw upon science out of a commitment to materialism per se, but, as Whitehead does with "organic science," in order to legitimate some non-reductivist project. Dahfu's claim that "What homo sapiens imagines, he may convert himself to" no more reflects the basic features of the scientific image than Robbe-Grillet's phenomenological dictum, "I do not transcribe, I construct." When he claims provocatively that "you are in the flesh as your soul is" (*HRK* 268), his choice of words is telling: "soul" is at least as embarrassing to the modern materialist as "spirit," the term Bellow calls "taboo" in his "Nobel Lecture."

Indeed, for all the interest he claims to have in science, Dahfu gives little indication that he finds any of the Wariri traditions far-fetched or preposterous. He just wants to make some of their odd beliefs—the reincarnation of the king's soul into a maggot, the transfiguration of the maggot into a lion, the heir's hunt for the lion—look properly Newtonian.

The sources for Dahfu's two-science visions are not Jamesian-Whiteheadian speculation or Husserlian phenomenology, but post-Freudian psychoanalysis. As commentators have noted, Dahfu's character is likely based upon Wilhelm Reich, the psycho-revolutionary whom Bellow read in the 1950s with great interest, and who magnified to illuminating extremes the Freudian mixture of voluntarism and scientism.[22] Enthralled early on with Freud's technical vocabulary (blocks, cathexes, displacements), Reich in the 1940s and '50s pushed Freud's hypotheses about "sexual energy" to their logical extremes, identifying the physical reality of the libido with so-called "orgone energy," which he saw as *"a visible, measurable and applicable energy of a cosmic nature."* ("Visible": Reich said it was green in color.) In human beings, orgone manifests itself in plasmatic currents and propels them to expressive movement. But in most people this energy is clogged by human muscular structure or "armor," which blocks against "the breakthrough of emotions and organ sensations." Only with orgone therapy—which, by the time of Reich's death in 1957, could happen in specially designed "orgone boxes"—could muscular armor be broken down, plasma re-mobilized, and one's "potency" fulfilled. Challenging Freud's distrust of the instincts, he saw the *vis animalis* as a therapeutic ideal, one epitomized in the "svelte, soft bodies of the girls of the South Seas." Should this ideal be unattainable, he added, another model of "genital character" might serve in its stead: "That which is 'natural' in man, which makes him one with the cosmos, has found its genuine expression in the arts, particularly in music and painting."[23]

---

[22] On Bellow's interest in Reich, see Atlas, *Bellow,* 162–65, 272; Hal Cohen, "A Secret History of the Sexual Revolution: The Repression of Wilhelm Reich," *Lingua Franca* 9.2 (March 1999): 30–31; Eusebio L. Rodrigues, "Reichianism in *Henderson the Rain King,*" *Criticism* 15 (1973): 212–33; Daniel Fuchs, *Saul Bellow: Vision and Revision* (Durham: Duke University Press, 1984), 115–16. Atlas and Fuchs also suggest the influence of Paul Schilder, another post-Freudian analyst prominent in the 1950s.

[23] On the visibility of orgone, see Reich, *Character Analysis,* 3rd ed. (New York: Farrar, Straus and Giroux, 1971), 341. On "armor," see Reich, *Selected Writings: An Introduction to Orgonomy* (New York: Farrar Straus Giroux, 1970), 10. On the South Seas and artists, see Reich, *Character Analysis,* 161. For more on Reich generally, see Philip Rieff, *The Triumph of the Therapeutic* (New York: Harper and Row, 1966), chap. 6; Paul Robinson, *The Freudian Left* (New York: Oxford University Press, 1969), chap. 1. Interest in Reich's work has diminished since his death, but has not gone away entirely: the therapeutic movement known as "bioenergetics" was developed by followers of Reich, and still claims some adherents.

Given such flattery, it is unsurprising that Reich was well-liked and oft-cited among artists of the day.[24] The particular source for Dahfu's ideas, however, is ultimately less important than the role they play in the text, in particular, the way they seem to add a scientific luster to the idea of an "inner" presence. "The spirit of the person," says Dahfu, "is in a sense the author of his body" (*HRK* 238). Or again, in a more seemingly analytic idiom: "Body and face are secretly painted by the spirit of man, working through the cortex and brain ventricles three and four" (*HRK* 268). A *res extensa,* that is, only temporarily takes the form that it does. More powerful than any material body is the presence within that can sustain, alter, and redeem it. What readers have long seen as the most central scenes in the book—the scenes in which Dahfu introduces Henderson to Atti, the lion whom Dahfu visits daily in the den—revolve around the "transformation of human materials" that such an inner spirit purportedly engenders. "I intend to loosen you up," Dahfu tells Henderson, "... because you are so contracted... The tendency of your conscious is to [be] extremely contracted and self-recoiled..." (*HRK* 264). Getting Henderson to roar, breathe, and walk on all fours is an effort to uncoil what Dahfu calls "the flow of vital energies" (*HRK* 268), so that he can rise to "high conduct." Only when Henderson can "be the beast" that lives "within" him, only when he can "snarl greatly" and "feel the lion," will he learn to "experience with deliberate luxury" (*HRK* 260).

From this argument about the determination of outside by inside follows at least one major corollary, and this is the conflation of metaphoric and literal that Dahfu's theories imply. "Now look, Mr. Henderson," says Dahfu at the beginning of their tutoring with Atti, "I wish you to picture that you are a lion. A literal lion" (*HRK* 267). This demand is particularly important when we recall "the disturbance" that drives Henderson to Africa, the "voice that spoke there and said *I want, I want, I want!* It happened every afternoon, and when I tried to suppress it it got even stronger. It only said one thing, *I want, I want!*" (*HRK* 24). Henderson presents this voice as a quasi-independent being, an *it* with its own set of beliefs and desires that have never found adequate expression in the material world. The great attraction of, in Dahfu's terms, an "imagination" that converts to "actual" is that the ontology identified by this *it,* the riot of fantasy and longing that it expresses, might

---

[24] See Cohen, "A Secret History," 30–31, for a summary of Reich's influence on Mailer, Ginsburg, Burroughs, Bowles, and others. One might note, too, that Reichian meditations (ironized) float through the mind of Moses Herzog as well: "The erotic must be admitted its rightful place, at last, in an emancipated society which understands the relation of sexual repression to sickness, war, property, money, totalitarianism. Why, to get laid is actually socially constructive and useful, an act of citizenship." See *Herzog* (New York: Viking, 1964), 166.

replace the ontology embedded in Henderson's ordinary language. Our past accounts of ourselves and the world might be overcome by an entirely new store of sentences and stories. In endorsing this picture of "imagination" becoming "actual," Dahfu is, once again, only updating a common way of speaking in his tribe. When appointed Rain King (or Sungo) of the Wariri tribe, Henderson sees himself, following a long line of secular anthropologists "explaining" African religious practices, "dressed up as the Rain King" (*HRK* 211). As Dahfu makes clear, however, the Rain King garb does not make Henderson merely *like* the Rain King, some figurative image of a holy being. "It is not merely dress," he tells Henderson. "You are the Sungo. It is literal, Mr. Henderson" (*HRK* 211). For Robbe-Grillet in his phenomenological moments, the gull in his mind's eye could be "more real" than the one seen with his actual eye, just as, for the Freudian Reich, art could reveal a psychic reality deeper than mere physical appearances. Similarly, for Dahfu, "becoming a lion" or the Sungo entails more than an inventive way of speaking. One is transformed; we commit ourselves to the ontology of religious and spiritual entities as readily as we commit ourselves to spatiotemporal ones.

Dahfu clearly sees Henderson as a fellow traveler—a "companion mind," he calls him after their first day in the lion's den (*HRK* 271). And Henderson, too, is clearly attracted to Dahfu's visions. He is "swayed," "thrilled" by Dahfu's "genius," his promise of a "nobility" that seems not only unassailable by modern science, but actually grounded upon it. And not without reason. For the same reason that Bellow himself likely found in Reich (at least initially) a liberation from WASPish postwar social and sexual convention, Henderson finds in Dahfu's theories an affirmation of human power, assurance that human beings are in some mysterious way more than "junk." Dahfu upholds Henderson's hope that "Becomers" can be "Be-ers," and that these "Be-ers" are potentially forms of life only dimly imagined in the past. As Marcus Klein once noted in discussing the Nietzschean dimension of *Henderson,* the "exercise of personality is everywhere in Bellow's world an act of courage," especially when his heroes start out from "a position of individuality imperiled."

Yet as Klein also noted, "the rocks upon which simple exulting personality would founder" were also discovered from the start of Bellow's career.[25] While Mailer—not only the arch-Hipster, but also the arch-Reichian—could see in Dahfu "a profoundly sophisticated man with a deep acceptance of magic, an intellectual who believes that civilization can be saved only by a

---

[25] Marcus Klein, *After Alienation: American Novels in Mid-Century* (New York: World Publishing, 1964), 220, 218, 220.

voyage back to the primitive," a figure through whom "Bellow succeeds in telling us more about the black man's psyche than either Baldwin or Ellison,"[26] Henderson himself ultimately has grave misgivings. First and most generally, Henderson clearly comes to lose whatever faith he may have had in Dahfu's mind-body theories. Whereas Dahfu sees science buttressing his vitalistic vision of the inner transforming "human material," Henderson admits that, after going to the lion's den with Dahfu, he "didn't have full confidence in the king's science":

> Down there in the den, while I went through the utmost hell, he would idle around, calm, easy, and almost languid . . . Sometimes as we lay on the trestle after my exercises, all three of us together, he would say, "It is very restful here. Why, I am floating. You must give yourself a chance. You must try . . ." But I had almost blacked out, before, and I was not prepared to start floating. (*HRK* 273)

This unwillingness to "start floating" is emblematic of Henderson's consistently materialist stance, his awareness that, to recall his remark, "the physical is all there and it belongs to science." "True, inside," he says after several visits to the den, "my heart ran with human feeling, but externally, in the rind if you like, I showed all the strange abuses and malformations of a lifetime" (*HRK* 273). Even when deep in his performance of the lion, the "human longing" he feels through "the hot noise" of his roaring (*HRK* 267) never lapses. He must always "long" to transform his body into a lion's in a way that a lion itself never needs to do. In the end, Henderson has to conclude that Dahfu's "enthusiasms and visions swept him far out" (*HRK* 235).

The most conspicuous evidence of Dahfu's being swept away comes in his death. In accordance with the tribal custom, Dahfu goes out to capture his father, the old king Gmilo, now allegedly (according to custom, once again) in the form of a lion. But as with the Arnewi who refuse to touch the frogs or—Henderson's comparison—the Jews who refuse to fight on the Sabbath, the adherence to certain scientifically groundless beliefs jeopardizes the very survival of the believer. The lion in the scene is violent and uncontrollable, and in Henderson's eyes is absolutely "real":

> I then tried to tell myself because of the clearness of those enraged eyes that only visions ever got to be so hyperactual. But it was no

---

[26] Norman Mailer, *Cannibals and Christians* (New York: Dell, 1966), 127. "Wilhelm Reich as a mind" is classified under "Hip" in "The Hip and the Square," *Advertisements for Myself*, 424. ("Wilhelm Reich as a stylist" falls under "Square.")

vision. The snarling of this animal was indeed the voice of death. And
I thought how I had boasted to my dear Lily how I loved reality. "I love
it more than you do," I had said. But oh, unreality! Unreality, unreality!
That has been my scheme for a troubled eternal life. But now I was
blasted away from this practice by the throat of the lion. His voice was
like a blow at the back of my head. (*HRK* 307)

The "blow" here can be read as cousin to the "blow" Henderson receives
when chopping wood, and it suggests how the brute force of this non-
intentional matter represents a more robust "reality" than any of the inner
spirits and vital energies that Dahfu tries to conjure. The passage exposes
how Dahfu in his den ignores what Henderson calls the untameable, "more
cruel aspect of the lion" (*HRK* 316). He overlooks that Atti is a *pet* lion, a
domesticated creature who, compared to the raging lion in the field, was "no
bigger than a lynx" (*HRK* 307). Dahfu, that is, studies only one side of the
lion's nature—its elegant manners, its poise, its self-assured strength—and
succumbs to the fatal fault Philip Rieff once ascribed to Reich: he overlooks "the cruel imbecilities of nature."[27] Death in Henderson's account of
the lion attack is an event difficult to redescribe, and the "force of nature"
represented by the lion is far more consequential than the "force of nature"
that Dahfu attributes to the spiritual presence painting the face and body.
Next to the quite undeniable, and quite alarming, causal powers of the
blood-thirsty lion, the powers of the imagination look suspiciously like
mere human projections. One could perhaps try to go a step further here
and appeal, as Dahfu himself does, to the concept of immortality, and suggest that death to the materialist is a kind of birth for the non-materialist,
the final casting aside of our embodied form in favor of another. But this
description is bound to seem merely poetic and quaint for someone as committed to the scientific image as Henderson, for whom Dahfu is simply
neglecting the natural imbecilities that are difficult for the modern mind to
out-imagine—say, the bacteria that will eat up one's body upon death. The
mind and its purposes do not reside in an inner ether, but are exhibited in
the worldly acts of specific embodied persons. And as we learn when we
acquire the vocabulary of physical objects, these embodied persons are forever subject to a world of causes.

The intuition that Dahfu's theories "swept him far out" from the condition of embodied persons ultimately compels Henderson to question the
understanding of metaphor that I identified above as a corollary to Dahfu's

---

[27] Rieff, *Triumph,* 159.

position. Henderson's wariness is most noticeable near the end of the book. He and his guide Romilayu are imprisoned with a tiny lion cub by a group of priests who, after the death of Dahfu, seek power in the tribe. As the two of them make their escape, Henderson addresses the cub as the Wariri would, as the embodiment of the next king, a form ultimately of Dahfu himself: "Goodbye, King." But he immediately reverses himself. Not only does he decide to bring the cub along, but he also, most significantly, de-poeticizes his description: "This animal is coming with us" (*HRK* 325). This shift from "King" to "this animal" is echoed when, on the plane back to New York, Henderson describes the cub to a flight attendant not as his friend, or even "an enigmatic form of that friend," but as something altogether more attenuated: "a souvenir of a friend" (*HRK* 333). Moments later an analogous linguistic shift is played out even more explicitly, as Henderson looks out the plane's window at "these upside-down sierras of the clouds": "Like courts of eternal heaven. (Only they aren't eternal, that's the whole thing; they are seen once and never seen again, being figures and not abiding realities; Dahfu will never be seen again, and presently I will never be seen again; but everyone is given the components to see.)" (*HRK* 333). The distinction here between "figures" and "abiding realities," and the passive voice of the final clause—"everyone is given"—registers Henderson's distrust of Dahfu's world-making theories of metaphor, and more generally toward the claim that "a man is really the artist of himself" (*HRK* 268).

 ## THE PROSE OF PERSONS

My reading of *Henderson the Rain King* here has treated it as a kind of philosophical dialogue, with Dahfu representing the temptation-voice of vitalistic internalism and Henderson that of Montaignian skepticism, self-conscious but wary of self-celebration. If "dialogic" means various voices engaged in a moral or metaphysical argument, then Bellow's book would surely qualify, and it is hard to deny Bellow's reverence for and similarities to Dostoevsky, the figure most commonly associated with the term "polyphony."[28] In the end, however, emphasizing the different positions in *Henderson* makes the book more schematic than it actually is. Bellow's books percolate with arguments and reasoning, but they are not dialectical exercises. They are instead

---

[28] On Bellow's relation to Dostoevsky, see Fuchs, *Saul Bellow*, chap. 2. The long-standing dichotomy between the "monological" Tolstoy and "dialogic" Dostoevsky has been questioned by various Bakhtinian scholars, and the latter's dialogic virtues have as a result come to seem less paradigmatic. But I ignore this debate here as secondary.

what we normally think of as narratives, especially those expansive narratives we call novels. "Every time I worked on my thesis," Bellow once said in explaining why he dropped out of graduate school, "it turned out to be a story."[29] Asking why Bellow rejected theses in favor of stories, and what kind of stories he took to writing, will allow me not only to fill out the contrast I've been tracking in this chapter between him and Robbe-Grillet. In the process it will also provide a fitting way to tie together many of the claims that have been made over the course of part I generally.

The matter is particularly interesting in the case of *Henderson the Rain King,* a book readers have long seen as the most adventurous in Bellow's oeuvre—"a screwball book," as Philip Roth says, "a stunt of a book, but a sincere stunt."[30] At the level of the sentence, Bellow is as free-wheeling and unconstrained as he is in *The Adventures of Augie March,* his breakthrough novel published six years earlier. And the passages I have quoted are enough to suggest how the chaos of Henderson's mind bestows a manic touch to the fusion of vernacular and high-brow that critics always note when describing Bellow's prose. Even more obviously screwball is the ontological level of the text, the kinds of entities it treats as real or fictive. Clearly the most daring aspect in this regard is the way the scenes with Dahfu pressure the assumptions of scientific materialism. If Bellow has always had affinities with the Romantic tradition (Moses Herzog is, recall, a scholar of Romanticism), they are nowhere more evident than *Henderson.* In *Moby-Dick,* we are led to believe that the "spirit spouts" just *might* exist alongside the real ones; in *The Scarlet Letter,* the letter "A" just *might* have appeared in the night sky before Dimmesdale; and in *Henderson,* Dahfu's vitalistic visions look sometimes like they *might* turn out to be true. Contextualizing Bellow forwards rather than backwards, an analogous description would say his book provides an early glimpse of Postmodernism—its giddiness a rejection of plaintive Eliotic Modernism, its glimpses of irrealism an anticipation of Thomas Pynchon and Steven Millhauser. No less an experimentalist than John Hawkes has called *Henderson* "Bellow's finest work," and some readers have seen Henderson himself as a character worthy of John Barth.[31] Seen in these terms, *Henderson* might be said to answer Robbe-Grillet's call for a text that

---

[29] *Conversations With Saul Bellow,* ed. Gloria L. Cronin and Ben Siegel (Jackson: University Press of Mississippi, 1994), 4.

[30] Philip Roth, "Re-Reading Saul Bellow," *New Yorker,* October 9, 2000, 86.

[31] Hawkes's assessment is from *The Contemporary Writer: Interviews With Sixteen Novelists and Poets,* ed. L. S. Dembo and Cyrena N. Pondrom (Madison: University of Wisconsin Press, 1972), 9. On Barth and Bellow, see Beverly Gross, "The Anti-Novels of John Barth," in *Critical Essays on John Barth,* ed. Joseph J. Waldmeir (Boston: G. K. Hall, 1980), 30–31.

resolutely "renounces used-up formulas" and "prefabricated schemes," that "invents quite freely, without a model."

Such descriptions, however, forget Bellow's frequently expressed admiration for Dreiser and (Robbe-Grillet's elected nemesis) Balzac, and overlook just how and where the funhouse experiments of *Henderson* come to an end. Henderson's inability to forget what he is like "externally, in the rind" is enacted in the text's basic commitment to the inherited grammar and ontology of our ordinary language. Unlike Stein, Bellow never decomposes sentences into strings of words, and never implies, unlike Robbe-Grillet, that most of the things identified by his sentences are the constructions of a single mind. As a result, Dahfu's theories never stop seeming fantastical, and the supernatural spirits of the African tribes are ultimately presented as nothing more than superstitions. Earthly facts of a disenchanted world—the world in which, as Sellars puts it, the wind "does" things only in a poetic sense—have long been the bread and butter of the novel as a genre, and this is a tradition that Bellow has embraced. Using a fabulist like Dahfu as narrator is a strategy that Bellow never attempted to carry out. Even his most deeply introspective novels (*Herzog,* say) rely upon some potential gap between the way one person perceives and describes the public world and the way that world really is. And within this shared vocabulary, there is as little room for assertions about Rain Kings as there is for the kind of assertions that fill most fantasy and science fiction. *This man can make rain fall from the sky* is not a sentence we would know how to fit into our web of beliefs any more than, to take a Lockean-flavored case made famous by Derek Parfit, *My two brothers both became me after receiving half of my transplanted brain.* The latter sentence flaunts the inferences usually made between concepts like hemispherectomy, neural severing, physical disability, and mental malfunctioning, just as the former sentence doesn't cohere with what we would ordinarily say about things like weather fronts and gulf streams.[32] Endorsing certain beliefs about gravity makes it harder to endorse other beliefs about human beings floating. By the same token, *Henderson* describes no dramatic revolution in consciousness that would require its own Uncaused Cause. Not only is Dahfu never said to transform into a lion, but Henderson never undergoes any decisive spiritual transformation. An effusive letter of reconciliation to Lily is written

---

[32] The brain-transplanting brothers are described by Parfit in *Reasons and Persons* (Oxford: Oxford University Press, 1984), 254–61. In citing this case, I mean to endorse Quine's criticism of thought experiments (quoted by Parfit, 200) that imply that our words and sentences have logical force beyond the past uses to which they have been put. For a brief Wittgensteinian criticism of Parfit precisely along these lines, see Grant Gillett, "Brain Bisection and Personal Identity," *Mind* 95 (1986): 224–29.

when he is drunk, part of it is lost by Romilayu in transit, and, as Roth puts it, Henderson winds up on the final page a happy man—"where?"—in the Arctic.[33] In short, Bellow's stylistic and narrative choices resist Robbe-Grillet's claim that sentences and stories could be intelligibly written "freely, without a model," with no relation whatsoever to any previous sentences and stories applied to ourselves and the world. Indeed, Dahfu himself might be considered a kind of emissary sent from Robbe-Grillet's theoretical essays into Bellow's fictional world, a foreign ambassador arriving to promote visions that, to recall Robbe-Grillet's remarks about the *nouveau romancier,* begin "from nothing, from the dust."

There are reasons, then, that Bellow is frequently characterized as a "realist." As we saw in chapter 2, however, "realism" is a notoriously murky term. Realism of the kind that claims physics will someday provide a final description of the universe has been the target of various sorts of attack over the last few decades. Whether or not such attacks are pertinent to Balzac or Dreiser, there is little reason to think that this realism is the kind that informs *Henderson the Rain King.* The laws of gravity are acknowledged in *Henderson,* but there is little evidence that Bellow aspires to what Rorty has ironically called "Nature's Own Language." Nor is there much evidence to suggest that the realism of Bellow's work is due to his having identified a set of universal narratives generated by the underlying, common, and innate features of the human mind. *Henderson* is, after all, as much about the *fragility* and *fracturing* of stories as it is about their coherence. Narrative self-descriptions are continually threatened by the loss of the cultural norms that would give them whatever sense and force they have. As in Wittgenstein and Sellars, the "realism" of Bellow's novel emerges, instead, from his careful attention to the habits of our folk psychology and our folk physics. Its interest is with the kinds of languages, concepts, beliefs, and social practices by which we moderns typically, if also provisionally, make sense of the world, including most especially ourselves and each other. For all of Henderson's respect for science, Bellow's concern is, as Michael André Bernstein puts it, "not with deducing a universally valid formula" of any kind, and it is "always the charlatans and self-deceivers who pride themselves on having discovered the unique code, law, or pattern that supposedly governs the multiplicity and heterogeneity of human

---

[33] Philip Roth, *Reading Myself and Others* (New York: Farrar Straus Giroux, 1975), 133. "Transformation" is a word used in by Pifer in *Saul Bellow against the Grain,* chap. 6, which is a good example of a reader underestimating the complexities of the book. A similar overly optimistic response might be noted in Rodrigues, who claims the story shows how Henderson's psyche and plasma are now free of armor plates.

existence."[34] Hence the variety of destabilizing features found throughout Bellow's work: his complex use of free indirect discourse, his elegiac retrospections, his penchant for the picaresque. The result is a fine line: a fiction that is sensitive to the brittleness of human forms, yet a faith all the same that such forms are more than well-wrought self-delusions.

A negative way of unpacking this characterization would be to continue my contrast with Robbe-Grillet. After all, it is precisely *La jalousie*'s disruption of our ordinary language, both in its physicalist and phenomenological moments, that makes it so striking. But it is also what makes Robbe-Grillet's narrators unequivocally insane, as he himself admits. All his narrators are, to recall his description, "*always* engaged... in an emotional adventure of the most obsessive kind, to the point of often distorting his vision and of producing imaginings close to delirium" (*PNR* 118). So it is not surprising that, just as Michael Gold compared Stein's work to the "monotonous gibberings of paranoiacs in the private wards of asylums," critics have diagnosed Robbe-Grillet's speakers as sado-masochistic, obsessional, schizoid, with "no particular ties, no long-term purpose, no specific beliefs," "outside the concrete forms of his society, and at the same time, outside concrete history."[35] Such personalities are understandably important for an author who so aggressively endorses and dramatizes a version of internal disembodied presences. Any suggestion that two minds share a common world can only be made in bad faith. Weary with all "prefabricated schemes people are used to," Robbe-Grillet requires an extraordinary personality to act as his speaker, one who is profoundly detached from the norms of his or her inherited language.

From the perspective that I've attributed to Sellars, Wittgenstein, and now Bellow, it is not self-evident why such a personality should be the only one able to tell us about what is really real. One may of course balk at the clinical descriptions given of Robbe-Grillet's narrators and regard judgments like "sado-masochistic" or "schizoid" as a mere disciplinary effect of modern power. But presumably, as I said at the beginning of my discussion of Stein, nobody would deny that these narrators are in *some* way unusual or, analogously, that uninitiated readers will find the novels to be in *some* way jarringly strange. To assent to this claim is merely to say that our habits of intentional

[34] Michael André Bernstein, "Saul Bellow: Essayism, Allegory, and the Realistic Novel," *Salmagundi* 106–7 (1995): 90–91.

[35] John J. Clayton, "Alain Robbe-Grillet: The Aesthetics of Sado-Masochism," *Massachusetts Review* 18 (1977): 106–19; Didier Anzieu, "Le Discours de l'obsessional dans les romans de Robbe-Grillet," *Les Temps Modernes* 21 (1965): 608–37; Zevedi Barbu, "'Choseisme': A Socio-Psychological Interpretation," *Archives Européennes de Sociologie* 4 (1963): 137–38.

attribution are not used to dealing with the kind of unfamiliar personalities and language that Robbe-Grillet gives us. If we *did* encounter Robbe-Grillet's language everyday, if our folk psychology *were* well-equipped to cope with it, then the novels would not strike us as so peculiarly experimental. But, so Bellow and his philosophical contemporaries might point out, it is a long leap from this uncontroversial observation to the claim that Robbe-Grillet's stories reveal something definitive and universal about us as human beings, or that they arose from some historical and philosophical necessity. Indeed, the same could be said, *mutatis mutandis,* about any other picture of the mind that privileges madness, the endless indeterminacy of meaning, or the deep meaninglessness of the world as *the* central explanatory concept for understanding behavior. Explicit in the arguments of Sellars and Wittgenstein, and implicit in the fiction of Bellow, is the belief that such claims presuppose a vast background of understanding without which we—including the "we" reading these sentences now—would be unable even to *recognize* something's being indeterminate, misperceived, or unpredictable. To some readers, Robbe-Grillet's texts are bound to seem at best merely a bunch of idiosyncratic fantasies, self-important avant-garde ramblings. At worst they might even seem to be totalitarian ravings, an arrogant set of claims about the human invention of reality.[36]

The sort of aesthetic and philosophical stance that I have been associating with the manifest image over the last couple chapters remains largely agnostic about the ontological status of both material objects and mental states. It keeps in view both how we manage to make sense of ourselves and the world, as well as how this sense can grow tenuous and frail, how what we call a "human being" might suddenly seem better described as "junk." And it is this attention to such sense-making practices that leads Bellow to eschew the idea of agents as atomistic, self-constituting loci of thought and will, entities that are ready, in Henderson's description of Dahfu, to "float away." This is suggested in at least a couple different ways. For one thing, Bellow's novels rarely involve the kind of dramatic disconnection and incoherence—inexplicable time shifts, arbitrary connections, fragmented plot lines, obsessive repetitions—that we see in the work not only of Robbe-Grillet, but before him Stein, with her commitment to the "continuous present." As I've suggested, Bellow's novels focus on characters thrust precariously back on their own devices, without a foreordained or "innate" teleology. But they are also aware that human flourishing, indeed simple survival, depends upon how these characters overcome such local dislocations and build their lives into some kind of

---

[36] Clayton draws this conclusion in "Alain Robbe-Grillet," 116.

more or less coherent unity. When strange things occur, when unexpected happenings happen, Bellow's characters try to understand them by weaving them into the ongoing story of their lives as a whole. And "whole" here means the whole of a lifetime, or part of a lifetime, not just a few minutes or hours. So it is appropriate that Bellow's narratives typically occupy not just a few unusually intense hours or days, but months or even years. Again, systematic or universal teleologies are unavailable here. Sense in Bellow's novels is a fragile achievement, something that can be lost—lost not just after some damage has occurred to the brain or body, but also when our culture no longer has an established set of scripts, when we no longer know where to place ourselves in a larger narrative. But the impossibility of final systems does not mean that we are left drowning in the sheer flux of, in Stein's phrase, "living as we are now living as we have it and now do live in it" (*LA* 104). It simply means any given *telos* is fallible, that no way of joining a past, present, and future "I" is certain, and that maintaining a roughly unified identity over time requires *phronesis,* a know-how that is sensitive to particular situations. One could argue that the final chapters of *Henderson the Rain King,* in which Henderson successfully improvises an escape from the Wariri tribe, exhibit the rough-and-ready kind of practical reasoning that becomes necessary in lieu of larger, overarching structures of belief. I've suggested that "transformation" is too strong a term to describe Henderson's story, but "regeneration," with its connotations of reviving and renewing materials that are previously given, seems altogether appropriate.

Let's call this the temporal dimension of Bellow's fiction, the suggestion that one's practical identity is closely tied to the development of a body's behavior understood over time. More than that, however, I am not the only one able to give such an account of my life. For just as a description of a person as a collection of molecules will not help us understand his or her actions, it would also be impossible to make sense of them if we pictured persons as utterly self-standing egos. This is the intersubjective dimension of Bellow's work. One of the most important contexts within which we ascribe folk-psychological predicates to persons is the context of a personal history—which, since it is difficult to tell a story with just one character, includes a person's relation to a family and community and species. As Dennett puts it, when you address me, you are addressing not just the entity *I* have constituted, but also what over the years has been constituted by my parents and siblings and friends, among others.[37] Addressing me in this way

---

[37] Daniel C. Dennett, *Consciousness Explained* (Boston: Back Bay Books, 1991), 429.

is certainly not addressing something as fixed and firm as a Cartesian ego. But if our commitment to these loosely interlocked interpersonal ascriptions were to break down completely, whether forgotten or rejected, an agent might begin to seem to us curiously empty, as with *La jalousie,* or perhaps wildly self-deceptive, as in the case of Dahfu, fatally "swept far out" by "enthusiasms and visions." More generously understood, such an agent might appear to us as a prophet, supernatural figure, or god. The line between these different interpretations is thin. But the instructive point in each case is the same. If the stability and usefulness of our folk psychology depend upon the web of beliefs we accrue and revise over the course of a life, surely some of the most stable and least-easily-revised beliefs would be those that say persons act in ways typical of other mortal, non-omniscient, non-soothsaying persons. Anything that countermanded these truisms would be on the verge of something we do not currently refer to as an earthly agent. If, despite the anti-intentionalist, we really *do* ascribe beliefs and intentions to entities around us, it is also true that these beliefs and intentions are those befitting a fragile, dependent, finite, embodied creature embedded in the history of a particular species, environment, culture, and language.

One final point will allow me to conclude my description of Bellow's distance from the tradition of internal presences, and that concerns the kinds of characters that his stance leads him to describe. Unlike a great many post-Romantic writers, including Robbe-Grillet, Bellow's work consistently shuns not only the psychotic and the deity, but the artist as well. His protagonists are not characterized first and foremost as having a uniquely creative inner life that allows them to withdraw from or transcend their time and place. They are active participants in an intersubjective world. To be sure, Babbitts earn little sympathy in his fiction, and his main characters are often brilliantly inventive minds. To recall one Dubliner's assessment of Leopold Bloom, another hero of the ordinary, there is "a touch of the artist" about most of Bellow's protagonists.[38] As also with Bloom, however, this "touch" is never directly from the hand of God. Artists who, like Robbe-Grillet, "construct" when others merely "transcribe," who seek, like Dahfu, to "sustain" and "redeem," are rarely the focus. More rarely still do they receive our complete sympathy. For all their inventiveness, Bellow's characters are not poets or prophets or madmen, but biographers and historians and scholars who reject the palaces of art in favor of contemporary events and historical developments. That these characters remain the focus throughout his work

---

[38] James Joyce, *Ulysses,* ed. Hans Walter Gabler (1922; New York: Penguin, 1986), 193.

contributes to Bellow's writing loose, baggy monsters rather than refined post-Flaubertian gems. This habit has perhaps cost him a certain amount of attention among some academic readers, who often prefer to put their specialized training to use on more densely allusive texts. But for whatever biographical reason—his being the grandson of a rabbi, his training in the social sciences, his resistance to the highbrow world of the East Coast literary establishment—Bellow always resists venerating or divinizing the poet-maker. When Abe Ravelstein complains that Chick, his novelist friend and biographer-to-be, has absorbed the infantalizing modern obsession with "distinctness of observation," and when he says that Chick forgets that the life of the *polis* rather than the self "had first claim on our attention," Chick's laconic response says much about Bellow's own aesthetic project: "His severity did me good."[39]

I have taken the liberty in these last few pages to use the pronouns *we* and *us,* and this is not entirely accidental. For just as in the debates between Dahfu and Henderson, what is at issue in Bellow's work are not only questions about the role art actually plays in our thinking, but also practical questions about how to conceive of agency generally. Is art the making of worlds, starting, in Robbe-Grillet's words, from the dust? Is it true, as Dahfu has it, that one is really the artist of oneself? In his thorough-going materialist vocabulary, in his attention to our folk psychology, in his choice of characters, Bellow ultimately suggests that the answer should be no. He answers this way not out of some puritanical or Platonic hostility; he is, just like Robbe-Grillet, a novelist himself, and his negative answer is always qualified. In his hands, however, art becomes less a celebration of the artist's singularity and genius than a sensitive display of the common words and practices that, as Henderson says while looking out the window of the plane sailing fantastically above the clouds, "everyone is given the components to see." And in doing so, Bellow points the way toward a substantially different picture of an agent than that given to us by figures such as Stein and Robbe-Grillet: one creative yet dependent upon the histories in which it is embedded; one inventive yet grateful for the words given to us. Foregrounding finitude, Bellow begins to clear space for mutuality. Setting limits to the prophet, to the poet, to the inner presence, he begins to make room for solidarity.

---

[39] Bellow, *Ravelstein,* 97–98. For a good assessment of this anti-aesthetic aspect of Bellow's protagonists, see Fuchs, *Saul Bellow,* chap. 1.

PART II

Agents Without

CHAPTER 4

Selves, Sentences, and the
Styles of Holism

How does one become "avant-garde"? The
term migrated from the military to the cultural arena with Saint-Simon in
the nineteenth century, but a classic image for it was given by Wassily Kandinsky at the start of the twentieth:

> The life of the spirit may be fairly represented in diagram as a large
> acute-angled triangle divided horizontally into unequal parts with the
> narrowest segment uppermost. The lower the segment the greater it is
> in breadth, depth, and area.
>
> The whole triangle is moving slowly, almost invisibly forwards and
> upwards. Where the apex was today the second segment is tomorrow;
> what today can be understood only by the apex and to the rest of the
> triangle is an incomprehensible gibberish, forms tomorrow the true
> thought and feeling of the second segment.[1]

For Kandinsky, those committed to "the life of the spirit" are the vanguard
of history. But their brilliance also destines them to a life of solitude and

---

[1] Wassily Kandinsky, *Concerning the Spiritual in Art,* trans. M. T. H. Sadler (1912; New York: Dover, 1977), 6. Henceforth cited parenthetically as *CSA*. On Saint-Simon's initiation of the term *avant-garde,* as well as its role in Kandinsky and beyond, see Luc Ferry, *Homo Aestheticus: The Invention of Taste in the Democratic Age,* trans. Robert de Loaiza (Chicago: University of Chicago Press, 1994),

disdain from the rest of the triangle, the masses who "have never solved any problem independently" and are "dragged as it were in a cart by those the noblest of their fellowmen who have sacrificed themselves" (*CSA* 6). Although responsible for a society's evolution, the true avant-gardiste necessarily stands scorned and misunderstood, remote from his or her contemporaries: "Even those who are nearest to him in sympathy do not understand him. Angrily they abuse him as charlatan or madman" (*CSA* 6).

It is roughly this sense of "avant-garde" that could be applied to Stein and, a few decades after her, Robbe-Grillet. As part I argued, both Stein and Robbe-Grillet trace the sources of their work to a form of agency residing "inside," estranged from the public world of material bodies and the ordinary words describing them. And the result of this internalism is in each case, as in Kandinsky, a strongly progressivist view of the history of the arts (as if artworks of the past were not just out of fashion, but false) and an attendant belief that intransigent experimentalism, a relentless challenging of settled habits, is the only option for writers who don't want to see themselves condemned as common.

Recently, however, Houston A. Baker has described the experimentalism of Ralph Ellison not in order to praise the author's progressivism but in order to explain, as his essay's subtitle declares, why Ellison "was *never* avant-garde."[2] For Baker, the critical shift that allowed Ellison to replace Richard Wright as the central figure in twentieth-century African-American literary history is "disturbing," for one of the conspicuous aspects of Ellison's career is his "utter failure as a 'Prophet of Tomorrow'" ("Failed" 5). Though more stylistically elegant than anything Wright ever wrote, Ellison's *Invisible Man* nowhere hints at the emergent "black southern public sphere" that "would lead a cataclysmic rights revolution" through Dr. Martin Luther King and others in the decade after it was published ("Failed" 5). Whereas Wright engaged in strict scientific critique of capitalism, Ellison hibernated in an effete literary world, relinquishing an analysis of "the intimate horrors of racism" for "a mess of Eliotan or Hemingwayesque allusions" ("Failed" 8). Wright was "an embattled, public, activist, black intellectual," whereas Ellison

---

197ff. Some major considerations of the concept in recent decades include Peter Bürger, *Theory of the Avant-Garde*, trans. Michael Shaw (Minneapolis: University of Minnesota Press, 1984); Matei Calinescu, *Five Faces of Modernity: Modernism, Avant-Garde, Decadence, Kitsch, Postmodernism*, 2nd ed. (Durham: Duke University Press, 1987).

[2] "Failed Prophet and Falling Stock: Why Ralph Ellison Was Never Avant-Garde," *Stanford Humanities Review* 7 (1999): 4–11. Henceforth cited as "Failed." A revised version of this essay appears in Baker's *Critical Memory: Public Spheres, African American Writing, and Black Fathers and Sons in America* (Athens: University of Georgia Press, 2001).

remained blind to "the nascent energy of Civil Rights and Black Power," believing that "intellectualdom is both colorblind and capable of effective, non-engaged, philosophical intervention in the terrors of 'race' in these United States" ("Failed" 8). Like his nameless narrator, he stayed aloof and uninvolved, a mere "existentialist intellectual" ("Failed" 10).

Whatever one thinks of Baker's assessment, his comments illuminate a second way of understanding Kandinsky's triangle. Stein and Robbe-Grillet count as avant-garde insofar as the internalism motivating their work alienates them from the social sphere populated by the masses. By contrast, Baker withholds the term from Ellison precisely *because* he lacks the common touch. In Baker's eyes, an avant-garde earns its laurels less from the idiosyncratic visions of the gifted artist—Wright's importance lies, of course, not in any formal innovations—than from the unity and breadth of the collective it cultivates. The stylistic complications and abstruse theorizing that make Stein and Robbe-Grillet "avant-garde" would disqualify them for Baker, who reserves the term for writers whose work seems to foster solidity in the triangle's base rather than writers whose eccentricities drive them toward the apex.

One lesson we learn from juxtaposing Kandinsky and Baker is that, unless the use of the term is further stipulated, "avant-garde" obscures more than clarifies, in spite of (or more probably because of) its obvious romance. But I begin with their comments because the rival versions of "avant-garde" they employ—what we might call the individualist and collectivist senses—crystallize the transition I want to make here in part II. The end of part I arrived at an idea of agency that ascribes intentional states and actions first and foremost to bodies, especially human ones. And I argued there that accepting this picture means seeing agents as deeply embedded in a particular time and place, an embedding that characterizes both their physical and intentional aspects. The character of Dahfu in Bellow's *Henderson the Rain King,* I claimed, cannot transform himself into a lion, despite his highest hopes and grueling exercises, and the meanings of our words are similarly bound to the public practices within which our lives take place. "Not prepared to start floating" is the way Eugene Henderson describes this embedding, and this sentiment, I suggested, is what links Bellow to the contemporaneous philosophical accounts of Wittgenstein, Sellars, and Quine, with their common emphasis on (Quine's phrase) the "essentially dramatic idiom" of intentional explanation.

No sooner do we feel at ease with these conclusions, however, than we recognize the questions that they generate. It is these further questions that will be at the heart of the discussion in part II. One way of posing these questions is to ask whether the position described at the end of part I is the one implied by Baker in his attack on Ellison's novel and career. Surely "embedding," our rootedness in a place and time, is precisely the kind of thing that Baker accuses Ellison of neglecting in both his work and life. The author's comfy Manhattan clubs and rarefied Modernist allusions are all symptoms of estrangement, even a self-deceiving atomism. Given their emphasis on the ways agents can be identified and understood only amid other agents, and given their suggestions about the languages, histories, and conventions shaping us within a communal triangle, would Bellow, Wittgenstein, Quine, and Sellars therefore agree with Baker's attack? Do they mean to endorse the collectivist picture that Baker wants us to adopt? Framed in slightly different terms, the question left unaddressed at the end of part I is whether the holism described there has, as it were, only a single style, whether there are stronger and weaker versions of it, and if so, just what these versions might look like. If we claim that a narrative background is always needed to understand an entity, just how much narrative do we need? If we claim that actions and actors are intelligible only as part of a larger whole, how big does this "whole" have to be?

To introduce these questions, I want to look carefully in this chapter at *Invisible Man,* the object of Baker's hostility. Ellison's novel is clearly "about" race in America. But my hope is that, against the backdrop of part I, and read as a book preoccupied with questions of mind and meaning, the novel will look somewhat more wide-ranging than this obvious description allows. As I'll be arguing, the novel is akin in many respects to Bellow's *Henderson the Rain King,* in that each text associates agency closely with the condition of embodied persons. Indeed, the fact that Ellison and Bellow themselves shared a house in the mid-1950s, shortly after the appearance of *Invisible Man* and shortly before that of *Henderson,* is indicative of the common space their different works occupy.[3] Eugene Henderson is not, however, the same kind of character as Ellison's Invisible Man, nor do the two share anything like a common background, and this difference will allow me to refine the claims about persons and presences that were made in part I. Like Bellow's novel, *Invisible Man* thematizes the tension between persons and presences, but Ellison is concerned with different types of disembodied forms of life than Bellow, which means that the dynamic between

---

[3] For Bellow's take on Ellison as a housemate, see his "Ralph Ellison in Tivoli," *Partisan Review* 65 (1998): 524–28. On the friendship between Bellow and Ellison, see James Atlas, *Bellow: A Biography* (New York: Modern Library, 2000); Arnold Rampersad, *Ralph Ellison: A Biography* (New York: Knopf, 2007).

persons and presences changes from what we've seen thus far. Confronted by presences "without" rather than "within," different aspects of personhood come to the fore. This shift makes for different sorts of anxieties about what it means to "possess a mind" (*IM* 3), and motivates the particular theoretical and practical themes that will occupy the next several chapters.

GIVING THE WORLD A NEW SHAPE

Let's start by looking at two very different passages published within a few months of one another. The first comes about two-thirds of the way through *Invisible Man*. The retrospective narrator has recounted how he left college after an embarrassing episode with a trustee, and how he has moved north to find work in New York, ostensibly with the support of his college president, Mr. Bledsoe. Upon arriving in New York, he learns that Bledsoe has actively hindered him from finding work in the city. Betrayed and alone, he takes a job at a paint factory, becomes a tenant at the house of a kindly old Harlemite, Mary Rambo, and eventually, after speaking up spontaneously for an elderly couple he sees being evicted one day from their apartment, he is hired as a spokesman and activist for the Brotherhood, an organization that Ellison based on the Communist Party. In chapter 17, he recounts some of his early successes organizing in Harlem for the Brotherhood, and in the final paragraph of the chapter, he pauses to reflect on his newfound power:

> Thus for one lone stretch of time I lived with the intensity displayed by those chronic numbers players who see clues to their fortune in the most minute and insignificant phenomena: in clouds, on passing trucks and subway cars, in dreams, comic strips, the shape of dog-luck fouled on the pavements. I was dominated by the all-embracing idea of Brotherhood. The organization had given the world a new shape, and me a vital role. We recognized no loose ends, everything could be controlled by our science. Life was all pattern and discipline, and the beauty of discipline is when it works. And it was working very well. (*IM* 382)

The passage is the only moment in the novel when the narrator describes himself as wholly incorporated into a wider social body. The driving aspiration of his early life is to penetrate the various communities and institutions he encounters: his hometown, the college, the world of Bledsoe and the trustees, the world of New York City business, the Brotherhood. In the later chapters, as he becomes entangled in and disillusioned with the vicious internal politics of the Brotherhood, his alienation is to varying degrees

self-imposed. He understands his early desires as symptoms of empty conformity, and sees all of these communities and institutions as a sham. The
end of chapter seventeen, then, coming as it does immediately before the
unsigned warning ("*Do not go too fast*") appears on his desk, represents a
unique reconciliation between the narrator and his world, and serves as the
main intersection of the novel as a whole. All roads lead to this moment of
harmony beforehand and away from it afterward.

The second passage is a well-known moment in Quine's "Two Dogmas of
Empiricism," an essay that, as Rorty notes, is a landmark of twentieth-century
philosophy. Near the end of the essay, Quine summarizes his critique of
reductionism, one of the "dogmas" he wants to undermine. Reductionists
had claimed that individual observation statements are verifiable on a one-
by-one basis, and that, as Quine puts it, "each statement, taken in isolation
from its fellows, can admit of confirmation or infirmation."[4] Thus, for example, the statement *This water boils at one hundred degrees Celsius* was said to
be true or false purely on the basis of observing certain events that "correspond" to this sentence. As Quine sees it, however, this puts the cart before
the horse. No unique range of sensory experiences could possibly verify a
statement, for "our statements about the external world face the tribunal of
sense experience not individually but as a corporate body" (*LPV* 41). He then
provides two images for how this corporate "body" might be conceived:

> The totality of our so-called knowledge or beliefs, from the most casual
> matters of geography and history to the profoundest laws of atomic
> physics or even of pure mathematics or logic, is a man-made fabric
> which impinges on experience only along the edges. Or, to change the
> figure, total science is like a field of force whose boundary conditions
> are experience. A conflict with experience at the periphery occasions
> readjustments in the interior of the field. (*LPV* 42)

Verified in an observation, in other words, is not a single sentence, but an
entire theory. The sentence *Pluto is not a planet,* when surprisingly asserted
by astronomers in 2006, could suddenly be counted as true even though the
object in the sky did not behave any way it hadn't behaved before. Adjustments had been made to other sentences in the scientific theory as a whole,
especially the ones informing the use of the term "planet." ("A" and "not"
are far too close to the interior of our linguistic field to be put to other
uses in such quick and dirty ways.) In short, the sentences of a language are

---

[4] Quine, *From a Logical Point of View: Logico-Philosophical Essays* (1953; Cambridge: Harvard University
Press, 1961), 41. Henceforth cited parenthetically as *LPV.*

inter-animating, and any statement, claims Quine, "can be held true come what may, if we make drastic enough adjustments elsewhere in the system" (*LPV* 43).

Quine and the Invisible Man are obviously worlds away from one another in temperament and theme, but they are articulating analogous claims. What Ellison's narrator says about the things in Harlem is what Quine says about sentences within a language or theory: understanding one item requires understanding a great many others. Both authors similarly describe these wholes as entities in physical space, reminiscent of Kandinsky's triangle: a "new shape," "man-made fabric," "field of force." These figures restate in more vivid terms what Sellars means by the "all things considered" background necessary for intentional explanation and the "dramatic idiom" to which Quine himself refers. They are designed to emphasize how, as in a car engine, any single piece has its particular function only relative to the whole of which it is a part. Within the narrator's holistic "shape" and Quine's "fabric" or "fields," urban objects and sentences are as closely related as piston and axel, no matter how far-flung they may seem at first glance.

Something more should be noted about these images: each does the explanatory work in describing an entity's behavior that in part I was done by Stein's inside, James's pure experience, Pinker's Mentalese, Robbe-Grillet's imaginary seagulls, Reich's energy of a cosmic nature, and Dahfu's soul that authors the body. They are the imperceptible things that explain the meaning of what *is* perceptible—though now, in Ellison and Quine, the imperceptible entity that helps do the explaining is larger, not smaller, than the perceptible entity being explained. And as in part I, this gives rise to unavoidable questions. Are these explanatory "shapes" and "fabrics" mere metaphors? Do they identify existent beings of some kind? Do they disclose an ontological domain as stably identifiable as that of physical objects? Ellison's novel is a good place to lay out these questions because it is a kind of sourcebook for such supra-personal presences. All of the groups encountered by the narrator are held together by a set of keywords organizing the field of inferential connections in a given vocabulary and thus providing the world with a particular "shape." At the college, the Brotherhood's concepts *class* and *history* remain at the periphery while those of the Founder, the Booker T. Washington figure whose epic is sung by Reverend Barbee, are given the central role: *hope, faith, endurance*. For Ras the Exhorter, the world is interpretable only in terms of the Garveyite racialists: *white enslaver, black intelligence, your pahst*. Whatever the differences between these groups of keywords, each of them hopes to grant precisely the degree of precision and lucidity that the Brotherhood's terms are described as providing at the end of chapter 17. In theory this means that the linguistic field of a given language defines the boundaries of what a group of speakers know and how they understand themselves. If, that is, all *my* inferences about clouds, trucks, and everything else in the world accorded with all *your* inferences, our self-descriptions and practical reasoning would overlap perfectly, and *who we are* and *who I am* would be answerable in the same terms.[5] Such a possibility is glimpsed at the end of chapter 17 in the quick leap from "I" to "we" in the middle sentences of the passage, a leap that, for one lone stretch of time, allows the Invisible Man to become what Houston Baker claims Ellison himself failed to be: a Prophet of Tomorrow, a figure seeing past and future, recognizing a common destiny.

But an important difference between the passages from "Two Dogmas" and *Invisible Man* must be borne in mind. The units in question in Quine's case are wholly intentional: words embedded in sentences, sentences embedded in theories. His concern is with things about things, semantic entities of one size or another. The units making up the Invisible Man's "new shape" are by contrast a far more motley assortment of items. Comic strips and dreams could be said to be "about" something much in the way that Chartres Cathedral is "about" something for Henry Adams, and in this way they resemble the sentential entities that interest Quine. They might reasonably seem to say something about, for instance, social history: a Popeye comic may seem roughly as expressive of twentieth-century American society as Daumier's sketches are of nineteenth-century France. But there are problems with this comparison, too, since, next to sentences about twentieth-century American society, it is not obvious which aspects of a Popeye cartoon represent which aspects of society. Does his spinach represent something about American war preparations, international policy, labor strife, or even something about spinach? How do we know? Another type of item on the narrator's list is what we might call artifactual: trucks and subway cars. These are objects that have been made by human beings and used within their social practices, but it is even harder to say what these things "picture" or are "about" than it is with comic strips and dreams. They are useful instruments, but semantically impoverished. (What does a truck *not* say about contemporary culture?) The final type of thing on the narrator's list is the clouds and "dog-luck fouled on the pavement." Here worries about intentional ascription are most acute, since these items not only don't represent any states of affairs, but they also

---

[5] I draw this phrasing from Tracy B. Strong, "Nietzsche's Political Misappropriation," in *The Cambridge Companion to Nietzsche*, ed. Bernd Magnus and Kathleen M. Higgins (Cambridge: Cambridge University Press, 1996), 123. I return to the case of Nietzsche, and Strong's reading of him, in chapter 5.

aren't in any obvious sense "made." One could, of course, adopt an intentional stance toward these entities and construe them as being "creations" of a kind. But if we could do so with these things, we might as well consult a stalactite in a cave for our socio-economic prognostications.

The narrator's catalogue of "clues," then, rubs up against two related problems. One is that different levels of semantic content are typically attributable to different types of entities, and none of the ones he lists, not even the comic strips and dreams, are as fine-grained and relatively determinate as the ordinary sentences of a language. (Recall here that a similar issue arose in chapter 1 with claims about Steinian "sound patterning.") A second and more general problem is that, in eliding the differences between representational, artifactual, and natural items—and I take the randomness of his list to suggest this elision—the narrator collapses the distinction between *Geist* and *Natur* that is an essential feature of intentional explanation. What he describes is an atavistic world, one far from both the manifest and the scientific images, and closer to the Sellarsian "original image of man-in-the-world," where *all* objects are capable of the full range of activity associated with persons.

These problems are not, of course, lost on Ellison the author. His narrator is ascribing this style of holism to the impressionable and deluded younger version of himself, and the irony of the passage becomes clear when we realize that the non-sense expressed here is not characteristic of the text generally. The non-sense here isn't grammatical or stylistic; the sentences of the passage do not fragment ordinary English syntax, do not fabricate new words, and do not crumble into imagistic fragments. But the passage does describe a moment in which our folk psychology and folk physics is lost or suspended. The narrator's use of *cloud* is as estranged from ordinary modern usage as the Wariri's use of *rain* in Bellow's *Henderson the Rain King:* both float free of closely related concepts like *natural phenomenon, weather fronts, non-intentional events.* The larger irony of the passage, and the reason it is worth considering carefully, is that its non-sense is not merely a momentary slip in the narrator's development. It enacts the very dynamics that generate the narrator's own "invisibility" within early- to mid-twentieth-century American society. The clouds and subway cars of the passage are treated by the narrator as he himself is treated every day. Like them, dark-skinned persons in the society Ellison describes are treated as propositions, sentences within a larger "field" or "system" of sentences. They are made to play a role in the social field much in the way that, as Quine suggests, a word plays a role in a sentence or a sentence plays in a theory or language. Read in these terms, *Invisible Man* is as toughly naturalistic as anything produced by Richard Wright. The dominant symbol in the text—the narrator's not being seen by other members of his society—points at the literal level not to a failure of imagination or even intelligence, but a failure to recognize what Francis Bacon called "the evidence of the sense." The symbol of invisibility is meant to expose what Kant would refer to as *dogmatism,* the uncritical use of concepts unchecked by intuitions. To say this is not to insist that concepts are a veil and that the racism of the narrator's society would vanish if its members could get "behind" them to some "pure" perception of reality. But it is to insist that we scrutinize our distinctions between intentional and non-intentional orders. It is to ask whether epidermal systems deserve to be called purposive any more than weather fronts and clouds. The narrator of *Invisible Man* is reflective, intellectual, and meditative, but he is not a full-blooded philosophical Idealist, and he continually uses the vocabulary of dreaming to describe the people who do not "see" him in the right terms. This is most aggressive in the opening pages, when he recalls his assault on a man who bumped into him on the street: "He, let us say, was lost in a dream world. But didn't *he* control that dream world—which, alas, is only too real!—and didn't *he* rule me out of it?" (*IM* 14). The "dream world" spoken of here, and the active powers of conceptualization attributed to the stranger (he "controls" the dream and "rules out" the narrator), is the not-so-distant cousin to the metaphysical entities defended by the Platonist, who, in Kantian terms again, seeks to venture beyond the limits of sense solely on the wings of ideas.[6]

Roles, Wholes, Propositions, and Persons

I have been claiming that something important distinguishes the kinds of things grouped together by Quine from the kind of things grouped together by the society Ellison depicts, and that one of the dominant themes of *Invisible Man* is the distinction between semantic and non-semantic entities. But the particular way in which the text draws this distinction forces us to ask what may seem an unusual question. What exactly *is* the difference between a person and a proposition? What precisely makes one semantic and the other not? It may seem obvious enough on the face of it. But both human lives and sentences unfold over time, and "meaningful" is an adjective we often apply to each; they are each the kinds of things that potentially "don't make sense." How then could a person ever seem to mean in the

---

[6] Immanuel Kant, *Critique of Pure Reason,* trans. Werner S. Pluhar (Indianapolis: Hackett, 1996), 50 (A5/B9).

way a sentence can? Or, better put, how could someone *not* mean in such a way?[7]

Answering these questions requires that we spell out the different uses of "role" implied in the passages from Ellison and Quine, the difference roughly between roles in a social sense and roles in a semantic one. In particular, we need to make explicit the distinction running throughout Ellison's novel between non-linguistic types of "roles," on the one hand, and what we can call "selves," on the other. These categories signal two types of descriptions under which a given embodied person could be placed, two sorts of answer to the question, *Who is such-and-such a person?* "Roles," let's say, are the identities enacted in the performance of relatively well-defined social undertakings, so that the *who one is* question requires naming, say, an occupation or position or status: lawyer, father, American. "Self" here is somewhat more nebulous, and has traditionally been coupled with other nebulous concepts such as "mind," "soul," or "subjectivity." But a relatively less obscure way of using the term would be as shorthand for the salient parts of a person's self-description that aren't coextensive with those referring to the various functions one plays in the course of a life—e.g., one's particular dispositions, one's particular capacities, character, memories. The metaphors of interiority or depth often used to describe this aspect of persons—how one is "inside" or "deep down"—are vulnerable to philosophical deflation when reified in the manner of Stein, James, Pinker, or King Dahfu. But they are useful if they mean the sentences of one's self-description that are largely independent of those describing the social scripts one enacts. The question of *who one is* in these terms involves reference to a personality or biography: "Well, I'm shy but sometimes temperamental and impatient," or "An important thing happened when I was twelve." There is no census category of the shy-but-sometimes-temperamental-and-impatient in the way there is for the lawyer, father, or American. A "self" from this point of view describes not a set of quasi-objects like "spirits" or "subjectivities," but a more or less idiosyncratic constellation of qualities and experiences that constitutes some sort of substantive identity independent of one's roles.

We need to be careful in introducing such distinctions, for they can encourage fantasies.[8] On the basis of such distinctions arose, for example, the

---

[7] For a somewhat different formulation of and response to these questions, see Brett Bourbon, *Finding the Replacement for the Soul: Mind and Meaning in Literature and Philosophy* (Cambridge: Harvard University Press, 2004), chap. 7.

[8] We should also avoid implying that the terms "self" and "role" are being used here in a novel way. The distinction is a commonplace in contemporary political and moral theory, though also much less than universally accepted.

dubiously sharp Sartrean gulf between "facticity" and "transcendence," as well as the more embellished visions of a Wilhelm Reich. And accordingly, the distinction has been subject to frequent criticism—that it upholds belief in "separate spheres," as if we could segment our lives into different pieces without some diminishment or fragmentation; that it underestimates the forces constructing all aspects of knowledge, as if we could think outside specific matrices of culture and history. Nevertheless it is worth noting how self-evident the distinction frequently is. When I ask "Who are you?" to a man with a toolbox who appears suddenly at my door, I'm confused when he answers, "Well, I tend to be nervous around strangers, and I remember as a kid when...." But I know perfectly well how to go on when he answers, "I'm the plumber your wife phoned about the sink." By the same token, when, in the midst of a heated argument, a wife says to her husband, "I don't know who you are anymore!" it would be inappropriate or worse for him to hand her his *curriculum vitae.* "Roles" usually preexist us and are often easily demarcated from other roles: the ways of performing them are relatively well established. I didn't invent the practice of medicine, nor can I be a surgeon any way I choose, and being one may have little to do with my weekend activities as a Little League coach. The self-aspect of persons does not preexist us to the same degree, is relatively less scripted, and can persist through the performance of many particular roles. While I know the kinds of things doctors typically did before my birth, I couldn't say with certainty what my personality was before I was born, even if I happened to believe in reincarnation. And my characteristic quick temper and superciliousness will likely be evident whether I'm performing an operation or teaching how to field ground balls (though these specific traits may be liabilities in both cases).

From this basic distinction between the role- and self-aspects of persons arise many of the important asymmetries between first- and third-person perspectives, avowal and attribution, how I understand myself and how others understand me. A role, on this view, is always available for a self to reflectively endorse or reject. Or at the very least, a role can always be enacted in various ways, depending on the decisions or dispositions of a self. Some doctors perform their tasks cheerfully, others with a touch of melancholy. These dual aspects of persons are among the things that distinguish them most sharply from words and sentences, and that differentiate our understanding of one from the other. Put simply, sentences lack anything comparable to the self-aspects characteristic of persons.[9] Sentences can often be

---

[9] I recognize that "language" as I'm using it here, and in my analogy to the social roles depicted in *Invisible Man,* is chiefly referring to semantics rather than pragmatics. Such a use is justifiable in this

vague or ambiguous, but they form a "system" insofar as their constituent parts (words) can usually be defined in stable ways; their meanings animate one another in the way that Quine suggests. Indeed, the very possibility of compiling a dictionary or grammar book, texts recording the most common or socially sanctioned uses of words and sentences, rests precisely on the systematicity of semantic roles.

Invisible Man is a dramatization of what would happen if our criteria for understanding persons were equally systematic. Ellison's novel is absorbed with role-playing, settled public scripts, the conventions and systematic connections of social relations, and this concern expresses an anxiety over what would be lost or overlooked if the meaning of a person's life could be understood by reference to some sort of translation book. Clearly the narrator doesn't believe that he is actually invisible in the way that oxygen is invisible, and clearly the failure of "vision" he ascribes to his society is not some bizarre genetic deficiency. Though he describes himself in the final pages as being "without substance, a disembodied voice" (*IM* 581), he is enough of a *res extensa,* a thing of "flesh and blood, fiber and liquids" (*IM* 3), for other people to perceive and control his life in one way or another for most of the book. What *is* invisible in all this, however, is the dynamic interaction between *what I am* and *what we are* that is lost when the latter subsumes the former, when one aspect of personhood replaces another *tout court.*

There are at least a couple of ways that *Invisible Man* registers its wariness about the person-proposition analogy. One is the repeated capitalization of role-names: the Founder, the Exhorter, the Destroyer, Brother, Sambo. These labels usurp any sense of personal and familial identity in ways that anticipate the more hilariously deflationary names of Heller and Pynchon. More so than these later figures, however, Ellison maintains the possibility that something about a person exists beyond even the most tightly designated moniker. When, for example, Brother Tarp, the old man who works in the Brotherhood's Harlem office, describes his escape from the chain gang—the only story we hear from a Brotherhood member about his pre-Brotherhood days—the narrator observes that the old man addresses him as "Brother" only when he finishes his tale (*IM* 398). And Brother Jack's sudden "spluttering and lapsing into a foreign language" when challenged by the narrator late in the novel (*IM* 473) suggests that even his perspective is not fully

---

context, however, because my point of reference is Quine's account in "Two Dogmas" of the logical and semantic relations of a "theory." I am persuaded by Davidsonian arguments that the "uses" of language cannot be specified or constrained ahead of any particular occasion of use. Whether an analogy can be drawn between pragmatics and "selfhood" is a question I leave open.

identical to the function he stringently assigns himself.[10] A second expression of the text's skepticism about the equation of persons with sentences is the causal vocabulary it associates with institutions and social roles, a vocabulary that makes persons akin to the Sambo doll Clifton animates with an "invisible" "fine black thread" (*IM* 446). This vocabulary appears as early as chapter 2, when the old college trustee, Mr. Norton, describes how the school and its students represent his own personal "destiny": "*You* are important," he tells the narrator, "because if you fail *I* have failed by one individual, one defective cog" (*IM* 45). Shortly afterward, the old vet at the Golden Day inn describes the subservient young student to more caustic effect as an "automaton," the "mechanical man!" (*IM* 94). Similarly, Lucius Brockway, the longtime foreman of Basement No. 2 at Liberty Paints, describes his work with defiant pride as the engine of the factory: "They got all this machinery, but that ain't everything; *we the machines inside the machine*" (*IM* 217). When, as an increasingly admired figure in Harlem, the narrator tries to fend off an insistent journalist, he himself draws upon the same idiom to describe his role within the Brotherhood: "I'm no hero and I'm far from the top; I'm a cog in a machine. We here in the Brotherhood work as a unit" (*IM* 396–97). And this vocabulary of mechanization is not restricted to the narrator's own particular experiences. It is part of a chain of descriptions in which black labor is symbolically placed in the service of white socio-economic power: the "black powerhouse" that supports the college's "white Home Economics practice cottage" (*IM* 34); the "milky brown" drops used at the factory to reinforce the Optic White, the paint destined for national monuments (*IM* 200–202); the underground work of Brockway, who cooks "the guts" of the company's paints (*IM* 214); the three black horses on whom the white policemen ride outside the political rally (*IM* 337); the impression of the narrator, upon first meeting the Brotherhood, that he is being used as "a natural resource" (*IM* 303).

To the questions raised earlier, then, about the ontological status of the world's "new shape," about whether this is merely metaphorical or something more substantial, Ellison's answer seems relatively clear. The suprapersonal entities his narrator describes are not useful fictions, because they don't deserve to be seen as meaningful at all. Such "shapes" can *seem* to be purposive, but they're not: they're not animate, not intentional, not sapient. They are best described in the nomological terms of lawlike processes,

---

[10] For a good discussion of the role-playing common to Jack, Bledsoe, and Trueblood, see Andrew Hoberek, *The Twilight of the Middle Class: Post-World War II American Fiction and White-Collar Work* (Princeton: Princeton University Press, 2005), 58–59.

and they "do" things only as part of a rhetorical flourish that is at best picturesque and at worst debilitating and dangerous. One effect of such descriptions is that it is hard to make sense of Houston Baker's claim that Ellison, as opposed to his naïve young narrator, is awed by the "mysteries of American industry and industrialists" or that he had "utter faith in industrial democracy" ("Failed" 8). More importantly, the persistence of causal description reflects Ellison's fundamental concern with normativity, with what is required for something to be counted as an intentional agent in the most basic sense. The images of machinery, instrumentalization, natural resources, and so on suggest that the central problem of *Invisible Man* is what it means to be treated not as a norm-governed self-legislating entity, but as a non-intentional thing both subject to and embodying natural laws. The narrator's entire life is assigned, in Sellars's terms, to the space of causes rather than the space of reasons.

More needs to be said about the link implied here between the space of reasons and what I'm calling "selfhood," and how the narrator could gain the perspective needed to recognize this difference. But before doing so we should note how close we have come to the territory charted in my discussion of Bellow, who, more than Stein, understands the disenchantments of modern science and the exact nature of the threat it represents to the vocabulary of agency. To say, with Henderson, that the "physical is all there and it belongs to science" is to say that we are all potentially described as "junk" in just the way that the death of his maid seems to prove. In Ellison, the domain of the non-intentional is less physical than social or historical; the lawlike forces against which he struggles are primarily institutional and cultural. Hence the typical *bête noir* of his essays is not the reductive natural scientist, but the generalizing sociologist, who by the middle decades of the twentieth century had achieved a new level of authority.[11] If, however, sociology has thrived less over the last half-century than the physical sciences, and if the causes of behavior are for many people today better traced to genes and neurons than to schooling and class structures, the idea of (in the narrator's phrase) an "all-embracing" supra-personal system hasn't wholly lost its grip. With a slight shift from "society" to "culture," the claim that our lives are wholly determined by a historically created system of meaning and significance, "a system of beliefs and practices in terms of which human beings understand, regulate and structure their individual lives," has

---

[11] On the rise of sociology in the decades before *Invisible Man,* see Robert C. Bannister, *Sociology and Scientism: The American Quest for Objectivity, 1880–1940* (Chapel Hill: University of North Carolina Press, 1991).

in some quarters continued to seem as truistic as it sometimes seemed in Ellison's day.[12]

ANGUISH AND AUTONOMY

To say more about the contrast between persons and propositions I want to tie Ellison's famous retort to Irving Howe to an important formal feature of the book, namely its curious starting point. Making this connection is one way of cashing in on the suggestion made above that the concept of a "self" can be retained if we detach it from some of its traditional imagery, and use it to designate the portions of a self-description relatively separable from the descriptions in which one fashions oneself a surgeon or Little League coach. Certain things matter to me, I have certain dispositions and experiences, and these matterings, dispositions, and experiences accompany me in the performance of both kinds of roles. It is Ellison's sustained interest in the selfhood of persons that has led many critics, both before and after Houston Baker, and in various tones of commendation and condemnation, to describe him as an "individualist." This is not so much wrong as incomplete, since it overlooks Ellison's interest in more basic questions about what counts as a so-called "individual," what the grounds are for identifying and re-identifying such an entity, and what sorts of skills are required for a thing to talk about itself in the first person.

Howe, recall, had argued that the black writer must feel "a constant pressure" from the "sociology of his existence," an existence inevitably scarred by a "pain and ferocity that nothing could remove." Such scarring, he claimed, was best represented not by Ellison's complex and comic novel, but through the "clenched militance" of (once again) Wright.[13] In response, Ellison claimed that Howe's statements rested upon crude metaphysical assumptions about "Negroness." Howe's claims about the "sociology of a writer's existence" made a formulaic and all-too-easy equation between the politically marginalized condition of blacks in America and the lives led by particular black people: "Note that this is a condition arising from a *collective* experience

---

[12] On Ellison's relation both to the sociology of his day and to the sociology implicit in later readings by Baker and Henry Louis Gates, Jr., see Kenneth W. Warren, *So Black and Blue: Ralph Ellison and the Occasion of Criticism* (Chicago: University of Chicago Press, 2001), chap. 6. The brief account of cultures as "systems" comes from Bhikhu Parekh, *Rethinking Multiculturalism: Cultural Diversity and Political Theory* (Cambridge: Harvard University Press, 2001), 143.

[13] Howe's essay is reprinted in *Ralph Ellison: A Collection of Critical Essays,* ed. John Hersey (Englewood Cliffs, NJ: Prentice-Hall, 1974), 36–38.

which leaves no room for the individual writer's unique existence."[14] And this "unique existence," Ellison said, could be identified, in particular, with "that intensity of personal anguish" experienced by any given writer: the anguish, for example, "which might take the form of an acute sense of inferiority for one, homosexuality for another, an overwhelming sense of the absurdity of human life for still another," or "the experience that might be caused by humiliation, by a harelip, by a stutter, by epilepsy" (*SA* 130).

One could argue that Ellison's essay falls short of adequately answering all the questions that Howe poses.[15] But his remarks about "anguish" are worth considering. Nowhere does Ellison deny degrees of anguish; if these things were quantifiable, a stutter may be proved to cause less than a gesture or physical threat. Nor does he deny that some degree of suffering will be felt by huge numbers of people within a country as frequently racist as the United States. Nor is he arguing that, in response to such suffering, coalitions and groups cannot be formed to force a change in legislation or initiate a public riot. His point lies instead in his examples of "anguish." "Anguish" is a concept closely connected to bodily pain, and so at first seems applicable to any animal with a nervous system. But this isn't quite how the term is actually used. It would be hard to attribute anguish to, say, an ant or a pigeon. And Ellison captures this nuance in his examples, which refer chiefly to psychological and emotional suffering, hence to something largely restricted to human beings as a species. In this latter usage it is, as Wittgenstein was saying in the same years that Ellison was writing his novel, a part of the natural history of human beings—akin to commanding, questioning, storytelling, chatting, or playing—a distinctive part of "this complicated form of life" (*PI* §25). Ants and pigeons do not experience "anguish" in this sense; humans do. Moreover, as Ellison argues, anguish is experienced first and foremost by individuals. It is the members of a group who suffer, specific persons in specific ways within a specific context, and only by extension "the group." Groups and classes are obviously useful posits, but whatever else these entities are, they are not, he implies, a coherent neural, cognitive, and emotional economy in the way that an individual human person is. In any given group of stutterers, some will suffer more than others, depending on a host of other issues, and anguish in the face of racism won't be evenly distributed across all African-Americans. As K. Anthony Appiah put it almost thirty-five years after Ellison's response

---

[14] Ralph Ellison, *Shadow and Act* (New York: Random House, 1964), 130. Henceforth cited parenthetically as *SA*.

[15] See the questions raised by Darryl Lorenzo Wellington, "Fighting at Cross-Purposes," *Dissent* (Summer 2005): 101–5.

to Howe, we seldom respond to a discriminatory remark or situation in the name of an abstract universal principle, or in the name of *all* black people or *all* women or *all* homosexuals, etc. We usually respond in the name of a particular person who is grossly disrespected at a specific moment. The property of *feeling humiliation* is applicable first to embodied singular persons, and only thereafter to collectives: "It is not black culture that the racist disdains, but blacks."[16]

Ellison's reference to "anguish" in his response to Howe reminds us of the extent to which *Invisible Man* is a recital of humiliations. From the early scene at the Battle Royale until the final discovery that he has been a pawn of the Brotherhood, the book is studded with scenes of cruelty and embarrassment for the young narrator. What is important about these situations is how such moments of anguish are largely external to the specific roles the narrator is playing at any given moment. In the Battle Royale, for instance, he is thrown into the boxing ring with a group of boys who are both his age and from his hometown. But these "boxers" no more speak with one voice than each and every certified doctor acts jovially: the narrator is, in fact, the only one who seems to recognize the full extent of their abuse. The others, "tough guys who seemed to have no grandfather's curse worrying their minds" (*IM* 18), acquiesce to their roles in the ridiculous match, and indeed, when he suggests to one of them that they fake a knock-out in order to end the brutal spectacle, he is coarsely rejected.

This observation about the Battle Royale, and the asymmetries of perspective that it displays, brings us to the question of why Ellison would choose this episode, rather than something from the narrator's boyhood, for the starting point of the Invisible Man's memoir. The fact that *Invisible Man* takes off from the narrator's late teenage years, and says virtually nothing about his family or childhood, is oddly overlooked by Ellison's many commentators.[17] But it is intimately linked to the types of anguish that Ellison identifies in his response to Howe. One way of making this link is to say that anguish is the flipside of autonomy. Otherwise put, anguish of the type that interests Ellison is attributable only to creatures who can also recognize themselves in a certain way, who can pursue life projects that they have determined for themselves, and who can understand what it means for such

---

[16] K. Anthony Appiah, "The Multiculturalist Misunderstanding," *New York Review of Books* (October 9, 1997): 36.

[17] One reader who recognizes the importance of the book's starting point is Kerry McSweeney, who rightly sees it as an example of how small a role love, familial or romantic, plays in the text. See his *Invisible Man: Race and Identity* (Boston: Twayne, 1988), 119–20.

projects to fail or be thwarted. Ants and pigeons cannot experience anguish in this sense, because their existence is wholly within the space of causes. Queen ants don't plan to mate any more than pigeons plan to storm a park bench. The narrative structure of *Invisible Man* suggests that the youth of a human person is similarly constrained, thus secondary. Ellison is clearly conversant with the symbols and idiom of Freudian theory, as the narrator's encounter in chapter 9 with Mr. Emerson's son makes clear, but unlike twentieth-century novelists from Proust and Joyce onwards, he traces little of anything significant to his protagonist's childhood; passing reference to his grandfather's curse is the exception that proves the rule. In this respect *Invisible Man* is a strikingly un-Freudian book. The novel displays no sustained interest in childhood for the same reason that it displays no sustained interest in—just as strikingly, given its African-American contexts—religion and the church. Most important to the narrator is the moment when the stabilities and certainties provided by family or God have washed away and no longer seem legitimate. What matters is the occasion when, in Kant's terms, we emerge from "self-incurred tutelage" into "maturity," a self-determined existence in which concepts like a "life project" make sense.[18]

Within Ellison's novel, the capacity for self-determination is vividly exemplified by a single character whom the narrator encounters well after the Battle Royale: Rinehart, the shape-shifter he inadvertently impersonates in an effort to evade Ras's angry disciples in chapter 23. In one of his many comments on the book, Ellison described Rinehart as "the personification of chaos" (*SA* 181), but this is the kind of misleading remark for which the distinction between teller and tale was designed. "Chaos" implies that Rinehart is a kind of moral hurricane, moved by arbitrary forces. But Rinehart's success as a conman deeply depends upon some prior achievement of autonomy. Ellison gets closer to the truth in the same interview when he says that Rinehart knows "how to manipulate" his desires and is close kin to Melville's Confidence Man: "He is a figure in a country with no solid past or stable class lines; therefore he is able to move about easily from one to the other" (*SA* 181–82). Rinehart's absence from the text means that we never learn about the particular deliberations that led him to adopt his particular roles—pimp, "the number man," briber, lover, and (most brilliantly) "Spiritual Technologist." But knowledge of how to manipulate oneself and the world would be impossible for a self conceived as "chaos" or, as Gertrude Stein has it, pure immediacy without identity.

---

[18] Kant, "An Answer to the Question: 'What Is Enlightenment?'" in *Political Writings*, ed. H. S. Reiss (Cambridge: Cambridge University Press, 1991), 54–60.

These claims about Ellison and autonomy need to be qualified, but it is important to recognize how, throughout his work, in the essays and the completed novel, sympathy is extended most consistently to characters who have a touch of Rinehart about them. Defending his speech at the funeral of Tod Clifton, another character who shows himself capable of Rinehart-ish multiplicity, the narrator rejects the Brotherhood's label for his dead colleague—"traitor"—in favor of a more complex group of predicates: "He was a man and a Negro; a man and a brother; a man and a traitor, as you say; then he was a dead man, and alive or dead he was jam-full of contradictions" (*IM* 467). Meditating on the "possibilities" opened up to him by Rinehart, the narrator imagines a similarly pluralistic biography: "If a sharecropper could attend college by working during the summers as a waiter and factory hand or as a musician and then graduate to become a doctor, why couldn't all those things be done at one and the same time?" (*IM* 509). One might also recall, in this context, the famous coal-heavers arguing passionately about opera in "The Little Man at Chehaw Station,"[19] or, for that matter, Ellison's own younger self, who with some friends in Oklahoma dreamed of becoming "Renaissance Men"—a dream of "self-cultivation" that involved, he says, "mastering ourselves and everything in sight as though no such thing as racial discrimination existed" (*SA* 7).

As Kenneth Warren has suggested, all this has made it easy for critics to identify a Ralph Ellison at odds with himself, and caused some of them mistakenly to seek the "real" Ellison residing behind or beyond the various positions he adopted over the decades.[20] And again, as I'll argue in a moment, the emphasis on fluidity and pluralism in Ellison never swells into formlessness and anarchy. But spelling out the criteria for autonomy as he displays it is important for several reasons. For one thing, doing so allows us to make an important point about the historical specificity of the nameless narrator's story. By this I mean to challenge the frequent claim that Ellison is writing in defense of something like "human nature" or, as he himself puts it in his 1981 preface to the novel, "human universals" (*IM* xxii). Such claims underwrite, for example, Martha Nussbaum's suggestion that Ellison offers a re-writing of Sophocles's *Philoctetes*, a text similarly concerned with "a refusal of acknowledgement, a humanity that has been effaced," most vividly in the brutal physical violence undergone by each of the title characters (the ulcerous sore that cripples Philoctetes, the Battle Royale experienced by

---

[19] Ralph Ellison, *Going to the Territory* (New York: Random House, 1986), 32–38.

[20] Warren, *So Black and Blue,* 97.

Invisible Man).[21] Overlooked in such a comparison, and in indiscriminate claims about the narrator's "humanity," is that Ellison's novel is concerned with a conception of selfhood that would have made little sense to Sophocles or Aristotle (who for Nussbaum is also part of Ellison's family). The "self" of *Invisible Man* cannot be identified by reference to nature, by what the gods think and do, or—a version of what I argued earlier about roles—by one's place in the *polis*. Appeals to such grounds can only be illegitimate, and this specific conception of *who one is* alters even something as basic as how one understands physical violence against a person. This hardly means that Sophocles and Ellison belong to different species, or that they don't share capacities common to a human form of life. But in Ellison, unlike in Sophocles, *who one is* is something that must be determined over and against both *Natur* as well as the social roles that, in some cases, can seem as determinate and alien as the non-intentional physical world. Unless we understand just how distinctly modern, post-Galilean a book it is, unless we understand that the objects of the non-human world are no longer "ways of being a person" (as Sellars puts it), the narrator's claims that he feels like a "natural resource" in the Brotherhood are unintelligible. What drives the narrator is accordingly not the Socratic "Know thyself," as if there were something to be found and examined, but the more modern "Become who you are." Pursuing such a goal is not easy, and in the narrator's repeated attempts to adopt the roles given to him, *Invisible Man* shows an awareness of the pleasures of remaining in tutelage. But self-legislation demands, at least in part, self-design and redesign. Ellison is, therefore, not so much "setting himself in the ancient tradition," as Nussbaum has it, as he is aligning himself with Wilde, Nietzsche, Proust, and—as people have often noted in discussing his inheritance of the American intellectual tradition—Emerson.[22]

Herein lies the significance of the book being a narrative memoir rather than any of the other kinds of books that the narrator obviously has the wherewithal to write. (He would, for instance, make a fine music critic.)

---

[21] Martha Nussbaum, "Invisibility and Recognition: Sophocles' *Philoctetes* and Ellison's *Invisible Man*," *Philosophy and Literature* 23 (1999): 257–83.

[22] On the link of Ellison to Emerson and James (via DuBois and Locke, among others), see Ross Posnock, *Color and Culture: Black Writers and the Making of the Modern Intellectual* (Cambridge: Harvard University Press, 1998), chap. 6. On the difference between "Know thyself" and "Become who you are" as I'm describing it here, see Robert B. Pippin, "On Becoming Who One Is (And Failing): Proust's Problematic Selves," in *The Persistence of Subjectivity: On the Kantian Aftermath* (Cambridge: Cambridge University Press, 2005), 307–38. Pippin also criticizes Nussbaum on similar grounds as I have here; see especially 274. In "Invisibility and Recognition," Nussbaum acknowledges that the stories of Philoctetes and the Invisible Man imply different conceptions of nature (265), but as I am suggesting here, she fails to recognize the full implications of this claim.

Self-legislation and self-design are impossible without self-representation, the ability to describe one's beliefs and desires in the form of a story. Herein, too, lies the significance of the style and structure of the novel. Like Rinehart donning the masks of pimp, lover, and Spiritual Technologist, the retrospective narrator performs all the voices, frames them, and moves between them with a degree of freedom that none of the other speakers could ever match. As critics have generally recognized, *Invisible Man* is a linguistic *tour de force,* and owes a considerable debt to Joyce and Faulkner, the greatest ventriloquists in twentieth-century English-language fiction. The condescension of the Yankee Mr. Norton, the vernacular musicality of Trueblood, the vatic voice of the vet, the high rhetoric of Reverend Barbee—these wildly different voices appear in the first few chapters alone. As Richard Poirier has argued, citing Kenneth Burke (one of Ellison's chief influences), troping may only be in words, but "it might also, as an activity, make us less easily intimidated by them, by terminologies inherited from the past or currently employed in the directives of public policy."[23] *Invisible Man* is saturated in inherited terminologies, and nowhere more so than in his Rinehart-like mimicry does the retrospective narrator illustrate his escape from the rigid structures they represent. To juxtapose them chapter by chapter is, in the Bakhtinian phrase, to dialogize them, and to draw attention to all the other words and attitudes lying beyond the forms of thought they embody and express.

Note here that among the inherited terminologies framed and dialogized is that of black folk culture. Ellison's relation to black folk culture has been a contentious topic at least since Larry Neal, writing at the height of the Black Arts movement, observed Ellison's mixture of "Black culture" and "concepts that exist outside of it."[24] My claim, however, that selfhood should be thought of as "becoming who one is" suggests that folk culture in *Invisible Man* can only represent another holistic system threatening to make the narrator into a kind of well-formed proposition. The point can be made by considering Jim Trueblood, the sharecropper whom the narrator meets in chapter 2 while driving the college trustee, Mr. Norton, around town during a visit. To some readers, Trueblood has seemed the central figure of folk culture in the text. Baker, for instance, calls Trueblood a force of unrestrained energy,

---

[23] Richard Poirier, *Poetry and Pragmatism* (Cambridge: Harvard University Press, 1992), 129. On the young Ellison's relation to Burke, see Lawrence Jackson, *Ralph Ellison: The Emergence of Genius* (New York: Wiley, 2002), 315–16, 352–54. For Burke's response to *Invisible Man,* see "Ralph Ellison's Trueblood *Bildungsroman,*" in *Ralph Ellison's* Invisible Man: *A Casebook,* ed. John F. Callahan (Oxford: Oxford University Press, 2004), 65–80.

[24] Larry Neal, "Ellison's Zoot Suit," in *Ralph Ellison's* Invisible Man, ed. Callahan, 103.

"the cosmic force of the phallus" producing further "Afro-American generations," a figure not bound by the ordinary high-art "rules of constraint" that
Ellison himself endorses.[25] But it would be a mistake to overlook Trueblood's
limitations. His narration is indeed, as Baker says, an "energetic, even ecstatic
expressive" act (*BI* 187), but it also displays nothing like the range of voices,
breadth of interests, and intensity of self-reflection featured in *Invisible Man*
as a whole. When Baker claims that *Invisible Man* is "governed by the conventions of the artistic system in which it is situated" (*BI* 181), he never
specifies in detail what "system" he means or what "rules" in particular
the text is blindly obeying. So it is unclear how Trueblood's story avoids
"constraint" more than Ellison's own book, unless one begins with some
primitivist clichés about how country folk exist beyond institutional norms,
unburdened by social impositions. It is telling, in this respect, that Trueblood,
unlike the narrator himself, seems to have gained no clearer insight into his
plight by the end of his tale, and that he ends on the same note of confusion
with which it begins: "But what I don't understand is how I done the worse
thing a man can do in his own family and 'stead of thing gittin' bad, they got
better" (*IM* 68). Trueblood may be duping Norton here by playing the role
of the ignorant sharecropper, as Baker implies, and this may all be in tune
with his role as the trickster. But if so, his subversion obviously makes little
lasting impact. If Mr. Norton's appearance in the final chapter of the book
is any indication, his encounter with Trueblood hasn't led to any substantial
epistemic or moral change. As he asks the now-underground narrator for
directions in the subway, the old college trustee is just as aloof and helplessly
insular as he was in the opening chapters.

Such a description of Trueblood may seem to smack of the very elitism
with which Baker credits Ellison. But we need not dispute that the sharecropper embodies energies and possibilities that are absent in Norton's musty
Brahmin world. Ellison would agree when Appiah says that much postwar
thinking about race has been designed to transform "the old script of self-
hatred" into a new one that refuses to assimilate to norms imposed by hierarchies of power, and he would concur when Appiah says: "If I had to choose
between Uncle Tom and Black Power, I would, of course, choose the latter."
But Ellison would also follow Appiah when he says that anyone who takes
autonomy seriously will "want to ask whether we have not replaced one kind
of tyranny with another" in revising these scripts. Such an individual will

---

[25] Houston A. Baker, *Blues, Ideology, and Afro-American Literature* (Chicago: University of Chicago
Press, 1984), 181–83. Henceforth cited parenthetically as *BI*.

prefer "not to have to choose": "I would like other options," says Appiah, ones that allow a person to be "not too tightly scripted, not too constrained by the demands and expectations of others."[26] The choice, in other words, is not between Trueblood and Mr. Norton. It is instead between the restricted, conventionalized, syntax-like forms that govern the lives and languages of both these characters, on the one hand, and, on the other, a self that is loose and unformulaic, that is not a dictionary entry, that is flexible, experimental, and open-ended in its range. And to imagine other avenues requires precisely the kind of self-reflexivity that *Invisible Man* as a whole embodies. The humiliations that Ellison's narrator experiences arise not only from people taking advantage of him, but also from his own failure to be an adult, to be "responsible"—a term almost completely absent in the early stages of the book, but prominent in later chapters.[27] Next to the growing self-awareness on the part of the narrator, neither Trueblood nor Mr. Norton has emerged from self-incurred tutelage. They are childlike and parochial, incapable of ever writing the mixed and motley, variegated, self-inquiring kind of book that Ellison's narrator himself composes. Baker would certainly identify such a failure in Norton, as well as in every other white character in the text; and in doing so, he would be wholly correct. But while yams may be sweet and hot, they are also susceptible to frostbite, and ultimately the freedom they represent is equally incomplete.[28]

 ## Speaking for You

Up to now I have identified two strands in *Invisible Man:* first its ironization of a strongly holistic conception of knowledge and, by extension, ethico-political communities; and second, its attempt to distinguish competing

---

[26] In Kwame Anthony Appiah and Amy Gutmann, *Color Conscious: The Political Morality of Race* (Princeton: Princeton University Press, 1996), 99.

[27] See his final conversation with Brother Jack (*IM* 463–64) or his rejection of the drunken Sybil (*IM* 525–26).

[28] For an analogous take on Baker's overly upbeat reading of Trueblood (by way of a comparison to Malcolm X), see Hoberek, *Twilight of the Middle Class,* 58–59. For an idealization of black folk culture similar to Baker's, see Susan L. Blake's "Ritual and Rationalization: Black Folklore in the Works of Ralph Ellison," *PMLA* 94 (1979): 121–36. Blake focuses on Mary Rambo and Brother Tarp as representatives of "a positive interpretation of the black folk perspective," as opposed to the "Sambo mentality" she fancifully claims the narrator endorses. These are surely important characters, but Blake misses the fact that Brother Tarp remains a loyal Brotherhood member until the end, as well as the narrator's final reason for leaving Mary's house: "I had been as invisible to Mary as I had been to the Brotherhood" (*IM* 571).

aspects of persons, aspects I have been calling roles and selves. The political impulses driving such an idea of agency shouldn't be underestimated. Ellison is not only, as I've suggested, continuing a literary and philosophical tradition that identifies who one is with becoming who one is. In the process he is also renovating the more distinctly African-American tradition of the slave narrative, life stories that in their very telling could be considered acts of personal liberation.[29] For all its voluntarism, however, Ellison's text is also marked by deep ambivalence. I have cast doubt on the analogy between persons and propositions, and I don't mean to go back on it. But I also don't mean for this doubt to be categorical. Just as the constituent elements of even the most inventively new sentences are the words familiar to us from previous usage, so too a self loosened from its roles potentially runs the risk of losing its intelligibility. Defining this ambivalence in this final section will allow me to forecast some of the themes to be picked up in the next couple chapters.

The ambivalence of *Invisible Man* arises because Ellison recognizes how an absolutist partitioning of "self" from "role" can disfigure our self-descriptions. A self whose roles seem mere appendages can quickly feel weightless, its commitments confined to the affections or impulses of the moment. Something like this happens not only in *Henderson,* whose manic narrator lacks any occupational, familial, ethnic, or other ties, but also, to a quite different effect, in Sartre, whose distinction between transcendence and facticity I've mentioned in both this and the last chapter. And indeed it wouldn't be hard to draw a line from Antoine Roquentin of *La nausée* to other mid-century American cousins, such as Cross Damon of Wright's *The Outsider,* Rabbit Angstrom of Updike's *Rabbit, Run,* and Sal Paradise of Kerouac's *On the Road.* In an essay written around the time that early portions of *Invisible Man* were being published, Ellison identifies this sort of estrangement in the population of Harlem. Newly arrived in the North, the African-American is without many of the institutional bulwarks that had existed in the South, and thus "surrenders and does not replace certain important supports to his personality" (*SA* 298). Like Henderson, Roquentin, and the others, the Harlemite is without the traditional institutions of church and family "to give him direction, and lacking a clear explanation of his predicament," he "feels that his world and his personality are out of key." This feeling is summed up, he says, in the phrase "I'm nowhere," which

---

[29] On this point, see Valerie Smith, "The Meaning of Narration in *Invisible Man*," in *Ralph Ellison's* Invisible Man: *A Casebook,* ed. Callahan, 191–92.

articulates the sense "borne in upon many Negroes that they have no stable, recognized place in society" (*SA* 300). Certain scripts of Southern black life, certain established institutions and customs, provided standards for one's practical reasoning, and the loss of such orientation is evidence that roles are not merely impositions on some free-standing ego lying deep "within." The relation of role to self can indeed be competitive at times; my life as a surgeon or baseball coach may get in the way of what I see as my self-development. But it can also be complementary. (Once again we note the historical specificity of Ellison's novel. It is concerned not only with a specific type of selfhood but also with the evolving social conditions in which this selfhood is valued or endangered—conditions far indeed from Martha Nussbaum's ancient Athens.)

Ellison's awareness of atomistic anomie is registered in *Invisible Man* in at least a couple ways. One is the underlying style of the book as a whole. For all Ellison's well-known debts to Eliot, Faulkner, and other early twentieth-century predecessors, his prose remains comparatively restrained. Like Bellow's, it is playful, allusive, at times eccentric, but the demands it makes upon the reader are far less imperious than those made by, say, *Finnegans Wake* or Stein's portraits. He doesn't consistently explode English syntax, invent neologisms, or compose run-on sentences. Behind this stylistic constraint is an appreciation of intersubjective agreement that in chapter 3 I identified in Bellow's work, the sense that our self-descriptions are partly dependent upon descriptions given by others. It also reflects Ellison's basic commitment to the manifest image, with its primary distinction between intentional and non-intentional objects. To be sure, *Invisible Man* often leans toward a non-naturalistic mode that blurs the distinction. Think here of the dream sequences of the Prologue, with the vision of the old slave woman, or the final dream of Ras, Jack, and other figures of authority castrating the narrator beside "the river of black water" (*IM* 569). But it is notable that both of these excursions into fantasy are marked off from the rest of the text by italics, which play the same role that the quotation marks play around the words of Trueblood, Dr. Norton, or the Reverend Barbee. They dialogize the passages, cordon them off from the ontological commitments demanded elsewhere. One could argue that these shifts into italics are clumsy or unnecessary on Ellison's part. But they suggest how reticent he typically is to forgo the past uses of our language in the way that his predecessors often were. Like Bellow in his depictions of Dahfu, he wants to maintain a distinction between merely private descriptions of the world and normatively sustained, publicly recognizable descriptions. Despite charges sometimes brought against him, Ellison never wholly fashions himself in his fiction as a heroic individual or rises to the apex of the avant-garde, and in his literary practice, he never really seeks to seclude himself in a well-enclosed aesthetic domain.[30] He tropes, but rarely in a way that suggests an all-out crisis in Western history or self-understanding. His artistic touchstone remained the loosely structured, good-humored popular art of Louis Armstrong that he discovered in his youth, not the more radically dissonant, unstable jazz that Charlie Parker and others had introduced in the years just before *Invisible Man*'s publication.

A second level at which *Invisible Man* acknowledges the social constitution of persons is at the level of plot and character. As I noted at the start, the narrator's days with the Brotherhood provide him a degree of coherence that had been missing in his earlier life in New York. "I had felt a wholeness about my work and direction such as I'd never known," he observes, "not even in my mistaken college days. Brotherhood was something to which men could give themselves completely..." (*IM* 406). This coherence is ultimately shown to be groundless, but its loss is clearly felt by the narrator as a wound and disruption—a disruption so great that it eventually sends him underground. And this life underground, this friendless withdrawal from ordinary social exchange, should hardly be understood as some kind of moral ideal for Ellison. There is no doubt something distorting in the claims of the Brotherhood or Ras, with their confinement of personhood to roles, but there is likewise something distorting about a self seeking to determine itself in a vacuum. *Invisible Man* has been so frequently read as a twentieth-century version of the self-reliant American ego, the self-trusting American Scholar, that we potentially blind ourselves to how debilitating the narrator's actual circumstances are at the start of the novel. Hibernating in a man-hole, surrounded by 1,369 lights, with only a phonograph and sloe gin for company, he is as much a *reductio ad absurdum* of the self-isolated "American individual"—Thoreau at Walden, Dickinson hiding away in Amherst—as an embodiment of it. Dostoevsky, recall, was Ellison's most important nineteenth-century model as he was writing.[31] For similar reasons, Rinehart, the figure whom I have identified as the Invisible Man's nearest kin, may embody a certain kind of radical freedom, but he does so at the expense of actually appearing in the book. His freedom is ultimately empty, that of

---

[30] In *Heroism and the Black Intellectual: Ralph Ellison, Politics, and Afro-American Intellectual Life* (Chapel Hill: University of North Carolina Press, 1994), a study that Baker cites admiringly, Jerry Gafio Watts criticizes Ellison for his heroic individualism. I would argue that Watts, like Baker, is led to wayward conclusions in part because he overemphasizes Ellison's non-fiction, as opposed to his actual aesthetic practice.

[31] For some reflection on Ellison and Dostoevsky, see Joseph Frank, "Ralph Ellison and a Literary 'Ancestor': Dostoevsky," *New Criterion* 2.1 (1983): 11–21.

a disembodied ghost, feared by the community and never able to rejoin it in any substantial sense.

So self-legislation only meaningfully occurs within a context, and Ellison suggests that one's ability to determine oneself and one's acts only makes sense against the background of a wider set of social scripts. A French *duc* is not a kind of person that I can be today; even if I wear powdered wigs, buy a chateau, and condescend to my perceived inferiors, the collapse of the social and moral structures in which such traits were intelligible would make me not a *duc,* but a jerk. Another way of putting this is that, despite the Kantian echoes in some of what I've been saying about Ellison, he is not an ethical formalist. He does not see practical reasoning as centering on what Iris Murdoch, characterizing the moral philosophy of Ellison's day, called "the individual as a solitary will," "monarch of all he surveys and totally responsible for his action."[32] When push comes to shove, the Invisible Man retains a degree of piety toward his black identity, and in order to live in the world he cannot, like Rinehart, don a series of masks whose internal relations are merely arbitrary and lack any integrity. What Ellison forces us to ask, then, is whether we can recognize both this piety toward others *and* the ability to wear a mask, whether we can draw the distinction between selves and roles in a way that will suitably acknowledge the force of each. The question is not whether there *are* things like "communities" that form the contexts or settings for the life of an "individual," but how to make sense of these terms together.[33]

We can approach this question by recalling the famous concluding sentence of the novel. The narrator has been winding up his account of his life, and has just discussed his plans to re-ascend to the outside world. "I'm shaking off the old skin," he says, "and I'll leave it here in the hole...Even hibernations can be overdone, come to think of it" (*IM* 581). In his final line, however, his focus turns abruptly away from himself and his own narrative, and he addresses the reader directly, asking whether the story he has just told has been more than the local narrative of one particular life: "Who knows but that, on the lower frequencies, I speak for you?" (*IM* 581). The sentence is unusual, for while the narrator addresses the audience frequently in the text, especially in the Prologue and Epilogue, it is usually to ward off skeptical

---

[32] *Existentialists and Mystics: Writings on Philosophy and Literature,* ed. Peter Conradi (New York: Penguin, 1997), 287–88.

[33] "Piety" is a term applied to Ellison by Jeffrey Stout in a discussion that makes use of the expressive-inferentialist vocabulary offered by Robert Brandom, whom I discuss in a moment. See Stout, *Democracy and Tradition* (Princeton: Princeton University Press, 2003), chap. 2.

questions about himself and his story. But in the final sentence, he addresses his readers in a way that implicates them more directly. Much hinges on "you," a perennially ambiguous pronoun in English. If the narrator is indeed moving beyond the condition of the alienated "existentialist intellectual" that Baker and others have taken him to embody, who precisely is he addressing?

One way to describe the final sentence is to invoke a distinction made in another context by Robert Brandom, a philosopher who counts himself among Sellars's most ardent disciples and who thus, perhaps not coincidentally, shares Ellison's partial inheritance of American Pragmatism. Brandom distinguishes between two models of sociality, one he calls an "I-we" model and the other an "I-thou" model. The former could be considered the analytic philosopher's version—Saul Kripke's reading of Wittgenstein is his target—of the radical holisms presented in Ellison's novel, and represents what Brandom calls the "communal-assessment" theory of normativity. On this view, an individual's actions and utterances are "assessed, responded to, or treated in practice as appropriate or inappropriate by the community to which the individual belongs."[34] For, say, a foreigner trying to discern if and how a given person's behavior is normative, what matters most are the "regularities of appraisals by the community as a whole" (*MIE* 38). As Brandom argues, however, the very idea of a "community as a whole" assessing a given member's actions and utterances is a misleading fiction. The problem with this way of speaking is that Kripkean "communal assessment theorists have a tendency to personify the community, to talk about it as though it were able to do the same sorts of things that individual community members can do—perform additions, apply rules, assess performances, and so on" (*MIE* 38). Actions such as "assenting, endorsing, accepting, and regarding as right" are undertaken, that is, first and foremost by individuals. It is a person who distinguishes between, say, *red* and *yellow* things, not the community as such. While many communities do indeed have meetings, authorized representatives, or other ways of officially settling on a communal view or act, this kind of communal action, says Brandom, "is the exception and could in any case hardly be what is wanted for explaining either norms in general or conceptual, intentional, or linguistic norms more particularly" (*MIE* 38).

Brandom's remarks mesh nicely with my observation earlier that, for Ellison, communities lack an organized neural, psychological, and emotional structure that would allow them to feel "anguish" in the way an embodied person does. In essence, he claims that the *I-we* model of sociality reincarnates

---

[34] Robert B. Brandom, *Making It Explicit: Reasoning, Representing, and Discursive Commitment* (Cambridge: Harvard University Press, 1994), 37. Henceforth cited parenthetically as *MIE*.

Descartes's dualism, with the "community" replacing "the object" as the thing opposed to (alien to, beyond) the "subject." But in real life we never actually encounter any entity called the "the community," and pieces of the holistic Quinean fabric can always be unraveled. To adapt what Achilles said to the Tortoise, there is no Community taking us by the throat and *forcing* us to draw any particular inferences from A and B to Z.[35] This isn't to say that a broad range of people don't share a broad range of overlapping norms, or that these norms don't have a kind of force. But this normative force isn't like the force of gravity, and the question is how one would disentangle the vast criss-crossing of norms that characterizes any cluster of individuals—how clear a boundary could be drawn between people who share certain norms and others who don't, and hence which particular set of norms would constitute an identifiable "community." "Assessing, endorsing, and so on are all things we individuals do and attribute to each other," and it is from clusters of these smaller social relations—dyads, partnerships, intersubjective groupings—that we ultimately come to constitute a wider community, a "we" (*MIE* 39).

"I-Thou" was a phrase made famous by Martin Buber, but Brandom's account of it lacks Buber's mystical air and is best understood as an inheritance from Mead and Dewey, the latter of whom also, as I'll suggest in the next chapter, criticizes the notion that persons are isolated agents acting according to abstract rules. Whatever its ancestry, the idea here is not merely that persons are always already embedded in a social whole. Steinian, Jamesian, and Pinkerian notions of an intentional system residing "inside" are no longer at issue. The point, rather, concerns the nature of these social wholes, the source of whatever stability they have, and the types of mutual involvement and collective engagement that sustain them. Communal life, from this point of view, is best thought of as a horizontal phenomenon rather than a vertical one: the norms of what we call a community are not imposed from above by some extra-human entity—God, Language, the Symbolic—but are sustained by us, between us, for a variety of purposes. And this "us" is ever-shifting; how one draws a line around a given "we" will depend upon the purpose of the line and the norms in question. As Brandom puts it, the pronoun may be said in many ways: "We may be thee and me. We may be all that talks and all that moves, all that minds or all that matters" (*MIE* 3). But however we give the word content at a particular time, we shall not be identifying some organically united or systematically functioning structure

---

[35] Lewis Carroll, "What the Tortoise Said to Achilles," *Mind* 4 (1895): 278–80. In Carroll's story, the entity taking one by the throat is, of course, Logic.

ruled by overriding determinant forces. As long as we can say "we" in these variety of ways, what we call a "culture" may seem less like a self-enclosed triangle than, to adopt a metaphor Wittgenstein uses to somewhat different purposes (*PI* §67), a segment of thread. Taken between my hands, the segment can be identified as *this* segment rather than *that*. Yet the individual fibers of the segment come in a variety of lengths, and not all of them ever touch each other directly. Different ones do different work within the whole, and those on the edges overlap fluidly with other segments that are not in my hand.

It is something like this "I–Thou" conception of a community—reciprocal, engaged, with indefinite edges and continuously shifting interlocutors—that the narrator hopes will emerge in the final sentences of *Invisible Man*. The temptation is for readers to see the "you" of the final sentence as a well-defined thing that we have seen described somewhere else in the novel: a strong political community, of whom the narrator is somehow offering himself as an authorized representative, or perhaps a cultural community in Ras's sense, of which the narrator may be taking himself to be an exemplary member. But such interpretive temptations should be avoided. After his experiences as a public orator on behalf of the Brotherhood, the narrator gives no indication that he is interested in being a political spokesman. And if he considers himself an exemplary member of a "culture," he doesn't go out of his way to specify which one. A better way of understanding the sentence is to see "you" here as deliberately underspecified, and simply as a *reader*—the kind of entity, that is, who by now has finished reading (and has perhaps appreciated) the text, who could make sense of (and perhaps identify with) what the narrator has just uttered, and who could comprehend (and perhaps endorse) the routes of interest and feeling that he has just described over the course of several hundred pages. The indexicality of the sentence is crucial: who counts as "you" will shift from context to context, depending upon the reader and the circumstances. In asking if he "speaks for you," the narrator is asking not whether we share his opinions, but whether we understand his words, not whether we agree with him, but whether his story is intelligible and his self-description something we are able to recognize. His life is his own and not anyone else's, a rich particularity. To this extent he remains a "Thou" to any "I." But he can likewise be part of "us." His self-description is something we are capable of recognizing as in some way—closely or distantly—analogous to ours, in some way characteristic of a human agent. To suggest that the readers of his text share a form of life is surely not gratuitous in light of American history, which has been marked by an inability to recognize even this much in large portions of its population.

There is of course no guarantee that a "we" of the sort I'm describing can actually be formed. *Invisible Man* ends not with "you," but with a question mark—a piece of punctuation that registers how fragile our communally sustained norms can be, how much work they require even in the best of circumstances. His plan to re-ascend from his hole suggests a renewed hope that he might be able to endorse the world and take responsibility for it, but he is never shown walking and working back on the streets of Harlem. Yet reading the ending in the terms I have suggested is one way to make sense of certain themes in Ellison's work that have not been fully appreciated. One is his attachment to the republican vocabulary of fraternity, evident in his narrator's otherwise sentimental-looking thought as he leaves the Brotherhood: "And could politics ever be an expression of love?" (*IM* 452).[36] This topic will be at the heart of my next chapter. But a second Ellisonian theme can be picked out by returning to Wittgenstein's metaphor of the thread for purposes closer to Wittgenstein's own, and in ways that return us to the analogy between persons and propositions with which I began. As we saw in the passage from Quine, languages have been described, like communities, as forming overarching holistic units. But just as we should be careful how we describe the relations of particular persons to their wider communities, so we should be careful how we describe the relation between particular language-uses within a given semantic web. What exactly is the relation of a novel such as *Invisible Man* to other territories of our language—to a historical treatise or lawyer's brief or newspaper article or scientific report or religious text? Such texts may all operate in the linguistic field of a given time and place, but to level the distinctions between these various language-uses is potentially as risky as leveling those between various persons. Leveling is perfectly appropriate in certain situations. Both persons and sentences can be placed side by side in various contexts for various purposes. But the particularity of a language-use is kin to the particularity of a person: full of family resemblances to other particularities, and understood against a background of comparable parts, but each with a different history, pursuing somewhat different goals, and with underdetermined relations between them. I raise this issue now because it is chiefly on account of the basic ambivalence of

---

[36] A question that Irving Howe, for one, found "portentous and perhaps meaningless" (*Ralph Ellison,* ed. Hersey, 38). For a sense of Ellisonian *fraternité,* see his 1981 introduction to the novel, in which "black and white fraternity" is described as central to "citizenship" and "the republic" (*IM* xvii, xx–xxi). On this topic, see John F. Callahan, "The Lingering Question of Personality and Nation in *Invisible Man:* 'And could politics ever be an expression of love?,'" in *Ralph Ellison and the Raft of Hope: A Political Companion to* Invisible Man, ed. Lucas E. Morel (Lexington: University of Kentucky Press, 2004), 218–29.

texts, rather than any well-formed theories of aesthetic autonomy, that Ellison tended to describe the political import of his work as indefinite rather than immediate and direct. One could argue that he sometimes took this indefiniteness too seriously, that, in public at least, he tended to fetishize aesthetic uses of language at the expense of other uses. But his stance cannot be dismissed by simple reference to a cultural system out of which he and his novel were straightforwardly produced, or in which they fit as well-defined pistons or axels. Ellison's novel does not belong in any separate sphere, but the relation between it and other writing is uncertain, varied, and ambiguous. Like other texts, his novel weaves itself into our language in various ways, in various contexts, but it would be impossible to say ahead of time how many ways and contexts and purposes there are, or which ones would be more definitive than the others. Like the persons who speak them, our words can find an indefinite number of interlocutors, an indefinite number of neighbors and friends.

CHAPTER 5

Embodiment and the Outside

The weekly newspaper *The Onion* once ran the following headline: "Report: U.S. May Have Been Abused During Formative Years." The report was issued, it said, by leading psychologists who claimed that the United States showed symptoms of childhood mistreatment: difficulty forming lasting relationships, deep paranoia, a penchant for intimidation in resolving disputes. Because of "trust issues" stemming from the abuse, claimed the alleged lead author of the study, "America has become withdrawn, has not made an ally in years, and often resents the few nations that are willing to lend support"—all dangerously immature behavior for a nation 230 years old. The report concluded by recommending that the United Nations renew "its efforts to organize an international intervention to help the U.S. get the counseling it needs."[1]

This is, I assume, funny, but pinpointing why isn't easy. One possibility is that, unlike real-life patients in therapy, nations lack psychological states that need excavation and examination. We can think of this response as the Thatcher Reduction, after the former British Prime Minister who once famously declared that "there is no such thing as society."[2] At other times, however, assigning patients to one corner and nation-states to the other might

---

[1] *The Onion,* June 22–28, 2006, 1, 8.

[2] Qtd. in Mark Mazower, *Dark Continent: Europe's Twentieth Century* (New York: Knopf, 1998), 335.

seem too blunt. Certainly *The Onion* wasn't the first to propose an analogy: Plato talked of the good city and the good soul in identical terms,
Hume compared the soul to a commonwealth or republic, and Hegel leaves
it ambiguous whether *The Phenomenology of Spirit* is a *Bildungsroman* or cultural epic. And our everyday speech ascribes person-like abilities to a host of
similar entities: streets are attributed moods, presidential administrations are
tight-lipped, and cities have inferiority complexes. If these expressions seem
innocuous bits of metaphor, do we really know what a non-metaphorical
description of these phenomena would look like? If countries don't have
mental states, what makes us so sure that persons do?

Perhaps, then, the humor of *The Onion* article arises not from the entities it discusses (let alone its obvious political satire), but from the specialized
intentional states it describes—a psychoanalytic type that has been peculiarly prone to trivialization. However we understand it, the article asks us
to articulate just how we conceive of the line between a person, on the one
hand, and a Kandinskyan triangle—nations, cultures, groups, *Gemeinschaften,
Gesellschaften*—on the other. Such a line is not necessarily any more self-
evident than the one separating a person from a cathedral. As I argued in
the last chapter, Ralph Ellison's *Invisible Man* is absorbed with such questions.
It is aware of the "pattern" and "discipline" that tight social systems would
ideally provide, and even after the narrator determines to "become who he
is," he doesn't pursue the Thatcher Reduction or celebrate a lonely Sartrean
ego confronting the facticity of existence. One way of describing the novel
is to say that it disenchants the intentionality of economic and racial systems
by recasting them in a causal vocabulary, all in order to re-enchant the kind of
local, fluid, undefined relations suggested by the ambiguous second-person
pronoun of the final sentence.

The first task of this chapter is to extend the reading of the Ellisonian
"you" that concluded chapter 5. The proposal there was to think of the
conclusion of *Invisible Man* along the lines of Robert Brandom's *I-Thou*
model of normativity, or more metaphorically in terms of Wittgenstein's
thread, which is held together not by a single common strand but several
strands overlapping at multifarious points. These are both versions of what
W. V. O. Quine, refining his own metaphor of the force field, once called
"moderate holism": in making sense of a given phenomenon, we need not
have "the whole of science," but simply a "big enough fragment... to imply
what to expect from some observation or experiment."[3] These analogies,

---

[3] "Quine Speaks His Mind," in *Key Philosophers in Conversation: The* Cogito *Interviews,* ed. Andrew
Pyle (London: Routledge, 1999), 22.

however, are only analogies, and to develop "you" in a more concrete way, it will help to extend the epistemological and linguistic models into more overtly practical vocabularies.

To do so, we can place Ellison next to two figures who belong on the same family tree as Wittgenstein, Sellars, and Quine, but who offer more detailed accounts of practical life and reasoning. The first is John Dewey, who at the start of the century was a kind of ancestor to these post-positivist figures, and the second is Stanley Cavell, who, at the end of it, is a kind of descendent. The goal of pausing to consider this pair is not to give a complete account of them (which would be impossible here), but to select a few moments in their work that will allow us to contextualize and clarify what we are hearing in *Invisible Man*'s concluding indexical. Neither Dewey nor Cavell is much mentioned in discussions of Ellison, but this critical void should strike us as curious when we reflect on the way that linguistic and epistemological views have practical consequences for each of them.[4]

As in chapter 2, however, the goal is not just to cast light backwards, but also to toss a flare forward. In the second half of the chapter, then, I'll consider two positions that push the holism of Dewey and Cavell in less moderate directions. Drawing these portraits again allows us to traverse both ends of the twentieth century, this time from Friedrich Nietzsche, whose gloomy final years coincided with Dewey's earliest writings, but whose influence on twentieth-century thought is unparalleled, to Niklas Luhmann, Cavell's close German contemporary. Here, too, the complexity of these thinkers makes them difficult to address economically. But underlying each figure

---

[4] A few words about the channels of affinity and influence running between these philosophers, since I won't be addressing them here. Of the three mid-century figures, Quine most openly acknowledges his debt to Dewey. Though his Augustan wit and background in logic obviously distance him from Dewey, he famously calls for a "more thoroughgoing pragmatism" at the end of "Two Dogmas of Empiricism," in *From a Logical Point of View* (Cambridge: Harvard University Press, 1961), 46, and tips his hat to Dewey in the opening pages of his essay "Ontological Relativity," which was originally given as a John Dewey Lecture at Columbia. Sellars seldom refers explicitly to Dewey, but would have found him an unavoidable presence. Dewey taught at the University of Michigan in the 1880s and early 1890s, just before Sellars's father, the philosopher Roy Wood Sellars, was a student there. One of Roy Wood's first published essays was on Dewey ("Professor Dewey's View of Agreement," from 1907), and by the time Wilfrid was himself a student at Michigan and Oxford, Dewey was the most celebrated living American philosopher. As for Wittgenstein, he is, as so often, the trickiest one to fit into this history. Wittgenstein was quite ambivalent about the term "pragmatism"; see, for instance, *On Certainty*, ed. G. E. M. Anscombe and G. H. von Wright (Oxford: Blackwell's, 1969), 54 (§422). At the same time, there is surely a strong pragmatist dimension in his writings, and his self-consciousness about the label can be read as testimony to this kinship. Similar things can be said about Cavell, the youngest member of the party I'm discussing. He shares Wittgenstein's ambivalence about pragmatism and shows little explicit influence of Quine or Sellars, but the pragmatic impulses running through Austin, his early formative influence, are hard to deny.

is the belief that the kinds of assumptions informing the work of Dewey and Cavell, and by extension Ellison, simply omit too much—that the intentional systems to which these figures devote their attention are illusions, or at least ontologically suspect. Nietzsche and Luhmann don't exactly claim that things like nation-states have things like "trust issues" or "repressed memories," but they do raise important questions about the picture of normativity and action with which their American counterparts operate. And in doing so, they forecast some of the tensions and conflicts that Don DeLillo's work will explore and extend in my final chapter.

Darwin and Democracy

Dewey's *Art as Experience* (1934) opens with a scathing attack on the idea of aesthetic autonomy. In the past, he says, painting and sculpture were "organically one with architecture, as that was one with the social purpose that buildings served," and dramatic productions were "a vital reenactment of the legends and history of group life."[5] Each of these things involved the "manifestation of group and clan membership, worship of gods, feasting and fasting, fighting, hunting" (*AE* 7). Today, by contrast, art resides in a "niche apart," cordoned off as a "spiritual" undertaking unrelated to the nitty-gritty world of industry and economic life. This compartmentalization encourages audiences to think that everyday life and aesthetic experience are entirely unrelated phenomena, and persuades artists to believe their work must "exaggerate their separateness to the point of eccentricity" (*AE* 9). Such a conception of the work of art finds its institutional embodiment in modern museums, which Dewey calls—beating Walter Benjamin to the punch by a half-decade—"memorials to the rise of nationalism and imperialism," devoted "in part to exhibiting the greatness of [a nation's] artistic past, and, in other part, to exhibiting the loot gathered by its monarchs in conquest of other nations" (*AE* 8). A more clear-eyed conception of art's significance, says Dewey, would place it back in the "stream of living," so that understanding, say, the Parthenon would require us to return to "the bustling, arguing, acutely sensitive Athenian citizens" in whose community the building was embedded (*AE* 4).

On the face of it, Dewey is defending the by-now familiar historicist claim about artworks reflecting or reinforcing dynamics of social power. And in certain respects he is. Dewey is everywhere hostile to thinkers and theories

---

[5] John Dewey, *Art as Experience* (1934; New York: Perigee, 1980), 7. Henceforth cited as *AE*.

that try to make "truth" mean something more than "revisable certainty."
Yet the title of the first chapter of *Art as Experience* implies a different train
of thought and hints at the particular "stream of living" that interests him:
"The Live Creature." The phrase is less historical than biological and reflects
Dewey's sense that humans are organisms engaging with specific physical
environments. "To grasp the sources of esthetic experience," he says, we need
"recourse to animal life below the human scale" (*AE* 18). Understanding a
work, in other words, requires that we return not merely to socio-economic
or cultural matrices but to a confluence of heterogeneous forces: a physical
environment of materials and pressures, a social world of public expectations,
a set of biological impulses, a critical intelligence initiating purposive action.
In the "live creature," none of these forces exist in isolation, and art is one of
the few remaining realms where such inherent unities are concentrated. The
alertness and vitality of animal life become our standard of aesthetic creation
and perception. "The activities of the fox, the dog, and the thrush," says
Dewey, "may at least stand as reminders and symbols of that unity of experience" that is broken when we cordon off work from play, thought from
feeling. "The dog," remarks Dewey in an ingenuously Emersonian *aperçu,*
"is never pedantic nor academic" (*AE* 19).

Mentioning Emerson here is a way of calling attention to the Romantic strains audible throughout *Art as Experience.* But while the book clearly
recalls Schiller and Wordsworth—the human soul has been deadened and
art will help revive it—its Romanticism is soaked in Darwin and cleansed
of any redemptive final unities. Indeed, Dewey's mature thought is as incom-
prehensible without the backdrop of modern biology as Descartes and Kant
are without the backdrop of modern physics.[6] Dewey's first influential essay,
"The Reflex Arc Concept in Psychology" (1895), argued that stimulus-
response psychology had merely repackaged older dualisms between sensation and idea, body and soul, and had encouraged the idea that human
interactions are a "patchwork of disjointed parts, a mechanical conjunction of unallied processes." An account of a child reaching for a candle
flame properly begins not with an abstracted "sensation" of light, but with
the larger background of the child's active looking, her perceptual engagement with the candle.[7] In Dewey's later work, these Darwinian lessons are
applied to virtually every stable category of traditional philosophy. The ancient

---

[6] On the difference between the physics-driven "first Enlightenment" and pragmatism's biologically
oriented "second Enlightenment," see Robert B. Brandom, "When Philosophy Paints Its Blue on
Gray: Irony and the Pragmatist Enlightenment," *boundary 2* 29 (2002): 1–8.

[7] John Dewey, "The Reflex Arc Concept in Psychology," *Psychological Review* 3 (1896): 357–70.

conception of a species as a fixed form and final cause, which keeps "indi-viduals distant in space and remote in time to a uniform type of structure and function," is replaced by a post-Darwinian view that posits no bedrock beneath nature's shifting sands. Questions once posed about the "wholesale essence back of special changes" are now asked in terms of "how special changes serve and defeat concrete purposes." Whereas we once sought a single form of intelligence, the common thread uniting morals and mathematics, today we seek "the particular intelligences which things are even now shaping."[8]

The Darwinian roots of *Art as Experience* are obvious enough in the first chapter's title. But less obvious is the fruitful ambiguity generated by the number of the title's noun: the phrase is "The Live *Creature*," not "*Creatures.*" On the one hand, the noun is a singular term designating a specific organ-ism in a specific setting. Just as Darwin's account allows for stark differences between particular creatures coping with an assortment of circumstances, so Dewey's aesthetics allow for variable relations to a work of art. This engen-ders what can sometimes seem a disturbing degree of instability in Dewey's picture of aesthetic reception: collective agreement about a particular reading, viewing, or listening is always fragile, if achievable at all. Aesthetic expe-rience, says Dewey, "is a matter of the interaction of the artistic product with"—and here the echoes of my preceding chapter are fortuitous but instructive—"the self. It is not therefore twice alike for different persons" (*AE* 331). Indeed, our relation with an artwork is so variable that the object itself is properly seen as a "strain in experience rather than an entity in itself" (*AE* 330). Originally the work was, as Dewey puts it, "called forth by something occasional, something having its own date and place," but "*what* was evoked is a substance so formed that it can enter into the experience of others and enable them to have more intense and more fully rounded out experiences of their own" (*AE* 109).

On the other hand, Dewey doesn't simply exult in the unending differ-ences of individual experiences, and the "creature" of "The Live Creature" is not just a token, but a type. A piece of marble or canvas may be, as Dewey says, an enduring object that lives *qua* art only "in some individualized expe-rience," "recreated every time it is esthetically experienced" (*AE* 108). But he also assumes that the members of a species share enough perceptual and cognitive capacities that "the basic pattern of relations of the live creature to his environment" will make his or her experience of the marble or canvas more or less representative. He assumes, too, that perceptual and cognitive

---

[8] John Dewey, *The Influence of Darwin on Philosophy and Other Essays* (New York: Henry Holt, 1910), 15.

stability are both achievable and often desirable. "In a world of mere flux," he notes, "change would not be cumulative," and we would never experience the "combination of movement and culmination" that marks life at its most intensely fulfilling (*AE* 16–17). My experience in an environment will roughly harmonize not only with yours, given our similar sensory, linguistic, and mental abilities. In most cases it will also harmonize with my own experience at other points in time, given the rough continuity of my own basic range of capacities.[9]

Now, art earned only one book in Dewey's mountainous oeuvre, so why does any of this matter? It matters first of all at the biographical level. Ellison may never have read Dewey first-hand, but he absorbed Deweyan thinking through Kenneth Burke, who enthusiastically reviewed the philosopher's work and who gave his Darwinian themes a rhetorical verve that Dewey's own writings largely lacked.[10] At a more conceptual level, Dewey's aesthetics matter because, in emphasizing the biological underpinnings of aesthetic reception, he crystallizes the balance between what we might call *rupture* and *representation* characteristic of all his work and, I would argue, Ellison's as well. The individual organism, human or other, confronts the world in particular situations and responds idiosyncratically to a host of specific factors and adaptive needs. Hence, as in Ellison, intentional states are properties first and foremost of embodied human beings: they are the coordinates allowing us to locate the particular beliefs and desires of any organism, the rupture between it and the rest of the world, and the asymmetries of perspective within any group of organisms. After Darwin, the idea of a "uniform type of structure and function" no longer holds, even among species-members; we all experience sunburn and sorrow in different ways at different moments. At the same time, responses to the world average out over a given cross-section of organisms, which is one reason why umbrella terms (human, dog, dolphin) remain indispensable. A species isn't a fiction simply because species-membership is

---

[9] For a sketch of Dewey's aesthetics in relation to "analytic aesthetics" and a variety of continental positions, see Richard Shusterman, *Pragmatist Aesthetics: Living Beauty, Rethinking Art,* 2nd ed. (Oxford: Rowman and Littlefield, 2000), chap. 1.

[10] For Burke on pragmatism, see the appendix of Burke's *The Philosophy of Literary Form,* 3rd ed. (Berkeley: University of California Press, 1974), 379–94; *Attitudes toward History,* 3rd ed. (Berkeley: University of California Press, 1984), 1–33. On Ellison and Burke, see Timothy L. Parrish, "Ralph Ellison, Kenneth Burke, and the Form of Democracy," *Arizona Quarterly* 51 (1995): 117–48. For some hints at the Deweyan context in Ellison's work, see Jeffery Stout, *Democracy and Tradition* (Princeton: Princeton University Press, 2003), chaps. 1–2; Ross Posnock, "Ralph Ellison, Hannah Arendt, and the Meaning of Politics," *The Cambridge Companion to Ralph Ellison,* ed. Posnock (New York: Cambridge University Press, 2005), 201–16; Posnock, *Color and Culture: Black Writers and the Making of the Modern Intellectual* (Cambridge: Harvard University Press, 1998), chap. 6.

no longer drawn up on a metaphysical blueprint. Hence the representativeness of any particular organism, its ability to stand in for others despite its distinct particularity. We humans can all experience sorrow and sunburn, whatever their variable manifestations.

This sort of balance between rupture and representation, between the behaviors of a specific body and the biological and social contexts within which these behaviors make sense, is what makes Dewey sound deeply historicist in some breaths and deeply universalist in others. Nothing is permanent, the human self-image is always contestable, yet humans typically share patterns of need, desire, thought, and action in ways that make the differences between you and me less metaphysically weighty than those between us and the dolphin or dog. And this balance leads Dewey to a strongly de-ontologized conception of social bodies. Implied in his account of art and its reception is the sense that, as in Ellison, a group is not as well-organized a neural and psychological economy in the way that a human being characteristically is. His claim about the art object captures the stance he adopts toward social entities: "nation," "race," "class" are terms designating important strains in experience more than things in themselves. Thus, for instance, Dewey's influential educational theories. If we start by contrasting the self-renewal of animate organisms with the passivity of inanimate things, then an emphasis on the engaged, interested, worldly quality of a particular student's learning is only a step away. Thus, too, Dewey's skepticism toward the idea that ethics is a matter of rule-following. The ethicist's traditional aspiration to find a fixed good, a good that will be endorsed universally, that will be expressible in a set of broad principles, principles that can act as the major premise of a syllogism—from Dewey's perspective, such a cluster of ambitions lead only to a cul-de-sac. Thinking, he says, always begins "from specific conflicts in experience that occasion perplexity and trouble,"[11] and this includes moral thinking, which is triggered by a unique constellation of principles, passions, and moral goods that are set against one another in specific situations. Again, Dewey is not celebrating a picture of unending flux. In practice, moral problems can often be generalized and principles can be pieced together as "intellectual instruments" (*RP* 162–63). But as organisms faced with ever-new quandaries, we shouldn't forget that these are *our* instruments, and shouldn't allow quasi-things like The Moral Law to distract us from the local occasions instigating our confusion. Terms such as *healthy* and *just,* says Dewey, do not name fixed properties, but are "adverbial," "modifiers

---

[11] John Dewey, *Reconstruction in Philosophy* (Boston: Beacon Press, 1948), 138. Henceforth cited as *RP.*

of action in special cases": "Not man in general but a particular man suffering from some particular disability aims to live healthily, and consequently
health cannot mean for him exactly what it means for any other mortal"
(*RP* 167). Moreover, these various adverbial modifiers cannot be arranged
into a determinate pecking order. To flourish as a particular organism, to
live healthily and justly, I must cultivate a range of virtues and recognize "a
plurality of changing, moving, individualized goods and ends" (*RP* 162).

The ultimate effect of conceiving the moral life in these terms, says Dewey,
is "to transfer the weight and burden of morality to intelligence"—a move
that, he says, does not "destroy responsibility" as much as "locate" it more
perspicuously (*RP* 163). By extension, what matters in discussions of politics
is "this or that group of individuals, this or that concrete human being, this
or that special institution or social arrangement" rather than undifferentiated discussion of "*the* state," "the nature of institutions as such, society in
general" (*RP* 188). (One can only imagine Dewey's reaction to *the political,*
the contemporary locution that remodels such black boxes.) There can be no
ready-to-wear body of maxims that will distinguish right from wrong action
in every case, at least none that remains plausible once we recognize ourselves
as the post-Darwinian particulars that we are. So, too, political and social
organization cannot be undertaken without acknowledging that "[i]nterests
are specific and dynamic" (*RP* 195). The failure to do so gives rise to the
search for what Dewey calls "some mysterious collective agency" operating
behind public events. Such failure leads, that is, to the notion of some unseen
super-entity magically directing a mob or political convention or corporation, rather than—and here we recall the narrator's realization at the end of
Invisible Man that Brother Jack had been priming the pump for a race riot all
along—the concrete persons who "are taking advantage of massed force to
conduct a mob their way, boss a political machine, and manage the affairs of
corporate business."[12] Choices and purposes, he claims, "have their locus in
single beings," not in "occult forces" (*PP* 22, 36). But this does not mean—
and now we swing again from rupture to representation—that "there is no
such thing as society." For people's choices and purposes always concern "the
consequences of their behavior upon that of others and that of others upon
themselves" (*PP* 24). And the boundaries of "others" here can be no more
clearly demarcated than are, to use Wittgenstein's image, the strands in a piece
of thread. Society "is many associations not a single association," and there are
"as many associations as there are goods which are enhanced by being mutually

[12] John Dewey, *The Public and Its Problems* (New York: Henry Holt, 1927), 17–18. Henceforth cited
as *PP.*

communicated and participated in" (*RP* 205): "gangs, criminal bands; clubs for sport, sociability and eating; scientific and professional organizations; political parties and unions within them; families; religious denominations, business partnerships and corporations; and so on in an endless list" (*PP* 69–70). Just as we are always firmly embedded in a physical environment from which we can also be distinguished, and just as some of my responses to a sculpture will resemble yours and some will not, so webs of affiliation will arise between distinct individuals, persons who are themselves never wholly equivalent to the webs of which they are a part. A social practice, says Dewey, is not to be judged by the degree of unity it engenders, but rather, in a phrase that would have caught Ellison's eye, its contribution to an "unhampered exchange of ideas, to mutual respect and friendship and love."[13]

 BODIES OF FRIENDSHIP

In recent years the fragile balances of Dewey's thought have led commentators to distinguish him from contemporary Deweyans who have sought to segregate public and private domains. "You," Dewey implies, covers the person in front of me as effectively as it covers my union, church, or nation, and the "us" that it implies is something I can embrace or disdain, but never fully relinquish.[14] But even in his own lifetime, Dewey's de-ontologized social thinking caused clashes and confusion. It was the source of his differences with, for instance, Walter Lippmann, who defended a firm distinction between the "experts" and "masses" of modern democracy, and it also generated friction with particularists, nationalists, and internationalists, all of whom were frustrated with Dewey's unwillingness to champion one form of affiliation over others once and for all. (This same emphasis on adaptability made him an intellectual hero for many in the New Left of the 1960s.)[15]

---

[13] *John Dewey: Lectures in China, 1919–1920*, ed. Robert W. Clopton and Tsuin-Chen Ou (Honolulu: University Press of Hawaii, 1973), 84.

[14] "Segregation" is the term Richard Bernstein uses to describe the public/private distinction endorsed by Rorty; see his *The New Constellation: Ethical-Political Horizons of Modernity/Postmodernity* (Cambridge: MIT Press, 1992), 258–92. For an analogous criticism of Rorty from another self-described pragmatist, see Cornel West, *The American Evasion of Philosophy* (Madison: University of Wisconsin Press, 1989), chaps. 5–6.

[15] On Dewey's shifting mix of national and international concerns, see Jonathan M. Hansen, *The Lost Promise of Patriotism: Debating American Identity, 1890–1930* (Chicago: University of Chicago Press, 2003), chaps. 3–4. On Dewey's relation to the New Left—via, in part, C. Wright Mills—see James Miller, *Democracy Is in the Streets: From Port Huron to the Siege of Chicago* (New York: Simon and Schuster, 1987).

The importance Dewey placed on the social, embodied, situated nature of practical reasoning likewise put him at odds with much of the moral philosophy of his day. Between the emotivism of early analytic philosophy and the radical voluntarism of continental existentialism, many of the leading philosophical voices in Dewey's middle and later years were fixated on, to recall Iris Murdoch's phrase, the individual as a solitary will and monarch of all he surveys. Not until Murdoch and others writing at the end of the century initiated the turn to so-called virtue ethics do Dewey's themes rise to the surface, though his name is seldom associated with this development.[16]

Here we can turn to the work of Cavell, who, like Dewey, shares many of Murdoch's concerns and who is also oddly ignored among virtue ethicists. (The reasons for this neglect are worth considering. One may be that both Dewey and Cavell each self-consciously places himself in an American intellectual tradition that often seems, misleadingly, to have room only for blind forms of liberal individualism. This one-dimensional historical picture has recently been challenged on several fronts, but old habits die hard.)[17] The relation of Ellison to Cavell clearly has less of a biographical foundation than that between Ellison and Dewey, but their development and work do exhibit interesting parallels: both began as musicians, work self-consciously after aesthetic Modernism, complicate easy distinctions between "high" and "low" culture, and see themselves as descendents of Emerson and nineteenth-century American intellectual culture generally. I want to begin, however, not with biographical-historical speculation, but by picking up the philosophical threads running through Cavell and Dewey. These are evident in, for instance, a distinction Cavell makes between two ways of taking Wittgenstein's term *Lebensform*. "Form of life" is most commonly taken to emphasize the social nature of language and behavior, against the atomism characteristic of post-Cartesian philosophy. Surely this "ethnological" or "horizontal" sense "is not wrong," claims Cavell, "and nothing is more important," but contesting it is what we might call the "biological or vertical sense":

> Here what is at issue are not alone differences between promising and fully intending, or between coronations and inaugurations, or between barter and a credit system, or between transferring your money or sword from one hand to another and giving your money or sword into the hands of another; these are differences within the plane, the

---

[16] A laudable recent exception to this generalization is Mike W. Martin, *From Morality to Mental Health: Virtue and Vice in a Therapeutic Culture* (Oxford: Oxford University Press, 2006).

[17] On the variety of moral traditions informing American culture, see James T. Kloppenberg, *The Virtues of Liberalism* (New York: Oxford University Press, 1998).

horizon, of the social, of human society. The biological or vertical sense of form of life recalls differences between the human and so-called "lower" or "higher" forms of life, between, say, poking at your food, perhaps with a fork, and pawing at it, or pecking at it. Here the romance of the hand and its apposable thumb comes into play, and of the upright posture and of the eyes set for heaven; but also the specific strength and scale of the human body and of the human senses and of the human voice.[18]

The passage echoes a remark I made in my own introduction, where I suggested that the plural in the phrase "forms of life" refers not to the spectrum of human practices and institutions, but the variety of entities to which we ascribe animate life and even mental states. What matters here is that Cavell begins from precisely the embodied condition that Dewey takes as his starting point in his account of aesthetic experience. Wittgenstein wasn't always sympathetic to Darwinian theorizing, but his later writings share the nominalist spirit that Dewey adapts from nineteenth-century biology, and the "vertical" sense of *Lebensform* that Cavell describes here reflects these shared roots.[19] As I argued in chapter 2, a self or soul does not, from this naturalistic point of view, "possess" a body as one might possess a piece of furniture or pair of shoes. One is "attached" to one's body no more than a smile is "near" one's face. As Cavell puts it, "I am not a piece of flesh," nor am I "in this flesh," nor am I "my flesh and blood," nor am I "of my flesh": "I am flesh."[20]

It is the attention Cavell pays to the embodiment of persons that give his readings of the *Philosophical Investigations* their particular power. Consider, for instance, his discussion of Saul Kripke, whose influential reading of Wittgenstein depends upon a certain understanding of rule-following. For Kripke, Wittgenstein gives a "skeptical solution" to the claim that we have no "ground" for acting and speaking as we do. What lisences our decisions to follow a rule one way or another on a given occasion is simply our "own confident inclination"—we act "without justification." What makes me endorse the claim that, say, 68 plus 57 equals 125? In Kripke's reading,

---

[18] Stanley Cavell, *This New Yet Unapproachable America: Lectures after Emerson after Wittgenstein* (Albuquerque: Living Batch Press, 1989), 41–42.

[19] For Wittgenstein's views on Darwin, see Ray Monk, *Wittgenstein: The Duty of Genius* (New York: Penguin, 1991), 537; G. E. Moore, "Wittgenstein's Lectures 1930–33," in Wittgenstein, *Philosophical Occasions 1912–1951,* ed. James Klagge and Alfred Nordmann (Indianapolis: Hackett, 1993), 107.

[20] Stanley Cavell, *The Claim of Reason: Wittgenstein, Skepticism, Morality, and Tragedy* (Oxford: Oxford University Press, 1979), 398. Henceforth cited as *CR.* My remark about the closeness of a smile and face is adapted from Cavell's previous paragraph on the same page.

I do so "unhesitatingly but *blindly,*" and when a language-learner is inclined otherwise, a teacher intervenes. A person "who is an incorrigible deviant" in adding 68 and 57 cannot be "admitted into the community as an adder," and will be "corrected and told" that he or she has "not grasped the concept of addition."[21] For Cavell, however, such a reading leaves no room for any distinction between inclination and judgment, between a rule and our power to subject ourselves to a rule, hence for the normativity of human thought that Wittgenstein seems everywhere to defend. In effect, Kripke transforms what Cavell calls Wittgenstein's "scenes of instruction" into scenes of domination, where the teacher exacts unthinking obedience from the student, making it a kind of stimulus-response training. Such a view, suggests Cavell, ossifies the teacher-student relationship and misses how Wittgenstein's writing continually puts the authority of adult speakers—their authority *as* speakers, as competent, norm-acknowledging agents—into question as forcefully as it does the authority of children. The "teacher's *confidence,*" says Cavell, "should be placed no more in himself (what he or she simply does) than in the child (what he or she does)—which is not to say that confidence should be shifted onto the child."[22]

I say that this reading turns on Cavell's sense of the human body because, as he notes, Kripke's "solution by 'confident assertion'" has a strong "air of power or violence" about it (*CHU* 76). Like Dewey, who recognizes the necessary rupture between embodied creatures, and like Brandom, whose response to Kripke I noted at the end of chapter 5, Cavell implicitly locates intentions first and foremost at the level of the person; no Community takes us by the throat and forces us to infer Z from premises A and B. And like Ellison, he wants to expose the actual or potential abuses that arise when we attempt to situate intentions elsewhere. Indeed, Kripke's account of what we do "unhesitatingly yet *blindly*" brings him remarkably close to the mechanistic vocabulary undermined throughout *Invisible Man.* "Inclination" is one of Kant's terms for *Natur;* it is a non-intentional property that human beings hold in common with what Ellison's narrator calls "natural resources." Kripke misses what a teacher actually wants a student to understand: not how to carry out lawlike regularities, but how to articulate reasons, to grasp the context within which one follows rules, including what one is *not* doing when carrying them out. If as a student learning a rule I fail "to take into

---

[21] Saul A. Kripke, *Wittgenstein: On Rules and Private Language* (Cambridge: Harvard University Press, 1982), 87–88, 92. With "blindly" and "justification," Kripke is mentioning the terms Wittgenstein uses.

[22] Stanley Cavell, *Conditions Handsome and Unhandsome: The Constitution of Emersonian Perfectionism* (Chicago: University of Chicago Press, 1990), 75. Henceforth cited as *CHU.*

consideration certain more or less obvious risks (of status, awkwardness, misunderstanding)," if I merely "give over responsibility for my actions," if I fail to see that any rule "can be taken another way" (*CHU* 71), then I have learned only how to perform an instructor's drills. What the teacher properly seeks to be is not the final authority, the final word, but a representative of the community into which the student is being "invited and initiated" (*CHU* 72).

Representative, not *voice of:* the teacher is herself, after all, never more than a particular embodied person, and therefore stands at some physical and epistemic distance from other members of the community. The group into which the child is "initiated" is constituted and renewed only through such initiations. When they fail, there is no *we.* Given the disjunction between our bodies, communities must be sought and reflectively endorsed, but never assumed. Kripke's reading, therefore, can be read as a parable for "the permanent crisis of a society that conceives of itself as based on consent" (*CHU* 76). The capacity that allows us to generate and endorse the norms orienting our speech and our lives, the capacity that allows us to bind ourselves to our own rules, is also the capacity to divest these norms and rules of their force.

What has been said so far is enough to indicate the extent to which Cavell brings us onto Deweyan terrain. Indeed, for many traditional educators, Dewey seemed to withdraw "confidence" from teachers in much the way that Cavell sees in Wittgenstein. But while Cavell has been as absorbed as anyone since Emerson with defining a distinctly American philosophical tradition, and while he understands philosophy "not as a set of problems but as a set of texts" (*CR* 3), the texts of Dewey are conspicuously absent from his discussions. For both Dewey and Cavell, the particularity of the biological organism makes the concept of a human agent less contentious than the concept of a collective agent. So why has Cavell self-consciously distanced himself from Putnam and Rorty, American contemporaries who have not been shy to embrace the Deweyan inheritance? Why does he see Dewey as a mere *philosophe,* someone impatiently righting the wrongs around him—not a transformative thinker but a schoolmaster or engineer?[23]

The best answer is to say that Cavell and Dewey are concerned with different degrees of what I have been calling "rupture"—how deeply, that is, the separateness of human bodies disintegrates shared features of the social body. In Cavell, rupture becomes estrangement, the asymmetries between

---

[23] For Cavell on Dewey, see *CHU,* 13–21, as well as "What's the Use of Calling Emerson a Pragmatist?" in *The Revival of Pragmatism: New Essays on Social Thought, Law, and Culture,* ed. Morris Dickstein (Durham: Duke University Press, 1998), 72–82.

first- and third-person knowledge widen, and in certain moments he can even seem to approximate the Thatcher Reduction. To be sure, the Cavellian student does often successfully learn a word, even if such learning isn't a matter of reinforcing Kripkean inclinations. Cavell is keen to probe, as he says, the "background of pervasive and systematic agreements among us, which we had not realized, or had not known we realize" (*CR* 30). "Agreements" here doesn't mean that we call the same judgments true and false, but as Wittgenstein says, that we share the language forming these judgments (*PI* §241). We largely agree about what distinctions are worth making, about what counts as *red* and what counts as *blue,* at least enough to recognize our disagreements, and we usually learn how to project expressions like *feed the kitty* into future contexts like *feed the swan* and *feed the meter* (*CR* 172–83). And these sorts of agreement, says Cavell, are "intimate and pervasive," the source of our "attunement" to one another: not "coming to or arriving at an agreement on a given occasion, but of being in agreement throughout, being in harmony, like pitches or tones, or clocks, or weighing scales, or columns of figures" (*CR* 32). If the search for criteria is also the search for community, the search is often successful, enabled by "the stability of the human frame," the "uniformity of all human bodies" (*CR* 395). Our biology can sometimes make us, as Dewey recognizes, representative of one another.

But more than in Dewey, such attunements are for Cavell always precarious, and while embodiment in the former is grounds for a happy pluralism, it engenders an anxious skepticism in the latter. In Cavell, the distinctiveness of my body makes my life more fatedly mine than it is in Dewey, and divesting the social body of its ontological force produces a kind of anguish. That I am my flesh, that you are your flesh, is for Cavell what motivated "the ancient interpretation of human separateness as a message of human incompleteness" (*CR* 399), and he is less confident than Dewey that this longstanding longing has been obviated by modern science and technology. This emphasis on separation is what makes his response to Kripke so emblematic of his work. Wittgenstein's *Investigations* constitutes, he admits, a response to skepticism, but its back-and-forth circling, its constant struggle with conflicting voices, reveals not a triumph over skepticism but what Cavell calls "the truth of skepticism" (*CR* 7). Such "truth" is evinced in the fragility of our shared criteria. What counts as *red* or *blue* might be clear enough, but what counts as *courage* or *recklessness, humility* or *feebleness,* are not judgments that even the best-trained adults always hold in common. Should someone remark—Wittgenstein's example (*PI* §177)—that he or she "experiences the because," we would have to conclude "that on this point we are simply different; that is, we cannot here speak for one another" (*CR* 19). This threat is precisely what haunts the relation of teacher and student. Before the child has been "initiated," he or she cannot identify something *as* something—as a table, as a pumpkin, as good or evil or beautiful, or even what it means to "identify" something at all. Learning the word for "father" or "love" is learning what a father or what love *is*. Yet such initiations can prove local or otherwise unbinding: the older child may learn that, for others, love is not a conditional agreement, or that the leading property of a father is not bullying intimidation. In such circumstances we may no longer be sure how to "correct" one another, or even how we ourselves are "inclined." Adding 68 and 57 may begin to seem an impoverished model for other regions of our language.[24]

Recognizing this condition, says Cavell, can make us feel "terrified that maybe language (and understanding, and knowledge) rests upon a very shaky foundation—a thin net over an abyss" (*CR* 178). Such a remark is a measure of his distance from Dewey: language and knowledge may lack firm foundations for Dewey, but no word could be less Deweyan than "abyss." It is these sorts of remarks that have made Cavell seem the most continental of non-continental philosophers and that partly explain his affinities to aesthetic Modernism.[25] It is also, most important for us, what shapes the particular kinds of social relationships that Cavell sees fit to highlight. If the social body is not a full-blooded intentional system, Cavell also does not want simply to succumb to skepticism. The deep ruptures between us make us less representative of one another than we are in Dewey, but Cavell wants also

---

[24] Cavell has considered similar "inclination" claims in, for instance, Norman Malcolm and Hanna Pitkin; see *CR,* chap. 2. It should be clear, too, that this reading of Wittgenstein in some ways informs my references to his work in my own second chapter, where I presented him as an argumentative philosopher continuous with Sellars and Quine. As I noted there, however, I was deliberately limiting my interpretation somewhat in order to avoid a hive of issues, which is precisely what Cavell rightly undertakes to explore.

Here I might also note a certain divergence in my description of Cavell from that given in Cary Wolfe's *Animal Rites: American Culture, the Discourse of Species, and Posthumanist Theory* (Chicago: University of Chicago Press, 2003). Wolfe claims that Cavell's horizontal/vertical *Lebensform* passage betrays "a palpable nostalgia for the human," a "slippage from human to human*ist*" that is ethically questionable (48, 51). But in calling Cavell a "humanist" (a characterization that, he admits, is made "much too quickly"), Wolfe misses the significance of the "ruptures" that I'm identifying here in Cavell, ruptures that arise less from bodies being *human* than from them being simply *bodies*. In Cavell's picture, the lion who could talk is liable to express just as much alienation, disorientation, and restlessness as any human being. I return to Wolfe's very interesting book briefly in my conclusion.

[25] Comparisons to Derrida arise from their shared dissatisfaction with what "works" pragmatically and their shared in interest in J. L. Austin—a theme Cavell addresses at length in *Philosophical Passages: Wittgenstein, Emerson, Austin, Derrida* (Oxford: Blackwell, 1995), 42–90. Cavell's relation to Modernism manifests itself in, among other places, his discussions of modern music and Beckett in his first book, *Must We Mean What We Say?* (New York: Scribner's, 1969), and in his ongoing dialogues with Michael

to emphasize the ways we are drawn beyond ourselves, as in the *Symposium*. Enacted throughout Cavell's work, then, is a movement between the language games in which we feel naturally at home *and* our drive to step outside these games, to "consider expressions apart from, and in opposition to, the natural forms of life which give those expressions the force they have" (*CR* 207). As the political theorist Andrew Norris has suggested, such a dynamic can be figured as a debate carried on at the gates of a *polis* that the interlocutors will never completely enter—an image, Norris suggests, of Cavell's "existential politics of anti-hegemony."[26] Something like this, I have argued, could also be said of Dewey: the *polis* can never be fully entered because there is never any *thing* to be entered, as opposed to relationships endorsed or undertaken. But in Cavell these conversations are carried on further away from the city gate, and whereas Dewey can give what he calls an "endless list" of meaningful associations—gangs, criminal bands, clubs for sport, and so on—Cavell concentrates on two relations that, for him, display both the fragility and the depth of our shared criteria.

One is friendship. This is of course a major theme in Aristotle, who identifies my friend as "another myself." Given the weight Cavell places on the separateness of human bodies, it is unsurprising that he should find Aristotle's remark dubiously self-assured, and in its place he adopts the more agonistic claim, which he associates with Emerson, that my friend is also my enemy, someone "contesting my present attainments" (*CHU* 59). The friend, from this perspective, represents a new "standard" by which I direct my conduct, offers an image of a "higher self," shaming me in my current state and making me recognize how I have failed to follow my "higher and happier aspirations" (*CHU* 51). Through friends the world is renewed "one person at a time," yielding, in Cavell's adaptation of Emerson, "an illustrious monarchy of two" (*CHU* 60). The claim seems straightforward enough. We have all probably had the experience, alternately exhilarating and humiliating, of meeting someone who continually demands the wittiest or most adventurous versions of ourselves. But Cavell describes such a figure in more philosophically pointed terms. As he conceives of it, the friend who

---

Fried. On this topic, see the intellectual-biographical sketch in Stephen Mulhall's editorial introduction to *The Cavell Reader* (Oxford: Blackwell's, 1996), 2–3. For a sense of what Dewey might have said to Cavell's talk about "the truth of skepticism," see Rorty's review of *The Claim of Reason*, reprinted in his *Consequences of Pragmatism: Essays 1972–1980* (Minneapolis: University of Minnesota Press, 1982), 176–90. Cavell responds directly to this review in *Contending with Stanley Cavell*, ed. Russell B. Goodman (Oxford: Oxford University Press, 2005), 158–61.

[26] Andrew Norris, "Political Revisions: Stanley Cavell and Political Philosophy," *Political Theory* 30 (2002): 838.

initiates my sense of self-dissatisfaction occupies the role assigned by Kant to the noumenal self, the "I" that is not coextensive with my body, that acts as a regulative ideal, that resides in the "intelligible world" over and against the domain of the senses. The "higher self," that is, represents the standpoint of perfection that Kant claims can never be part of the phenomenal world. The "true man" (Emerson, again) discloses the realm of ends and "constrains" us in precisely the ways the moral law is supposed to do. Once again we recall the quarrel between Brandom and Kripke: systems of rules do not make, apply, and enforce themselves, but are maintained *by us*. Taking Emerson as his own higher self, Cavell pictures the friend as embodying—and all senses of "embodying" are relevant here—the standard by which we judge the rightness of these rules and the rightness of the actions they allow. The friend awakens us to new ideas of personal and communal existence, a vision of human nature in whose light our own current conditions become visible (*CHU* 63).

The second, analogous relationship to which Cavell attends is marriage. Marriage, Cavell says, consists neither in a ceremony nor in what a ceremony represents to church or state, but rather in "the willingness for marriage itself, for repeating the acknowledgment of the fact of it" (*CHU* 104). Consent freely given is consent that can be withheld. Marriage thus models in miniature the kind of "contract" on which early democratic theories founded modern society. Mythical contracts may be mythical, but they express for Cavell something important about our modern self-understanding, our sense that we are both within yet not determined by our practices, that we are not wholly encompassed by our various roles as doctor or Little League coach or American, and that institutions can lose their legitimacy when they no longer seem to express enough of who we are. Ideally, says Cavell, quoting Milton, one of the earliest social contract theorists, a marriage is a "meet and happy conversation." It cannot occur without mutual consent, and thus represents a small-scale "commonwealth" (*CHU* 104). But like Ibsen's Nora, we can also come to feel violated or compromised by a given order and unwilling to participate any further. One may even feel that one's sense of violation is "representative" of something more general, that it encapsulates "society's distance from the reign of perfect justice" (*CHU* 110). All bonds are built on the sorts of identifications that a marriage models, yet such identifications are also always, of course, unstable.[27]

---

[27] For more of Cavell's account of marriage, see his *Pursuits of Happiness: The Hollywood Comedy of Remarriage* (Cambridge: Harvard University Press, 1981)—the title of which, again, indicates his interest in the analogy between political and romantic unions.

As in Ellison, then, Cavell's concern is to highlight relations of normativity rather than necessity: the nature that binds us is replaced by affiliations that we can endorse or reject. What matters moreover for Cavell is
that, as in Ellison, these norms are undertaken and sustained by embodied
beings. One does not, in Cavell or Ellison, befriend or wed a language,
nation, culture, or anything else that cannot (say) sip coffee, draw a picture, examine a map, laugh at a joke, love a grandchild. To say this is
to justify part of Cavell's philosophical style in much the way that he
justifies Wittgenstein's. The anecdotes, internal dialogues, and autobiographical interludes that fill his work, not to mention what he calls his
"tendency toward elaborately detailed acknowledgements" in the prefaces
to his books (CR xxii), reflect his sense that philosophical problems manifest themselves among particular persons coping with particular situations.
Such a sense also explains the seriousness with which Cavell has taken
literature. The history of literature is the place where "the idea and fate
of the human body" is made visible (CR 478), the place where both the
separateness of the human body and the bonds established in the face of
this separateness—the themes of epistemological and linguistic theories, of
moral and political philosophy—are each put on display. Reading fictions,
plays, films, and narrative poems means reading the history of our mutual
attunements, the achieved harmonies that have bound us to one another.
It is also the history of the conflicts and confusions that arise when such
attunements are forgotten or refused, the anguish that is as uniquely human
as our capacity for hope.

A Great Sublime Chorus

Whether the Invisible Man's *you* refers to Deweyan associations, relations
in which his various goods can be communicated and sustained, or whether
it implies that he is offering himself as a "higher self" in Cavell's Emersonian terms, is a question that Ellison largely leaves open. One could
argue that the ending shows his narrator has renewed the confidence in
communal life that he showed during his days as a public speaker, a confidence recast now in Pragmatist terms. Or one could argue that his life in
the manhole has made him more of a skeptical Cavellian figure, seeking
not associations but a social contract, agreements whose very constitution
acknowledge a deeper sense of rupture than Dewey, the former Hegelian,
allows. Both readings would sanction the distinction of "self" and "role"
than I attributed to Ellison in chapter 4, but they would differ on the
degree to which these terms are reconcilable with one another. Whichever

reading we pursue, it is worth explicating what precisely the options are. The different kinds of relationships that Dewey and Cavell describe are not always well-understood in contemporary culture, where "friendship" is usually defined not in the ancient sense of *philia,* but as a matter of personal inclination or affection—"liking" someone. And this limitation is in turn often reflected in contemporary literary studies, which, when it takes an interest in ethical questions, often focuses upon (either to defend or dismantle) contentious notions of absolute autonomy, self-consciousness, and a nameless, abstracted "Other."[28] Placing Ellison side by side with Dewey and Cavell is a way of suggesting that *Invisible Man* may be operating with a practical vocabulary that we are sometimes ill-prepared to understand or even notice.

It may seem fitting that, in sketching challenges to the kinds of moderate holism and intentional systems assumed and examined in the work of Dewey, Cavell, and, as I'm arguing, Ellison, we move away from the American intellectual tradition and toward two Europeans. This isn't to say that the tremendous mobility, relative youth, and strong liberal traditions of the United States have entirely spoiled the soil for the social models I will be identifying in Nietzsche and Luhmann, especially given the influence that American thinkers had on both these figures (Emerson for the former, Talcott Parsons for the latter). Nor should we be under any illusion that Nietzsche and Luhmann capture the whole of European thought over the last century. But the shift in geography here isn't wholly accidental, either. And while even a fantastically condensed genealogy of Nietzsche's and Luhmann's ideas is impossible here—a perfunctory history would have to go back to Montesquieu, Herder, Vico, Hegel, Comte, Marx, Weber, and Durkheim, and would need to encompass, to name some obvious twentieth-century names, Heidegger and Foucault[29]—the vocabularies that they offer can stand in for at least some prominent portions of contemporary thought, and will eventually be important for coming to terms with DeLillo.

Placing Nietzsche into this mix may seem unusual, given how many readers in the postwar years have tried to assure us that Nietzsche would have been

---

[28] For some reflection on this shortcoming in literary studies, in relation to a more recent figure than Ellison, see my "Fictions Public and Private: On Philip Roth," *Contemporary Literature* 46 (2005): 707–13.

[29] Overviews of this history include Maurice Mandelbaum, *Reason, Man, and History* (Baltimore: Johns Hopkins University Press, 1971), chap. 10; Josef Chytry, *The Aesthetic State: A Quest in Modern German Thought* (Berkeley: University of California Press, 1989); J. W. Burrows, *The Crisis of Reason: European Thought, 1848–1914* (New Haven: Yale University Press, 2000), chaps. 2–3.

disgusted with his fascist admirers, that responsibility for his early twentieth-century reception rests with his vile sister Elisabeth, and that the heart of his work is his exorbitant individualism—his emphasis on poet-makers, insane prophets, and so forth. For Robert Pippin, for instance, Nietzsche sees one's identification with others as "a kind of weakening, homogenization, or flattening of any 'vital' self." His "suspicions of sociality," says Pippin, bring him ultimately "close to liberal sentiments," sentiments so extreme that it is not clear how any kind of communal or political life would be possible at all.[30] Such a reading certainly highlights how many things beyond Nietzsche's writings had to be happening for fascism to take hold when and where it did. But it is clearly a mistake to say that he was interested only in private perfection. As Bernard Yack has noted, Nietzsche never simply turns his back on the cultured philistines and uncultured mobs that he claims to disdain; he addresses them incessantly. Like Marx, he wants to raise all people out of their debilitated situation, wants to claim, as he says at the start of *The Gay Science,* that "every human being, as human being," has the capacity to question the "wonderful uncertainty and ambiguity of existence."[31] And he implies throughout his work that certain social arrangements foster this questioning better than others.

Indeed, Nietzsche's very first work, *The Birth of Tragedy* (1871), usually celebrated for its account of Dionysian and Apollonian artworks, deserves a place next to *Capital* and *On Liberty* among the major works of political philosophy in the second half of the nineteenth century. Among the questions motivating the book are the staples of social theory. What is a good community? What holds a group together? What are the causes of a society's disintegration or flourishing? Nietzsche's answer to these questions focuses not on governmental institutions or economic histories, or on any of the associations and friendships sketched by Cavell and Dewey, but on what he regards as something more primal. Without *myths,* he says,

> every culture loses the healthy natural power of its creativity: only a horizon defined by myths completes and unifies a whole cultural movement. Myth alone saves all the powers of the imagination and of the Apollonian dream from their aimless wanderings. The images of the myth have to be the unnoticed omnipresent demonic guardians, under whose care the young soul grows to maturity and whose signs help the

---

[30] Robert B. Pippin, *Modernism as a Philosophical Problem,* 2nd ed. (Oxford: Blackwell, 1999), 109–11.

[31] Bernard Yack, *The Longing for Total Revolution: Philosophic Sources of Discontent from Rousseau to Marx and Nietzsche,* 2nd ed. (Berkeley: University of California Press, 1992), 320–21; Nietzsche, *The Gay Science,* trans. Walter Kaufmann (New York: Vintage, 1974), 76–77.

man to interpret his life and struggles. Even the state knows no more powerful unwritten laws than the mythical foundation that guarantees its connection with religion and its growth from mythical notions.[32]

Myths are not the disposable vestiges of superstition that the *philosophes* had proclaimed them to be, but a fundamental feature of any functioning community. When they disintegrate, the society is sure to follow. And for Nietzsche, this is precisely the threat posed by Socrates, the theoretical man whose self-reflection and optimistic drive to knowledge distance him from the kinds of cultural stories necessary to survive the "primordial pain" of reality. The Socratic human being "untutored by myth" is impoverished by "abstract education; abstract morality; abstract law; the abstract state," and thus "stands eternally hungry, surrounded by all past ages, and digs and grubs for roots" in a disenchanted universe (*BT* 135–6). "Knowledge kills action," which "requires the veils of illusion" (*BT* 60), and these enabling veils are precisely what myths provide. They give us a "concentrated image of the world" (*BT* 135) situating an individual within an ordered narrative, celebrating certain ideals, and thus providing the ends that structure practical life and reasoning. These ends cannot ultimately be justified with any proof-like assurance, or even examined without their force withering away. But binding ourselves to the norms they engender is the only reliable bulwark against what Nietzsche sees as (the echoes of Darwin and Schopenhauer are hard to miss) nature's blind, primal chaos. Myths foster what a century later would be called "imagined communities"—the "deep, horizontal comradeship" that restores the "unselfconscious coherence" of pre-modern communities, a coherence lost with the scientific revolution, the rise of industrial capitalism, and the demystification of religious life.[33]

After more than a century of commentary, and heavy borrowing on the part of others, such ideas are by now familiar. But readers have said far less about Nietzsche's strategy in developing them. For a book ostensibly about classical tragedy, *The Birth* offers surprisingly few sustained discussions of any particular plays. Nietzsche's focus instead is more on what happens off the stage than what happens on it; the book is, in effect, an early instance

---

[32] Friedrich Nietzsche, *The Birth of Tragedy and The Case of Wagner,* trans. Walter Kaufmann (New York: Viking, 1967), 135. Henceforth cited as *BT*. Other Nietzsche texts will be cited as follows, using the abbreviations indicated parenthetically: *The Genealogy of Morals,* trans. Walter Kaufmann (New York: Viking, 1967) (*GM*); see *Beyond Good and Evil,* trans. Walter Kaufmann (New York: Vintage, 1989) (*BGE*); *Untimely Meditations,* trans. R. J. Hollingdale (Cambridge: Cambridge University Press, 1997) (*UM*).

[33] Benedict Anderson, *Imagined Communities: Reflections on the Origin and Spread of Nationalism* (1983; London: Verso, 1991), 7, 16.

of reader-response criticism. From its opening pages, the text fixates on the event of Greek theater itself, on the rituals of performance, and only secondarily does it show interest in the staged depictions of characters, actions, and events. In the Dionysian celebrations from which tragedy historically originates, narcotic potions or the approach of spring shatter "the *principium individuationis*" (*BT* 36), the individual "forgets himself completely" within the "glowing life of the Dionysian revelers," the "union between man and man [is] reaffirmed," and even "nature which has become alienated, hostile, or subjugated, celebrates once more her reconciliation with her lost son, man" (*BT* 37). The tragic chorus, when eventually introduced into the production, does little to diminish this self-forgetting. Intoxicated by passion, the reveling throng makes no distinction between itself and the satyrs, who were symbols of "the sexual omnipotence of nature," jubilantly greeting their god. The chorus, says Nietzsche, is introduced into theater precisely to enact this intoxication: it is used as an "artistic imitation of this natural phenomenon" (*BT* 62). At first glance the term "imitation" seems to imply a distinction between spectator and chorus, off-stage and on-stage, and thus seems to grant some room for exactly the kind of self-reflection that Nietzsche claims to undermine. Yet even these distinctions, he insists, are permeable, for the audience always "found itself in the chorus of the *orchestra*," where the "votaries of Dionysus jubilate under the spell" of the god's power (*BT* 62). As a result, chorus and audience were never fundamentally set over and against each other: "everything is merely a great sublime chorus of dancing and singing satyrs or of those who permit themselves to be represented by such satyrs" (*BT* 62). Such unities, he claims, were fortified by the very architecture of the Greek theater, with its terraced structure rising in concentric arcs, designs that enabled each spectator to "*overlook* the whole world of culture around him and to imagine, in absorbed contemplation, that he himself was a chorist" (*BT* 63).

All this is, to put it mildly, quite far from Dewey. Dewey's aesthetics are also a kind of affective theory, and also seek to remove the work of art from a cordoned-off sphere, but what "interacts" with the painting, sculpture, or text for Dewey is what he loosely calls "the self," something which makes a work "not twice alike for different persons." The whole point of tragedy, for Nietzsche, is that such experience *is* alike for different persons, that boundaries between different audience members are dispelled, and that the experience of one viewer is significant only insofar as it plays a role in the emergent system of the audience as a whole. Nietzsche's distance from Cavell is still more illuminating, since Cavell also writes at length about tragedy and for some of the same reasons. Like Nietzsche, Cavell appreciates tragedy because it dramatizes a struggle against the boundaries of what we know, and thus displays the essential feature of being human. But the kinds of limitations that concern Cavell say a great deal about why and how Nietzsche pursues the claims that he does. In Nietzsche, the unknowable on which tragic drama turns are the governing forces of the universe, its *Urschmertz* and *Urwiderspruch,* "primordial pain" and "primordial contradiction." And the experience of the Attic theater doesn't so much reinforce the limits imposed by these forces as much as overcome them temporarily: the boundaries of the embodied human are dissolved within the terraced arches of the theater. Cavell's chief concern, by contrast, is other-mind skepticism, the uncertainty that arises when the leading feature of the mind is privacy rather than (as it mostly was before Descartes) rationality. What his argument requires, then, are self-conscious characters prone to experiencing, as he puts it, "problems of trust and betrayal, of false isolation and false company, of the desire and fear of both privacy and union" (*CR* 453). When tragedy is defined in *these* terms, then claims about one grand chorus singing and dancing, or about the reunion between man and man in the Dionysian rite, or about the symbolic sexual omnipotence of the satyrs, will seem distinctly out of place. Hence Cavell's *The Claim of Reason* concludes with an extended discussion not of ancient tragedy but an early modern one, *Othello,* a play in which anxiety about what the human body veils or doesn't veil—Othello's race, Desdemona's sexual history—is the pivotal problem.[34] Moreover, and appropriately, Cavell's focus is almost Aristotelian in its concern with character and plot at the expense of music, spectacle, and the other things that Nietzsche implies are central to bona fide tragic experience. Characters in Cavell's account are treated as living persons, as when, for instance, he remarks of Othello that if "such a man" is rendered impotent and murderous by human sexuality, "then no human being is free of this possibility" (*CR* 492). Cavell does not quite, as Nietzsche damningly says of Euripides, conceive of tragedy as an optimistic dialectic that "celebrates a triumph in every conclusion and can breathe only in cool clarity and consciousness" (*BT* 91). But tragedy as he describes it does take place on stage more than off, and his attention is far more on embodied figures than the disembodied excitations, powers, and currents running through the reveling throngs of the audience, stirred by the Dionysian spirit of music. Tragedy for Cavell springs from and enacts precisely the *principium individuationis* that Nietzsche claims should be, and can be, shattered.

---

[34] See also, in this context, Cavell's essay on *King Lear* that concludes *Must We Mean What We Say?*

Nietzsche grew, of course, to be displeased with what in a subsequent edition of *The Birth* he called this early "questionable book" (*BT* 17). In his later work, he casts aside the Schopenhaurian metaphysics that had led him to claim in *The Birth* that even the poet should "be conceived of only as the antagonist, not as the origin of art," since he "has already been released from his individual will, and has become, as it were, the medium through which the one truly existent subject celebrates his release in appearance" (*BT* 52). By the time he writes *Genealogy of Morals* a decade and half later, he is willing to ascribe agency at least to some persons, namely, the supermen who make the mores by which the masses live. Communities are now described as deliberately shaped artistic artifacts. Whenever a true political "creator" appears, he says, "something new soon arises, a ruling structure that *lives,* in which parts and functions are delimited and coordinated, in which nothing whatever finds a place that has not first been assigned a 'meaning' in relation to the whole" (*GM* 86). The cultural founders and leaders who "exemplify that terrible artists' egoism" are "the most unconscious artists there are," and their work is "an instinctive creation and imposition of forms" (*GM* 86–87). Whereas the young Nietzsche assigns responsibility for the Greek tragedies to nobody in particular, not even the poets themselves, the later Nietzsche, embracing the "aristocratic radicalism" attributed to him by Georg Brandes, rejects fantasies about "the true author" of the world and distinguishes continually between various hierarchies of humanity: masters and slaves, individual and herd.

One way of describing this change is to say that Nietzsche's loyalties shift over time from the Greek ideal of the *polis* to the Roman ideal of the *imperium.*[35] But in another sense, the model of agency presented in *The Birth of Tragedy* remains constant in Nietzsche's thinking. Enduring throughout his work is not only the assumption that a community—a true community—is founded on a "mythical foundation," but also that commitment to such myths give rise to a deeply coherent, self-subsistent union, a *Vereinigung.* The genesis of such high-level unities may change between different Nietzschean texts, but the assumption persists that, as Tracy B. Strong puts it, a political identity is intelligible only when *who I am* and *who we are* are answerable in the same terms, or, to adapt Ellison's terms, when you and I can "speak for" one another interchangeably, without remainder.[36] It is intelligible, that is, only when you and I are fully representative of one another, when no relevant rupture separates us, when our knowledge of one another's beliefs

---

[35] See Chytry, *The Aesthetic State,* 346–49.

[36] Tracy B. Strong, "Nietzsche's Political Misappropriation," in *The Cambridge Companion to Nietzsche,* ed. Bernd Magnus and Kathleen M. Higgins (Cambridge: Cambridge University Press, 1996), 123.

and desires is perfectly symmetrical. Such a view may seem to raise as many questions as it answers. Do *we* believe things about the sum of 68 and 57 simultaneously whenever a particular *I* calculates it? How could the sum ever be *mis*calculated? Is there any room for *you,* the second-person form highlighted at the end of *Invisible Man* and throughout Dewey and Cavell, the pronoun that implies some potential distance between a *me* and an *us?* However we answer these questions, it may have been the claim that cultures and historical epochs form coherent intentional unities that led one early commentator to say that, while Nietzsche shows little interest in the details of Hegel's arguments, he had "drunk the Hegelian philosophy with his mother's milk."[37] The image of the Dionysian spirit filling the Greek theater passes more or less away, but without *some* version of the collective agency that this group epitomizes, the entities scrutinized in Nietzsche's later work—the German Soul, the English Race, the French Nature, the Jewish Type, Peoples and Fatherlands—would make no sense.[38] This later work is informed not only by a belief that tables of value are constructed by us, that we determine the laws by which we abide, that even science, with its ideal of a non-perspectival account of the physical world, arises as much out of *our* impulses and desires as any artist's canvas. It is also informed by a belief that, once these tables of value have been established, they create a well-bounded set of believers, a unified body, much in the way that Dionysian powers unify the reveling throngs within the terraced theater. The unity of a culture remains, both in early and late Nietzsche, the unity of a Dionysian frenzy that disintegrates under the light of Socratic self-reflection. Our norms are human creations, works of art, none intrinsically "better" or "worse" than any others, but the moment they have been instituted, they bind us within our historical moment. Our myths are our *myths,* fictions that we create, but they are also *our* myths, communal structures of thought without which we would dissolve in the chaos of nature.

 ## CELLS AND SYSTEMS

The Birth of Tragedy still earns readers today in part because it is one of the main planks in the bridge joining Romanticism and twentieth-century intellectual

---

[37] The commentator was Karl Hillebrand, quoted in Yack, *Total Transformation,* 340. The remark is cited in the context of Yack's discussion of the affinities between Hegelian and Nietzschean conceptions of culture and the fate of art, 329–41.

[38] "Peoples and Fatherlands" is the title of part VIII of *BGE,* where the other phrases on this list are also prominent. Throughout this section, Nietzsche chastises himself for having once been seduced

culture. Not only does Nietzsche renew Herderian and Vicovian complaints about rootless liberal democracies, but he updates the parallel tradition that views socio-political *Vereinigung* as being most powerfully expressed in theater—a connection championed by Schiller as early as 1784: "Whoever first observed that *religion* is the mightiest pillar of the state... has perhaps given us—without knowing or intending it—our best defense of the theater on behalf of its noblest side." Such an idea compelled Wagner, *The Birth's* original dedicatee, to develop the *Gesamtkunstwerk,* and with Nietzsche as a main channel, this association between politics and public art came to shape twentieth-century phenomena such as Futurism, mass political rallies, the Theater of Cruelty, and the Black Arts Repertory Theater, among other things.[39] Introducing Niklas Luhmann into the group portrait here will allow us to leave this oft-explored Nietzschean inheritance to one side and introduce a new set of terms that at first glance may seem entirely foreign to Nietzsche's thinking. In part, this sense of dissonance arises from the fact that Luhmann takes notice of Nietzsche even less than Cavell takes note of Dewey. And partly it has to do with their radically different intellectual styles—Nietzsche the impassioned aphorist and system-smasher, Luhmann the aloof and relentless system-builder. But like Dewey and Cavell, Nietzsche and Luhmann are in many respects exploring different branches of the same tree.

The range of sources from which Luhmann draws in his writing makes for both an impressive breadth of vision and dizzying degree of abstraction, but the salient points are brought into focus by *Social Systems* (1984), which, in the original German, was subtitled *A Sketch for a General Theory,* and which lays the foundations for the late series of works that are generally taken to constitute his mature thought.[40] The guiding claim of *Social Systems* is that

---

by "fatherlandishness" and extols the "good European" who avoids indulging in these "old loves and narrownesses" (*BGE* 174). As I'm suggesting here, however, his analysis of the condition of European culture is unintelligible without some idea of collective intentions and attitudes.

[39] Schiller, "Theater Considered as a Moral Institution," trans. John Sigerson and John Chambless, in *Friedrich Schiller: Poet of Freedom* (New York: New Benjamin Franklin House, 1985), 211. On the entanglement of politics, art, and religion that shaped Nietzsche's environment, see George S. Williamson, *The Longing for Myth in Germany: Religion and Aesthetic Culture from Romanticism to Nietzsche* (Chicago: University of Chicago Press, 2004). On the origins and development of the *Gesamtkunstwerk,* in particular, see Matthew Wilson Smith, *The Total Work of Art: From Bayreuth to Cyberspace* (New York: Routledge, 2007). My remarks here aren't meant to suggest that Nietzsche's influence was restricted to the theater. On his wider literary influence, see David S. Thatcher, *Nietzsche in England, 1890–1914* (Toronto: University of Toronto Press, 1972); John Burt Foster, *Heirs to Dionysus: A Nietzschean Current in Literary Modernism* (Princeton: Princeton University Press, 1982); *Nietzsche in American Literature and Thought,* ed. Manfred Pütz (London: Camden House, 1995).

[40] Niklas Luhmann, *Social Systems,* trans. John Bednarz, Jr., with Dirk Baecker (Stanford: Stanford University Press, 1995); henceforth cited as *SS.* The titles of the books in this later series suggest the

social systems are "autopoietic," or, as he also puts it, self-organizing and self-referential. What does this mean? The term was first used by the Chilean biologists Humberto Maturana and Francisco Varela, who used it to designate an entity whose organization separates it from its environment, forms an internally coherent network of transactions or behaviors, and defines it as the kind of thing it is. In their words: "It is the circularity of its organization that makes a living system a unit of interactions, and it is this circularity that it must maintain in order to remain a living system and to retain its identity through different interactions."[41] Consider, they suggest, how our experience of colored objects is independent of the wavelength composition of the light coming from anything we observe. The fact that the red is not "in" the apple nor the green "in" the grass suggests that our perception is shaped by the structure of our own visual system, as this is "triggered" (which, in their terminology, is not the same as "causally determined") by different light "perturbations."[42] So it is, they claim, with any living system. The classic case, and the basic model for Manturana and Varela, is a cell. A cell is composed of different biochemical components (proteins, nucleic acids, etc.) and organized into a nucleus, organelles, a cell membrane, and other features. What makes a cell a particular kind of cell is not its lower-level components but its emergent high-level organization, the maintenance of which requires nothing else "beyond" the cell itself. These structures, according to Varela and Maturana, maintain their bounded structure insofar as they can sustain their difference from their environment (including other cells). Just as important—for such systems are dynamic processes, not static structures—they maintain their boundaries by successfully responding to external forces, such as the flow of energy and molecules in its environment.[43] Not all systems are autopoietic

---

extent to which Luhmann's final years were spent methodically filling in the space that *Social Systems* had cleared: *Die Wissenschaft der Gesellschaft,* 2nd ed. (Frankfurt: Suhrkamp, 1991), *Die Wirtschaft der Gesellschaft,* 2nd ed. (Frankfurt: Suhrkamp, 1996), *Die Kunst der Gesellschaft* (Frankfurt: Suhrkamp, 1995), and so on, up to *Das Erziehungssystem der Gesellschaft* (Frankfurt: Suhrkamp, 2002). As a starting point for understanding the intellectual contexts from which Luhmann's thought emerges, see Eva M. Knodt's forward to Luhmann's *Social Systems,* ix–xxxvi; R. Keith Sawyer, *Social Emergence: Societies as Complex Systems* (Cambridge: Cambridge University Press, 2005), chaps. 2–3; William Rasch, *Niklas Luhmann's Modernity: The Paradoxes of Differentiation* (Stanford: Stanford University Press, 2000).

[41] Humberto Maturana and Francisco Varela, *Autopoiesis and Cognition: The Realization of the Living* (Dordrecht: D. Reidel, 1980), 9.

[42] Humberto Maturana and Francisco Varela, *The Tree of Life* (Boston: Shambhala, 1987), 16–23. Henceforth *Tree.*

[43] On the dynamism of autopoiesis versus that static nature of structuralist theories, see Ira Livingston, *Between Science and Literature: An Introduction to Autopoiesis* (Urbana: University of Illinois Press, 2005), 79–80.

in this sense. A fabric-machine, to take an example used by Varela and Maturana, is an organized and bounded domain that unifies various materials, but what it produces is fabrics, not more fabric-machines (*Tree* 45–46). The cell, by contrast, survives as a unity by responding to its environment and producing more of the components constituting it. On a larger scale, a plant remains the particular plant it is not by adding parts from non-plants, but by using its environment to produce more of its own roots and leaves, none of which are themselves, of course, coextensive with the plant as such.

Not all commentators, even those sympathetic to Systems Theory generally, have found such biological accounts persuasive, and not all have found them especially relevant to social life. I'll return to these criticisms eventually, but only after considering how Luhmann adopts and adapts Maturana and Varela's models. Social systems are not, he admits, "living" processes the way that cells are. But they are "systems" to the extent that, like the cell, they differentiate themselves from their infinitely complex environments and maintain themselves by producing more of their components. The components in the case of social systems are not physical structures such as cellules, but what Luhmann calls "meanings," which he construes in the phenomenological sense of a "focal point," a "center of intention" that shows everything else "marginally as the horizon of an 'and so forth' of experience and action" (*SS* 60). A system that uses meanings is one that can divide the world conceptually into X and not-X. "Legal" and "illegal," for instance: everything pertinent to what we identify as the legal system operates relative to these two terms. Other systems structure their horizons through different binary oppositions. The scientific system works according to the opposition "true" and "untrue," the economic system according to "payment" and "non-payment," the art system according to "beautiful" and "ugly," and so forth. And when we recognize the analogy between these kinds of distinctions and a cell's recursively operating inner principles, we understand how a cellular system can model a social system's self-maintenance and persistence over time. The role played by membranes in the case of cells is played among social systems by what Luhmann refers to as "meaning-constituted boundaries" (*SS* 194–97). Such boundaries designate different procedures for selecting relevant information from the world while at the same time relegating other information to the background. Like the human visual system responding to light in its environment, the social system uses energy and information from the outside, but it is an operationally closed system in that it makes use of them only according to its own principles.

It should be clear even from this preliminary sketch just how marginal human beings are for Luhmann's theory. It is the network of codes and distinctions, not persons or individual subjects, that constitute a system as the system it is. These networks determine what is relevant or irrelevant to the system, just as a cell will "see" a certain ion as something that it does or does not "want" to interact with. The economic vocabulary of payment and non-payment simply plays no role in, say, a Catholic mass. From the point of view of the mass itself (and if we find this phrasing strange, we have been seduced by the anthropomorphism that Luhmann puts into question), what matters is the distinction between mundane and transcendent—which is to say that the event belongs to the religious system. Similarly, a judge doesn't make a decision in a particular case according to what she is being paid, but according the criteria of legal and illegal at work in a given society (and when the judge does otherwise, hackles are raised).[44] Moreover, none of these varying criteria are mutually commensurate. That which is legal need not be beautiful, transcendent, or profitable. To survive, each system must maintain the tightness of the inferences that its meanings make possible, just as the plant needs to maintain the strength of its leaves and grow new ones when the old ones die. Doing so means always finding ways to reduce the ever-changing environment to the system's own tightly linked and exclusive set of terms, much as Ras's group in *Invisible Man* reduces experience to "your pahst" or the Brotherhood fixes the world with the terms of the class struggle. The system must continually decide anew what is beautiful/ugly, what is legal/illegal, and so forth. Not to do so is—and again, the physical-systems vocabulary is Luhmann's, not mine—to risk entropy, the state in which "connectivity is not straightened," because "everything comes into consideration" and "the system reproduces itself out of itself purely by chance" (SS 49). A critic might try to claim a higher perspective here and question whether these systems are as self-subsistent as they believe. We might ask whether, say, the religious or legal system actually reinforces the economic system of the capitalist order. But as the case of the Catholic mass illustrates, what matters to Luhmann is the self-understanding of the systems, how they conceive of themselves as "unrelated" to other systems, how they appear (phenomenology again) "from the inside."

For some commentators, Luhmann's account does away with the idea of agency wholesale. Hans Ulrich Gumbrecht, for instance, has argued that "subjecthood and agency are highly marginal attributes in the realm of living organisms," and that Luhmann's attraction to a biological vocabulary is an

---

[44] This is Luhmann's own example, given in the interview "Theory of a Different Order," in *Observing Complexity: Systems Theory and Postmodernity,* ed. William Rasch and Cary Wolfe (Minneapolis: University of Minnesota Press, 2000), 127.

outgrowth of his wish to expunge these terms altogether.[45] But this is deeply misleading. Agency would indeed be highly marginal to biological systems if they were described in the kind of nomological terms that Ellison's narrator applies to "natural resources." But this is not at all Luhmann's strategy. Luhmannian social systems may not be "living" ones, but they are depicted as thoroughly sentient and thoroughly intentional. Social systems for Luhmann can select meanings, refer to themselves, organize themselves, maintain their boundaries, and distinguish features. They are able to observe events, view things from certain perspectives, interpenetrate one another, learn their own habits of acting, decide the identities and differences that matter to it, detach themselves from physical systems. These predicates are no more figures of speech, no more bound in scare-quotes, than those used by the psychoanalysts diagnosing the United States in *The Onion*. It is thus more accurate to say, against Gumbrecht, that Luhmann's theory is an effort to expunge the *human* agent from our account of social systems and structures—if by "human" we mean, as I have over the last several chapters, the sorts of capacities typically associated with embodied human persons. It is this unwillingness to treat embodied entities as the sole loci of agency that makes Luhmann into Nietzsche's heir. The Kantian capacities of spontaneity are displaced from an "I" onto a "we" or, perhaps better, an "it." The self-enclosure that the young Nietzsche figures in the terraced Greek theater, and which in the later work becomes the unified set of practices that he calls *culture,* reappears in Luhmann in the form of the bounded social system, which stands apart from its environment by reducing that environment's complexity. Hence the "constructivism" often ascribed to Nietzsche and openly embraced by Luhmann: nature in no way dictates the terms of a system's self-understanding. A system "acquires freedom and the autonomy of self-regulation by indifference to its environment" and by an increased sensitivity to that which "is capable of being connected internally" (SS 183). Or, in more starkly Idealist terms: "Societies constitute worlds."[46]

The difference, then, between Luhmann's biology-talk and that of Cavell and Dewey could not be stronger. Dewey and Cavell would endorse the Sellarsian claim, which we saw in chapter 2, that terms like "spirit" and "soul" designate a "ghostly *person,* something analogous to flesh and blood persons which 'inhabits' them, or is otherwise intimately connected with them" (SPR 11). Luhmann has no truck with terms like "spirit" and "soul," but

[45] Hans Ulrich Gumbrecht, "Why Maturana?" *Journal of Aesthetic Education* 40.1 (2006): 23.

[46] Niklas Luhmann, *Essays on Self-Reference* (New York: Columbia University Press, 1990), 7. Henceforth *Self-Reference.*

from his point of view, Sellars's remark would still represent an outdated belief that human beings are the only meaning-making systems out there. He wouldn't question Dewey's claim that choices and purposes "have their locus in single beings," but he would pressure him to say why "single beings" should mean only individual human organisms. And Luhmann would be even less persuaded than Nietzsche by Cavell's effort to model society on the basis of smaller, local relations such as friendships or marriages. From Luhmann's perspective, Cavell and Dewey fail to face up to what in modernity lies beyond the ken and control of any of its members. By the end of the eighteenth century, as a phenomenon such as the Terror illustrates, "collective singulars"—"abstract ideas" that "replace concepts having concrete reference to what could individually be experienced"—had come to stand over and above face-to-face "interactions." Accordingly, he argues, efforts to ground social theories in the older, all-encompassing notion of *societas,* a term that once encompassed both personal relations and more general social institutions and associations, are merely wishful thinking (*SS* 425–32). And he would presumably say the same with respect to *philia*. The complex systems of modernity "outlast the death of individuals," and this stability and continuity makes them, not individuals, the proper focus for describing "the history of salvation, political history," "the rise and fall of ages and empires," and other features of socio-cultural evolution (*SS* 407). All this, he would argue, is largely glossed over by the Americans.[47]

Luhmann departs from Nietzsche over at least two issues that deserve attention. One becomes evident when we clarify something about my explication so far: his distinctions between legal, educational, political, economic, and other systems are not offered as lamentations. The differentiated spheres of modernity cannot be wished away, and understanding their various forms of rationality and sense-making is more urgent than simply critiquing them. Nietzsche strives early and late for a culture whose parts and functions form a "coordinated" whole, and bemoans modernity's mishmash of "styles." What matters for an individual life, he claims, is "*obedience* over a long period of time and in a *single* direction" (*BGE* 101). Analogously, a true culture "is above

---

[47] Systems Theorists may not criticize all Americans in the tradition that I'm describing. In *Social Emergence,* R. Keith Sawyer distinguishes Dewey from George Herbert Mead on precisely the theme I'm addressing here (35–37), and Luhmann himself occasionally lauds Mead as a predecessor who was on the right track (see *SS* 245, 536). I have implied in this paragraph, too, that Nietzsche was uninterested in the sort of local affiliations highlighted by the Americans, but this isn't the whole picture. On this topic as it develops in Nietzsche's career, see Ruth Abbey, "Circles, Ladders and Stars: Nietzsche on Friendship," *Critical Review of International Social and Political Philosophy* 2.4 (Winter, 1999): 50–73.

all the unity of artistic style in all the expressions of the life of a people," barbarism a "lack of style or a chaotic jumble of all styles" (*UM* 5–6). But Luhmann, like Weber, holds out no hope for recovering such single directions and unities, and the units he identifies are always the subsystems of a society, not the society in itself. Whatever unity is exhibited by modern society is not that of "social integration" or any kind of "pooled identity," let alone one of "common territorial boundaries," but simply the bland minimal unity of meaningful communication generally (*Self-Reference* 178–79). "Old European" society, the period before the late seventeenth century, was differentiated vertically, with strata that reflected clear notions of higher and lower or center and margin: nobles and commoners, priests and laymen. But, in Luhmann's view, modern societies differentiate themselves horizontally, according to the incommensurate functions played by the economic, educational, political, artistic, and other systems. Luhmann's modernity is "an acentrically conceived world and society" that can be accounted for only by a "polycentrically (and accordingly polycontextural) theory"—"a labyrinth more than a freeway off into the sunset" (*SS* li–lii). His goal is not to stitch the world back together, but to describe precisely how its former unities of territory and rank have given way in the course of social evolution, how "the starting points vary" between modern systems, and why "integrative formulas" have loosened (*SS* 92). Whereas Nietzsche focuses on the experience of Attic theater, Luhmann focuses, so to speak, on modernity's proliferation of theaters, each with its own dramas and choruses, each abutting (though never coinciding with) its neighboring theaters.

Luhmann's coolly neutral account of modern differentiation puts him at odds not only with Nietzsche, but has also caused friction among thinkers who position themselves specifically against the Nietzschean tradition. One frequent sparring partner has been Jürgen Habermas, who has claimed that Luhmann's theory all too conveniently vindicates technocratic instrumental rationality and obscures the historical and conceptual importance of the public sphere.[48] But Luhmann's second departure from Nietzsche is just as important as the first, and becomes evident when we recognize that, for Luhmann, there is a third kind of system standing between the level of the "living" system (the material processes described by biology) and the level of the economic, political, and other social systems. This is what he calls the "psychic system." The psychic system is roughly what has been traditionally called the "subject," though, as he does with other systems, Luhmann

---

[48] Habermas examines *Social Systems* at length in *The Philosophical Discourse of Modernity: Twelve Lectures,* trans. Frederick G. Lawrence (Cambridge: MIT Press, 1987), 368–85.

describes it in untraditional terms as maintaining itself by selecting "meanings." All these systems are, he says, "isomorphic," but in the case of psychic systems, the form of meaning is not "communication," as it is in social systems, but what Luhmann calls "consciousness." The term "consciousness" reminds us once again of Luhmann's roots in phenomenology, and indeed nowhere does *Social Systems* strike more Husserlian notes than chapter 7, "The Individuality of Psychic Systems." As an autopoietic system, consciousness is perturbed but not causally determined by the systems around it. And this includes not only other psychic systems, and not only the educational, political, and other systems of modernity. It also includes language, which Luhmann describes in terms that recall what we heard earlier from William James and Steven Pinker. "One need only observe," he says, "one's own groping thoughts, the search for correct words, the experience of failing to find them" in order to recognize "that much more is present [in any given situation] than the linguistic sequence of words with meanings that can be isolated for communication" (*SS* 272–73).[49]

The details of the "psychic system" and "consciousness" are less important here than the light they shed on Luhmann's conception of social systems. For mentioning them is a way of illustrating the extent to which Luhmann conceives of social systems as thoroughly *independent* beings. Social systems, he says, "are not composed of psychic systems, let alone of bodily human beings," but instead form themselves "autonomously and on the basis of their own elemental operations" (*SS* 255). The millennia-old way of conceiving a social body has been to say that individuals are "within" it or "compose" it. The *zôon politikon* and *animale sociale* coexisted alongside others within cities, which made society into "a body of its own type composed of bodies that are not joined physically" (*SS* 211). In such a scheme, accordingly, the *telos* of the individual and the *telos* of the community could, in theory, parallel one another. Nietzsche's celebration of the Attic throngs roughly follows this tradition: differences between individuals are erased as Dionysian heights are reached, but it is originally *as* individuals that the audience enters the theater. Luhmann recognizes no comparably disparate components, and gives no comparable story about how the emergent unities that he describes actually grew to be radically independent. He begins, as it were, with the *principium individuationis* already dissolved and with an audience that is already

---

49 The connection to James is more than implicit; Luhmann approvingly refers to James's description of "the fringes" of consciousness just prior to the sentence I'm quoting here (*SS* 268). It is this conception of language as an extra-added feature of consciousness that Habermas finds questionable; see *Philosophical Discourse*, 378–84.

strongly unified and already self-reproducing. The psychic system does not lose its individuality *tout court* (hence the title of chapter 7); it observes, makes distinctions, and performs all the tasks Luhmann attributes to autopoietic systems. But given the self-subsistent, self-referring, self-enclosed nature of all autopoietic systems, it does so always at some remove from any social systems. They observe it as much as it observes them.

And this suggests one powerful consequence of Luhmann's theory: psychic systems are incapable of altering the social systems that make up their environments. As in Dewey, the "concrete person" stands outside the crowd, convention, or corporation, but in a very un-Deweyan way he or she is also powerless to conduct, boss, or manage it. To be outside the meaning-constituted membrane of a social system is for Luhmann only to "perturb" it. The system itself will ultimately decide the extent of its interactions with the individual. To be sure, Luhmann recognizes that social systems would be no more possible without psychic systems than psychic systems would be without biological systems. But just as we can describe a person's mental states without knowing anything about the chemical events in his or her brain—this is, after all, what makes our folk psychology as efficient and effective as it is—so, Luhmann implies, we can describe the behavior of a social system without correlating it in any way to the lower-level behavior of persons. This is what Luhmann means when he says, in a statement that at first glance seems wildly counter-intuitive, "human beings are not part of society" just as "nerve cells are not part of the nervous system" (SS 229). If we want an account of what was acceptable in the "system of social interaction" in the eighteenth century—the exclusion of awkward political and religious themes, the avoidance of erudite topics, the ideal of rapid and witty exchange (SS 195–96)—we need not know anything about particular speakers, any one of whom may represent a dismissible deviation from the statistical norm. Similarly, to understand how "the theme complex of love and sexuality underwent a moral crisis" from about 1650 to 1800, we need to ask how this form of person-to-person interaction was detached from the ideas and institutions of continuity (e.g., marriage) and was reduced to a momentary, inconstant phenomenon that "signified total fulfillment for the participants—but only for the instant" (SS 238–39). Asking these kinds of questions doesn't require bothering too much with any one individual's emotional or romantic encounters.[50]

---

[50] The development of modern love is treated extensively by Luhmann in *Love as Passion: The Codification of Intimacy*, trans. Jeremy Gaines and Doris L. Jones (Cambridge: Harvard University Press, 1986).

A moment ago I drew an analogy between the efficiency of our folk psychology and the explanatory goals of Luhmann's systems theory. The force of the analogy lies in Luhmann's belief that emergent social orders are detectable in things like "statistical aggregates" (*SS* 255). These inform us about the beliefs and desires of a given social body just as the aggregate behaviors of an individual body inform us of a person's beliefs and desires, even when we know nothing about the particulars of his or her idiosyncratic biological make-up. But this analogy breaks down in at least one important way that we should make explicit before moving on to the final chapter. Unlike the folk psychologist, the Luhmannian theorist necessarily forgoes both the manifest image as well as the ordinary language through which the manifest image is expressed. And this is something Luhmann himself recognizes clearly. In the preface of *Social Systems,* he claims that our everyday habit of ascribing purposive action to embodied, perceptible persons involves deceptive ontological beliefs, and theories built upon these commonplace ascriptions are said to work with "imprecise concepts" (*SS* xliii). As sociologists, we have to renounce the essentially dramatic accounts of behavior that we use everyday, and we must avoid terms designating public, common, and conspicuous objects. We need to place entities like Economy and Politics on the same plane of our descriptions as entities like John and Mary. Doing so would allow us to avoid the mistakes of most of the classical authors of modern social theory, in whose works, says Luhmann, "one finds a regrettable carelessness in conceptual questions—as if ordinary language were all that is needed to create ideas or even texts" (*SS* xxxvii). Jettisoning this ordinary language, he asserts, is the first step toward finding a language with far greater "rigor and precision" (*SS* xxxviii).

Such claims are revealing, for they make Luhmann vulnerable to the questions that always emerge when theorists treat ordinary language chiefly as a source of mystification. They move Luhmann onto slippery ice, where, as Wittgenstein says, conditions seem ideal but there is too little friction to walk (*PI* §107). In what circumstances, we should ask, do we learn to say that something is *deciding, perceiving, drawing a distinction,* or carrying out any of the other sophisticated capacities that Luhmann attributes to social systems? Aren't meanings always meanings *for* someone, a person who can reflectively endorse or refuse the norms structuring our speech and behavior? Aren't meanings therefore always susceptible to the breakdowns that Cavell, for one, explores in such detail? To ask these questions is to notice that, for all the talk of "communication" in Luhmann's work, there is remarkably little attention paid to *mis*communication, to signals misinterpreted or signs applied inappropriately. A judge accepting a bribe is not, in Luhmann's eyes, a case of someone misunderstanding the rules or making a mistake. It is rather a case of one system (the economic) operating in circumstances usually structured by that of another (the legal). A Luhmannian could respond by arguing that the notions of "mistake" or "misunderstanding" simply have no application to social systems, that social systems simply perceive what they perceive and make the distinctions they do. But if this is true, then such systems are clearly not wholly "isomorphic" with systems at the personal level, as Luhmann implies. At *this* level, misunderstanding, both among judges and everyone else, is commonplace—at times merely irritating, at times embarrassing, at times tragic. In essence, Luhmann gives us a version of Kripke's claim that "the community" decides how to add numbers and apply *yellow*. But in suggesting this, both Kripke and Luhmann display a curious defect: neither the "community" nor the "social system" can ever be *wrong* relative to a certain standard in the way that a person can be in speaking or acting. In fact, Luhmann goes well beyond Kripke in this regard, since, unlike Kripke, he lacks even the notion of a teacher who "intervenes" to set the student straight about how to add. Despite the monumental density of Luhmann's prose, in other words, Luhmann's thinking is marked by a certain tidiness. He is keen to locate the ruptures that separate systems from one another, and emphasizes the proliferation of systems that characterize the course of modernity. But for all these complications, each system he describes behaves in the same fundamental way. The systems-theoretical model that he adopts from Varela and Maturana is applied unremittingly to every level of analysis, with the effect that all systems exhibit the same basic dynamics and the same basic interactions. Drastically different domains come to exhibit a strange uniformity—a uniformity that contrasts sharply with the heterogeneous descriptions of behavior offered by Wittgenstein and Sellars. For these figures, no "general theory" will adequately explain the doings of the world's many entities, whether this theory is reductionist or anti-reductionist in spirit. They agree with Luhmann that different phenomena are identified when observers adopt different stances, but unlike Luhmann, they suggest that these different stances entail different models and explanatory strategies. Sometimes these models and strategies mesh with one another in some rough way: the United States may indeed often behave like a person abused in childhood. But it would be formulaic and unenlightening to insist that *all* systems, from bacteria to the New York Stock Exchange, are at all times perfectly well analogous to one another. Social explanation no doubt requires reference to something other than the actions of this or that individual. But this is not the same as saying that individuals never play a role in such explanations.[51]

This line of questioning suggests others. Can we really be so sure that the different sorts of systems Luhmann describes—the scientific and educational, say—are as cleanly differentiated as he claims they are? Is his theory really applicable to a world (ours, for example) in which economic interests do not merely "perturb" other spheres of life, but often control them in unsubtle ways?[52] One might also note comparisons to some of the questions raised in part I. To what extent does Luhmann simply give an externalized version of the mental modules, lexicons, visuo-spatial sketchpads, and other talented internal agents posited by many cognitive scientists? Such systems can be analyzed on their own, but they are never *identifiable* on their own; they are always the systems *of* persons. Isn't a similar kind of conceptual dependence evident with Luhmann's systems? Still more pressing questions could be raised about the very scientific model on which Luhmann bases his entire account. Does the theory of autopoiesis have anything like the predictive power of a mature science? Or is it, as Alex Viskovatoff has suggested in an analysis that echoes my discussion of "poetic science" in part I, simply a *descriptive* enterprise, a way of talking that lacks any nomological clout? Systems Theory may, as one leading Luhmannian puts it, give up "the idea of the ordering of the world causally by attributing causes and effects to its different phenomena" in favor of describing the "unity of systems that are ecologically linked with one another." But if the behavior of an ecological system can be understood only as an emergent whole, and if therefore it cannot be neatly reduced to causal mechanisms, does this mean that lower-level causal analyses are entirely irrelevant? Paleoseismologists can make sharper predictions when chemists tell them about the composition of a given area's soil. Can similar linkages to neighboring disciplines be made by Luhmann's theory?[53]

---

[51] For further questions about the relation of folk psychology to social explanation, see part II of Bernard Williams's *Making Sense of Humanity and Other Philosophical Essays* (Cambridge: Cambridge University Press, 1995). Habermas also addresses Luhmann's use of scientific descriptions "remote from everyday experience"; see *Philosophical Discourse,* 384–85.

[52] On the problem of differentiation, see Erkki Sevänen, "Art as an Autopoietic Subsystem of Modern Society: A Critical Analysis of the Concepts of Art and Autopoietic Systems in Luhmann's Late Production," *Theory, Culture, and Society* 18 (2001): 75–103.

[53] Viskovatoff raises his astute questions in "Foundations of Niklas Luhmann's Theory of Social Systems," *Philosophy of the Social Sciences* 29 (1999), 481–516. The Luhmannian disciple cited here is Dirk Baecker, "Why Systems?" *Theory, Culture, and Society* 18 (2001): 64. For further questions about Luhmann's scientific model, see also N. Katherine Hayles, "Making the Cut: The Interplay of Narrative and System, or What Systems Theory Can't See," in *Observing Complexity,* ed. Rasch and

It is unclear to me how Luhmann would respond to any of these questions. As a set of arguments about modern culture and society, his descriptions raise as many questions as they answer, and any theory of a certain phenomena—literature, for example—that grounds itself in Luhmann's thinking will be persuasive only to the extent that such questions can be convincingly answered. We need to be careful in making this claim, however. For pointing to potential holes in Luhmann's theory does not mean that Luhmann's vision, like Nietzsche's, cannot exert a powerful influence over a writer's imagination, or over us in our everyday lives. Cavell has wryly remarked how many academic thinkers are "daily surprised" that Descartes, Rousseau, religion, or Romanticism have survived the confident refutations that repeatedly appear in their journal articles (*CR* 5). Hence his attention to the "truth of skepticism" that is acknowledged in Wittgenstein. Luhmann's theories, I want to claim, exhibit a similar kind of "truth." Whatever weak logic or sketchy evidence we may feel compelled to expose and purify as theoreticians, surely he isn't merely foolish in sensing that there are social dynamics whose staggering complexity makes them seem in *some* sense self-subsistent and self-generating. Many of us, I assume, have at one point or another been struck by how our grandest gestures can seem to leave even small-scale institutions untouched, or have shrugged in ignorance when a child asks us to explain why our schools or artworks look as they do, or have found the global economy a kind of unintelligible mystery. These phenomena can all seem, to use a phrase whose full force Luhmann would appreciate, *beyond me*. And it is this appeal, this sense that Luhmann's theory captures something about us and can have a hold over us, that I want to take seriously here.

To do so, however, I need to move away from the philosophical portraits I have been giving and consider some of the ways the positions and debates I have been describing are given literary breath. But it is worth noting that, in doing so, we will not be leaving Luhmann behind as much as following his lead. For the recent history of the novel plays a small yet revealing role in his descriptions of modernity and of his own philosophical account of it, much as tragedy does more extensively for Cavell and Nietzsche. In the English preface to *Social Systems,* he notes that, in the "classical novel," the notion of action has "the double function of characterizing actors and propelling the story forward" (*SS* xliii). This novelistic tendency, he claims, filtered its way into sociology, which has generally "held fast to action" in all

---

Wolfe, 137–62; as well as the responses to Varela's "The Emergent Self," in *The Third Culture: Beyond the Scientific Revolution,* ed. John Brockman (New York: Touchstone, 1995), 216–22, especially those by Stuart Kauffman, Dennett, and Christopher G. Langton.

the unexamined anthropomorphic ways that he seeks to expose. The genre of the novel, however, has abandoned this old idea and blazed a new trail: it has "renounced inferences about motives and returned to a 'flat' character-ization of persons," and has "concentrated the story in a single moment and no longer carried it forward, but only remembered" (SS xliii). Sociology, he says, has for the most part plodded along "without heeding the signals that an art intellectually often in the vanguard...was transmitting everywhere" (SS xliii). What exactly this "vanguard" looks like is the question to which we now turn.

❦ CHAPTER 6

The Culture and Its Loaded Words

In interviews Don DeLillo has insisted that the dialogues in his novels display speech as it actually falls from the lips of people, but readers haven't always agreed. Perhaps the most hostile, or at least well-publicized, disagreement was voiced by B. R. Myers in his 2001 "manifesto" against contemporary fiction. After describing DeLillo as a novelist of limited gifts, full of spurious profundity, and downright silly, Myers selected a slice of dialogue from *White Noise*—in which Jack Gladney and his wife say repeatedly that they want what's best for the other—as an example of the "long conversations of the who's-on-first? variety" strewn throughout DeLillo's work. The exchange, he said, "loses its logic halfway through" and gives rise to "the same queasy fatigue we can get from an evening of channel-surfing."[1]

Dialogues, however, aren't the only things in DeLillo that can seem to lose their logic halfway through. One can only imagine Myers's response to this passage from *Underworld,* where Nick Shay describes his life in suburban

---

[1] B. R. Myers, "A Reader's Manifesto," *Atlantic Monthly,* July/August 2001, 114. For a more appreciative discussion of DeLillo's dialogues, see Martin Amis, "Survivors of the Cold War," review of *Underworld, New York Times Book Review,* October 5, 1997, 13. DeLillo's claim about the strict realism of his dialogues is made in *Conversations with Don DeLillo,* ed. Thomas DePietro (Jackson: University Press of Mississippi, 2005), 69–70 (henceforth cited as *Conversations*).

Arizona with his wife, his disaffected son, his aging mother, and a baseball that may or may not have been hit by Bobby Thomson in 1951:

> I used to tell my kids when they were small. A hawser is a rope that's used to moor a ship. Or, The hump in the floor between rooms, I used to say. This is called the saddle.
>
> We set her up with the dresser and the air conditioner and a hard mattress that was good for her back. She brought forth names from the family passional, the book of special suffering, and we paused and thought. . . .
>
> After the riots in Los Angeles my son started wearing baggy shorts and a cap turned backwards and sneakers with bloated tongues. Before this he used to be nondescript, sitting in his room with his computer, a quiet kid just turned twenty. . . .
>
> We designed and managed landfills. We were waste brokers. We arranged shipments of hazardous waste across the oceans of the world. We were the Church Fathers of waste in all its transmutations. I almost mentioned my line of work to Klara Sax when we had our talk in the desert. . . . But something made me wary. I didn't want her to think I was implying some affinity of effort and perspective.
>
> Famous people don't want to be told that you have a quality in common with them. It makes them think there's something crawling in their clothes.
>
> My father's name was James Costanza, Jimmy Costanza—add the letters and you get thirteen.
>
> At home we removed the wax paper from cereal boxes. We had a recycling closet with separate bins for newspapers, cans and jars. . . .
>
> Sometimes we used the pauses to watch TV. We looked at reruns of "The Honeymooners" and my mother laughed when Ralph Kramden flung his arms and bellowed great complaints. . . .
>
> A hawser is the thing you tie around a bollard.
>
> I noticed how people played at being executives while actually holding executive positions. Did I do this myself? You maintain a shifting distance between yourself and your job. (*U* 102–3)

I have quoted at length here in order to highlight the range of topics over which Nick sweeps on any given page. Each paragraph is a self-contained unit, a riff on a given theme. Many of the riffs display DeLillo's gift for spying the small absurdities of contemporary American life: the suburban son's immersion in urban hip-hop culture, the unending replay of old sitcoms. But an obvious link between riffs is discernible only between the fourth and fifth paragraphs quoted. In one he writes about avoiding comparison to Klara Sax, who is a celebrated artist by the time he meets her in the desert, and he follows this up by explaining why "famous people" don't care for sycophants. Strict entailment this is not; the link is thematic rather than logical. But none of the other paragraphs in the passage seem to exhibit even this much rough-and-ready relation. In the course of a page and a half, the text cuts briskly between the son's identity crisis, the family's recycling, Nick's fixation with obscure nouns like *hawser,* life with his mother, his job, his missing father, his mother's television habits, some more about hawsers, and finally the role-playing of corporate executives. The voice is a curious mixture of Beckett and the U.S. Census, enumerating more than narrating—a lonely monologue that describes less a particular family with a particular history than the median late-century suburban household of the American Southwest.

We can ratchet up these observations: the disconnection between paragraphs here is felt also between the book's scenes and chapters. The first four sections of *Underworld* are divided into five to seven chapters, all consisting of scenes of three to eight pages, and all covering a wide assortment of characters and loosely measured periods of time: the mid-1980s to the early 1990s, summer 1974. This rapid veering between chapters and scenes grows most frantic in Part 5, "Better Things for Better Living Through Chemistry," which is subtitled "Selected Fragments Public and Private in the 1950s and 1960s." Here we find seven chapters scrupulously arranged into three scenes apiece, with each scene assigned a date—"November 3, 1952," "October 22, 1962," "July 12, 1953," and so on. A scene-by-scene breakdown is unnecessary, but it is important to note the medley of characters, settings, and activities that Part 5 unites: Nick in a Minnesota Jesuit correction facility in the early fifties; Lenny Bruce's monologues during the Cuban Missile Crisis (in LA, San Francisco, Chicago, Miami, New York); the Cold War family life of a boy who, years later, is a work colleague of Nick's brother Matt; race riots in Jackson, Mississippi; a day in an advertising agency with Charles Wainwright, who owns the alleged Thomson homerun ball; Chuckie Wainwright, son of Charles, flying a bomber over Vietnam; Nick's fiancé watching late-sixties protesters in Madison, Wisconsin; J. Edgar Hoover and his assistant preparing for Truman Capote's Black and White Ball in 1969; Nick and a girlfriend in Mexico, seeking an abortion in the late fifties; Janet, Matt's future wife, sprinting home from work in 1967; Nick during the New York City blackout of 1965; etc.

The paragraph, scene, and chapter-sized pieces assembled in *Underworld* exhibit what we might call, for reasons that will become clearer along the way, an aesthetic of the heap. A question we should ask about this aesthetic is: why do it? What's the effect of piling pieces on top of one another? DeLillo is hardly, of course, the first writer to work in such a mode. Dos Passos's *U. S. A.* trilogy is in many ways the grandparent of *Underworld,* bringing together comparably sized portions of text and encompassing a comparable swath of private and public lives. But DeLillo is a more speculative writer than Dos Passos, more given to asking what in such texts and such lives is, to recall two keywords of *Underworld,* "real" and "unreal." His concern is not just to compile a record of historical events, but to ask how we make sense of these events in the first place. The ambitious scope of the novel will allow me to extend and complicate the previous chapter's discussion of Nietzschean and Luhmannian strong holism, and, with some work, will help me round out the discussion of agency that we have been pursuing throughout this book.

 ## EVERYTHING IS CONNECTED

Why does this piece of *Underworld* follow that piece of *Underworld?* A version of this question has been raised here before. Stein's writing forces it on us continually, at least in her most radical moments, where single words are amassed with the same heaping effect of DeLillo's paragraphs, scenes, and chapters. Moreover, just as with Stein, some readers might be inclined to answer the question of what connects everything by saying: *nothing.* Such a response may be made with a slothful shrug, but it may also be part of a more metaphysically ambitious claim—a belief, say, that the text's disunity illustrates the non-teleological haphazardness of existence. "Reality," this argument would go, is really an array of unstructurable and endlessly heterogeneous particulars, and any seamless narrative is merely an effect of prejudice, a mistaken belief that we can understand actions without falling into parochial moralism or totalitarian politics. Seeing *Underworld* in such a light would be to say, as one reader of *Libra* has put it, citing Hayden White, that DeLillo's novel exposes history as a series of rhetorical maneuvers effacing certain events in favor of others.[2] What Donald Sutherland learns from Stein's resistance to "remembering" might, in this light, be equally well learned from DeLillo: "immediate experience in its real immediacy is not comprehensible, has no meaning, and when you do induce a meaning you falsify the essential immediacy."

---

[2] See Glen Thomas, "History, Biography, and Narrative in Don DeLillo's *Libra,*" *Twentieth-Century Literature* 43 (1997): 120–23. At the end of his essay, Thomas wisely notes that *Libra* complicates White's Barthesian theories at the same time that it embodies them.

This skeptical argument runs into at least three related obstacles, however. One is that it ignores an embarrassingly obvious fact: all the sentences appear between the same covers. Such physical unity may seem too trivial to need mentioning, but doing so is a way of reminding us that the book might have been published as eight novellas, or eighty short stories, rather than as the novel with the eight parts (counting Prologue and Epilogue) that it is.

A less obvious obstacle for the skeptic concerns a distinction between Stein and DeLillo that analogies between them can obscure. Stein, recall, is fragmenting sentences; DeLillo is fragmenting stories. This distinction makes a difference, because stories lack anything like the well-established syntax of sentences. Our criteria for knowing when strings of words form sentences are relatively stable and shared, at least enough that we can diagram them or struggle with the often puzzling grammar of a foreign language. But our criteria for knowing when strings of sentences form intelligible stories are far more unsettled, hence flexible. Nick's paragraphs about Arizona life are every bit as thematically disparate as I have described. But they don't undermine any well-entrenched structures, and readers will agree far less about where to locate the "breakdowns" of his monologue than they will with the "breakdowns" of Stein's quasi-sentences. The idea that a series of reported actions and events might have determinable elements and structures has guided various well-known theories seeking narrative codes, grammars, and logics. But the Aristotelian trio of beginning, middle, and end is an elastic conceptual structure compared to a well-fashioned sentence. If it weren't, then computer programs for identifying badly told stories would be as cheap and plentiful as ones for identifying grammatical gaffes.[3] Indeed, narratives are more elastic than a host of verbal genres, even ones that extend beyond the single sentence. When Alan Turing was staking out standards for artificial intelligence, one of his great intuitions was that we need enough leverage to distinguish well-formed but arbitrarily arranged sentences from well-formed sentences that "follow" from others. The benchmark he came up with—how well a system answers questions—is a suitably well-circumscribed format, since most of the time an answer to a question can be recognized *as* an answer. (The Delphic oracle's responses are the exception proving the rule.) A Turing Test consisting of a story-telling contest would lack these norms of appropriateness, and so wouldn't be able

---

[3] For a classic effort to make a program for understanding stories, see David E. Rummelhart, "Notes on a Schema for Stories," in *Representing and Understanding: Studies in Cognitive Science,* ed. Daniel G. Bobrow and Allan Collins (New York: Academic Press, 1975), 211–36. For more recent discussions, see the extensive bibliography compiled by Erik T. Mueller, "Story Understanding Resources," http://xenia.media.mit.edu/~mueller/storyund/storyres.html (accessed May 24, 2007).

to tell the enigmatic parable-maker or misunderstood genius from the stupid machine.[4]

In short, whatever "gaps" seem to mark *Underworld,* there are few rules about how to "fill them in," and thus an indefinite number of plausible ways to do so. And this leads to a third problem with the skeptic's account: it fails to describe what actually goes on in *Underworld.* The origins of the baseball in Nick's house do not remain a mystery to the reader, even if they do to Nick and the other characters in the text. This fact suggests just how keen DeLillo is to display something other than the unintelligible arbitrariness of historical events. If, after all, he were striving to illustrate the impossibility or naiveté of traditional linear narrative, the book could have been far more haphazard than it is. The very same scenes might have been placed in folders on the floor and then ordered according to which ones DeLillo's pet dogs most gnawed upon. Or the texts might have been written even more arbitrarily relative to space and time, with far-flung scenes set in ancient Carthage, on Jupiter in the year 3097, in twelfth-century Armenia, in California during the Gold Rush, and so forth. *Underworld* may be as wide-ranging and epic in proportion as virtually anything in twentieth-century fiction. But ultimately it, too, has its boundaries.

That there are indeed boundaries is moreover something that the charac-ters *within* the text emphatically ask us to recognize. There are no Hayden Whites in DeLillo's sprawling cast, which is full of characters who in one way or another endorse the dictum of Jesse Detwiler, the visionary "waste theorist" who appears briefly in Part 3: "everything's connected" (*U* 289). Describing his sorrow at the Bobby Thomson homerun in 1951, Nick Shay claims to have become a "budding numerologist" who wrote down "all the occult connections that seemed to lead to thirteen" (*U* 95). Marvin Lundy, who crisscrosses the country obsessively searching for the Thomson home-run ball, explains how two apparently unrelated clues each led him to one of the Texas Highway Killer's victims, a man who once owned the ball: "So the two rivers meet. Took a homicide to reveal the connection" (*U* 179). Sister Edgar, a nun in the Bronx, picks up a *Time* magazine in the 1990s and recognizes Klara Sax, whom she recalls from the old neighborhood: "All the connections intact" (*U* 250). Matt Shay, working in a military laboratory

---

[4] Alan Turing, "Computing Machinery and Intelligence," in *Mind Design II: Philosophy, Psychology, Artificial Intelligence,* ed. John Haugeland, rev. ed. (Cambridge: MIT Press, 1997), 29–56. It's also important to Turing's test that it checks a system's ability to respond to questions rather than pose them. The dangers of treating the latter ability as the mark of intelligence is illustrated in the 1960s computer program ELIZA, which acted as a respectable therapist by turning statements into well-formed questions.

in the 1970s, reflects upon how the numbers and symbols of mathematics might enter nature in the form of a nuclear explosion: "Everything connected at some undisclosed point down the systems line" (*U* 408). Matt again, recalling a drug-induced vision at a party the previous night: "He felt he'd glimpsed some horrific system of connections in which you can't tell the difference between one thing and another, between a soup can and a car bomb" (*U* 446). And at the end of the book, as the World Wide Web extends Sister Edgar's life into cyberspace, in a sentence that repeats Detwiler's phrase almost verbatim: "There is no space or time out here, or in here, or wherever she is. There are only connections. Everything is connected" (*U* 825).

The word "connection" is a close relative of other terms designating tight coherence, and *Underworld* calls upon just about every one. *Match,* for example: driving a Lexus through the desert in the early 1990s, Nick thinks that the car is "a natural match for the landscape" (*U* 63), just as, more speculatively, Marvin in the late 1970s wonders "what's the point of waking up in the morning if you don't try to match the enormousness of the known forces in the world with something powerful in your own life?" (*U* 323). Or *code:* a street preacher in 1951 Harlem describes the Freemason and Rosicrucian symbolism of the American dollar bill, announcing that he is "getting closer everyday to breaking the code" (*U* 354), just as Carlo Strasser, Klara Sax's neighbor and husband-to-be in the 1970s, says that money is "becoming very esoteric," a "higher kind of intelligence" made of "waves and codes" (*U* 386). Or *sign,* as when Marvin sees in Mikhail Gorbachev's birthmark the immanent secession of a Soviet republic: "Marvin saw the first sign of the total collapse of the Soviet system. Stamped on the man's head. The map of Latvia" (*U* 173). Or *link,* as when Sister Edgar reflects on the "faith that replaces God with radioactivity, the power of alpha particles and the all-knowing systems that shape them, the endless fitted links" (*U* 251), or when J. Edgar Hoover sees a vast conspiracy controlling the 1960s: "It's all linked. The war protesters, the garbage thieves, the rock bands, the promiscuity, the drugs, the hair" (*U* 577).

Writing about Foucauldian archeology, Manfred Frank once remarked that Foucault's claim to be interested only in the "dispersion" of statements and "discourses in their specificity" was betrayed by Foucault's actual practice. Archeology, Frank observed, cannot get off the ground without "the assumption of minimal unity and regularity," a kind of "supersystem": "Otherwise it would not even be a theory, but simply a conceptless and thoughtless list of singularities that are not the singularities *of* something."[5]

---

[5] Manfred Frank, *What Is Neostructuralism?* trans. Sabine Wilke and Richard Gray (Minneapolis: University of Minnesota Press, 1989), 173–74.

Luhmann, who shares Frank's background in German Idealism, strikes a comparable note in the opening sentences of *Social Systems*. "The following considerations," he writes there, "assume that there are systems. Thus they do not begin with epistemological doubt."[6] What I have been saying here up to now is that something like Frank's "minimal unity and regularity" and something like Luhmann's ontological assumption about "systems" lies behind the fragments of *Underworld* as well. Invoking these analogies to the German and post-Kantian tradition should remind us that Sergei Eisenstein—whose fictionalized lost film *Unterwelt* appears directly in the middle of DeLillo's novel, and who has been called a "cinematographic Hegel"—quotes Goethe at the start of his seminal 1931 essay, "A Dialectic Approach to Film Form": "In nature we never see anything isolated, but everything in connection with something else which is before it, beside it, under it, and over it."[7]

 NEURAL STRANDS, PARANOIA, AND ART

This engenders a new crop of questions. To say that parts can be connected and linked is not the same as saying precisely what kind of a whole these connections and links actually make. Eisenstein compared filmic montage with the Chinese ideogram, both of which, he said, are able to fuse "monstrous incongruities" into "one whole." The "independent 'mouth' and the dissociated 'child'" lock together to form "the significance of 'scream'" (*Form* 33–34). Can a similar kind of significance be said to arise from the pieces of *Underworld?* What precisely is the nature of DeLillo's "minimal unity and regularity," and exactly what kinds of "systems" are assumed?

Again we recall similar questions that surfaced during our encounters with Stein, whose fragments force us to ask what unifies her work once we give up regarding it as the straightforward outcome of efficient causes. To answer these questions in DeLillo's case, consider an episode in the narrative of Lenny Bruce's tour of 1962. The moment comes during Lenny's performance in Chicago, where he is telling jokes about condoms and Josef Mengele's nurse, punctuating his act with the line he has repeated throughout

---

[6] Niklas Luhmann, *Social Systems,* trans. John Bednarz, Jr., with Dirk Baecker (Stanford: Stanford University Press, 1995), 12. Henceforth cited parenthetically as *SS.*

[7] Sergei Eisenstein, *Film Form: Essays in Film Theory,* ed. and trans. Jay Leyda (Orlando: Harcourt Brace, 1977), 45; henceforth *Form.* "Cinematographic Hegel" is a phrase used by Gilles DeLeuze in *Cinema 2: The Time-Image,* trans. Hugh Tomlinson (Minneapolis: University of Minnesota Press, 1989), 210.

the Missile Crisis: *"We're all gonna die!"* At one point, Lenny stops his mono-logue unexpectedly, peers into the audience, and spits out a string of offen-sive words: "Mick spic hunky junkie boogie." A moment later he returns to the gesture, with a different concatenation of terms: "Fuck suck fag hag gimme a nickel bag" (*U* 585).

Bruce's lines are significant because they present in miniature the aes-thetic of the heap that *Underworld* displays at different levels everywhere. His eruption consists of discrete pieces that seem as non-purposively positioned as the larger arrangements of "Better Things for Better Living Through Chemistry." This isn't to suggest, as some readers have, that Bruce is simply DeLillo's alter ego. Lenny's story ends, after all, on a moment of failure that *Underworld* itself explicitly attempts to overcome. Performing in Carnegie Hall, Bruce struggles to dismantle a joke and tell a "realistic" story about a girl in the Bronx with a "real name," but when he can't invent anything adequate—"Let's tell the truth this time," he keeps repeating—he reverts to a predictable repertoire of Jewish-mother jokes and eventually leaves the stage "in his stupid white suit, small and remorseful" (*U* 633). The Epilogue of *Underworld* returns to this very same narrative in the bleak story of Esmer-alda, thereby distinguishing the powers of a novelist, on the one hand, from the slighter form of popular stand-up comedy, "show biz" (*U* 546), on the other. Lenny's one-liners can be assimilated into the office banter of Charles Wainwright, the advertising executive (*U* 528), in a way that DeLillo's own expansive novel never could be.[8]

Still, Bruce is clearly a crucial figure. His importance becomes visible, however, only when we listen to the interpretive gloss that DeLillo's narra-tor applies to his assembly of obscenities. "Mick spic hunky junky boogie," declaims Bruce, to which the omniscient speaker appends an extraordinary remark: "There was no context for the line except the one that Lenny took with him everywhere. The culture and its loaded words" (*U* 585). Bruce presents us, that is, with what seems to be mere noise, elements outside any intelligible pattern. But when read from the narrator's higher perspective, his arbitrary-looking strings are in fact no more arbitrary than any more rec-ognizably well-formed utterance. "Mick," "spic," "hunky," and the other terms are, as Manfred Frank says of Foucault's archive, the singularities *of*

---

[8] For a reading that sees Lenny Bruce as DeLillo's stand-in, see Timothy L. Parrish, "From Hoover's FBI to Eisenstein's *Unterwelt:* Don DeLillo Directs the Postmodern Novel," *Modern Fiction Studies* 43 (1999): 713–15. In *American Magic and Dread: Don DeLillo's Dialogue with Culture* (Philadelphia: University of Pennsylvania Press, 2000), Mark Osteen offers a more nuanced picture, noting that "Bruce runs out of fuel" and eventually succumbs to his heroin addiction; see 247–48. He says little, however, about how this reflects on DeLillo's own project.

something, namely, "the culture." The wildly disparate books of the Old and New Testament are taken by Christians to be the expression of a singular divine spirit, and so, in a similar vein, readers are supposed to regard the various pieces of Bruce's utterances as the expression of a single intentional system. This doesn't mean that Bruce himself is entirely cognizant of such a system. He is presented in the scene as *channeling* the culture's words more than selecting them on the basis of some well-articulated belief or theory. Nor do his utterances represent *all* the loaded words offered by the culture. Different sorts of terms are channeled elsewhere by different sorts of characters. The housewife Erica Deming, for instance, sees "nothing shrouded or walled or protected from the glare" as she reflects upon her list of "[w]ords to believe in and live by": "Breezeway," "Crisper," "Sectional," "Car pools," "Cookie sheet" (*U* 520). Next to this collection of anodyne terms, Lenny's scat is an "idlike wail" (*U* 547). The riot of ethnicity, sexuality, narcotics, and sonic effect suggested by his two word-strings evoke what Bruce himself calls the "secret history that never appears in the written accounts of the time or in the public statements of the men in power" (*U* 594). Just as we are meant to juxtapose his grotty and dangerous words with Erica's antiseptic and socially sanctioned ones, so we are meant to notice that Erica's sanitized home appears in the text immediately before civil rights protesters are clubbed by police in Mississippi (*U* 521–26).

If, then, Lenny Bruce and Erica Deming represent id and ego respectively, "secret history" and "public statements," we should ask just what sort of mind is being partitioned along these lines. It isn't the mind of Lenny or Erica. Nor is it the mind of any other character in the book. It is instead what DeLillo has called, in an essay that appeared when *Underworld* was published, the "deep mind of the culture," or what Bill Gray, the novelist of *Mao II*, calls "the inner life of the culture."[9] Taken jointly, Bruce's and Erica's roster of words exhibits the kind of unity expressed for Ellison's narrator in the clouds, passing trucks, and other accidental-looking "clues" he perceives during his early days as a Brotherhood activist. The "culture and its loaded words," the "deep mind" or "inner life" of the culture, the "inner nature of the age" (*U* 611), "the forces of the culture" (*U* 495), "the unknown energy" (*U* 19)—these things allow for as few "loose ends" as the "pattern and discipline" instilled by the Brotherhood's vocabulary. These images do the work that Quine does with his metaphors of the "man-made fabric" and "fields of force," which he uses

---

9 Don DeLillo, "The Power of History," *New York Times Magazine,* September 7, 1997, 62; henceforth cited as "History." Don DeLillo, *Mao II* (New York: Vintage, 1991), 41; henceforth cited parenthetically as *Mao.*

to explain why speaking about one thing requires being able to speak about many others, a semantic network that is readjusted with disturbances to the margins. In social terms, "the inner nature of the age" recalls Nietzsche's reveling throngs of the Attic theater or the "coordinated wholes" of *Genealogy of Morals,* "in which nothing whatever finds a place that has not first been assigned a 'meaning' in relation to the whole." Such phrases are *Underworld's* version—and here, to offer a final analogy, recall Luhmann's biological model of social systems—of what DeLillo has called the "neural strands" that link a social body and unite the "solitary writer" with "the public figure at the teeming center of events" ("History" 62). Tony Tanner, raising questions about the disjointed nature of the book as a whole, has complained that DeLillo's scattered narrative threads "do not collect around anything—unless you think that 'Cold War America' will do the gathering-in work" required by any artwork that is not "avowedly or manifestly aleatory." But this gathering-in is in fact precisely the job that DeLillo asks "the Culture" to do. To take DeLillo's neural image seriously is to see the unity of the Culture as akin to the unity of a brain. Its dozens of disparate characters "communicate" with one another in much the way that the disparate regions of the brain "communicate" with one another as information is processed. Tanner's error is to believe that the interest of a text lies, so to speak, in individual neurons more than in the emergent networks of which they are a part.[10]

The distributed presence of these "neural strands" in *Underworld* perhaps explains why critics have on the whole been as anti-skeptical in their interpretations as the characters within the novel. With Luhmann, they have assumed that there are systems and have not begun with epistemological doubt. Ten years before the novel was published, Tom LeClair explicitly characterized DeLillo as a "systems novelist" who analyzes how the vast economic, political, and cultural systems of contemporary globalized life interact.[11] Much commentary on *Underworld* can be understood as updating this description. One critic has defined the novel generically by saying that it is "most obviously a cultural biography," a story whose unity lies not in any

---

[10] Tony Tanner, "Afterthoughts on Don DeLillo's *Underworld,*" *Raritan* 17 (1998): 56. DeLillo's persons-as-neurons image is not without precedent: it is analogous to Ned Block's "Chinese Nation" thought experiment in "Troubles with Functionalism," in *Perception and Cognition: Issues in the Foundations of Psychology,* ed. Wade Savage, Minnesota Studies in the Philosophy of Science IX (Minneapolis: University of Minnesota Press, 1979), 261–326.

[11] Tom LeClair, *In the Loop: Don DeLillo and the Systems Novel* (Urbana: University of Illinois Press, 1987). LeClair's book, the first full-length study of DeLillo, makes no extended reference to Luhmann, but includes a good synthetic overview of Ludwig von Bertalanffy, one of Luhmann's chief inspirations. See especially his introduction.

particular person but in the society as a whole.[12] Others have tried to discern the narrative arc of this "biography," detailing the different kinds of loaded words that the Culture speaks over time. In these readings, the Culture in its Cold War stage is connected by the possibility of nuclear war, which is threatening in obvious ways but at least offers a recognizable set of ideological oppositions. As Klara Sax puts it, power in this period "was stable, was focused, it was a tangible thing" (*U* 76). By contrast, the Culture after 1989 doesn't collapse into fragments (as many commentators in the 1990s believed, pointing to the rise of ethnic violence and other phenomena) but is connected by what Nick Shay, visiting the former Soviet Union, calls a "method of production" that makes for "a certain furtive sameness, a planing away of particulars that affects everything from architecture to leisure time to the way people eat and sleep and dream" (*U* 785–86).

One conclusion to draw from this characterization is that *Underworld* undermines any potential triumphalism about American victory in the Cold War. The same novel that sets out from the symbolic starting point of the Cold War makes no reference at all to the fall of the Berlin Wall, its equally symbolic end.[13] For our purposes, however, what matters about the Culture's interlocking "connections" is less that they are made differently at different times than the fact that they exist at all, that the book remains "most obviously a cultural biography" rather than, like *Invisible Man* or *Henderson the Rain King,* most obviously the biography of a particular human person. The text can be understood as a *Bildungsroman,* albeit one in which the *Bildung* at issue is undertaken by something other than a particular human person. Unities evolve and stable Cold War dichotomies give way to post-Fordist connections of multinational capital, but nowhere does the text foreground a moment when such supra-personal connections are wholly absent. Later on I will qualify this description somewhat, since it is a *Bildungsroman* in other, more familiar senses as well. But for now we should recognize just how closely the basic development of *Underworld* parallels a claim Luhmann makes about the development of modernity as a whole: the world that behaved once according to rulers and ruled, priest and layman, now behaves "polycentrically" and "polycontexturally" (*SS* li).[14]

---

[12] Joseph Dewey, "A Gathering Under Words: An Introduction," in *UnderWords: Perspectives on Don DeLillo's* Underworld, ed. Joseph Dewey et al. (Newark: University of Delaware Press, 2002), 10.

[13] On this point, see Peter Knight, "Everything Is Connected: *Underworld's* Secret History of Paranoia," *Modern Fiction Studies* 45 (1999): 811–36, which I have been summarizing in the last few sentences.

[14] Compare the well-known kindred idea in Foucault that "we need to cut off the king's head" in political theory. See *The Foucault Reader,* ed. Paul Rabinow (New York: Pantheon, 1984), 63.

I have singled out Lenny Bruce here, but he is hardly the only artist in the book who operates according to an aesthetic of the heap reminiscent of *Underworld* itself. Eisenstein, as I noted earlier, is a major figure. "Arguments are raised and made," thinks Klara Sax as she watches *Unterwelt,* "theories drift across the screen and instantly shatter—there's a lot of opposition and conflict" (*U* 429). Ismael Muñoz, a. k. a. Moonman 157, thinks of his subway graffiti as "making your name and street number a kind of alphabet city where all the colors lock and bleed and the letters connect and it's all live jive, it jumps and shouts" (*U* 433). Nick sees the Watts Tower as "an idiosyncrasy out of someone's innocent anarchist visions," "a rambling art that had no category" (*U* 276–77), and Klara similarly regards it as "an amusement park, a temple complex and she didn't know what else," a "Delhi bazaar and Italian street feast maybe" (*U* 492). Klara's work expresses many of the same impulses, evolving from her "Bag Lady" phase—"We took junk and saved it for art" (*U* 393)—to the more expansive form in which she and her volunteer assistants re-paint hundreds of former military B-52s in the desert. Nick understands her project much in the way that Eisenstein understood Chinese ideograms and montage: "She wanted us to see a single mass, not a collection of objects," "those old weapons so forcefully rethought" (*U* 84). All these works seek in some way to channel "the culture and its loaded words," and each poses the question raised in the novel's prologue by J. Edgar Hoover, who uses precisely the biological image that DeLillo uses in his essay: "how many bundled links do we find in the neural labyrinth?" (*U* 51).

The mention of Hoover in this context suggests just how far *Underworld* is committed to the ontology of its "connections." The text never shies away from suggesting that the former FBI director is as sharply attuned to holistic patterns as any of the artists in the book and thus deserves a place among them. This attunement is the source of Hoover's phobias and fixations, and leads him into that most DeLilloan territory, conspiracy.[15] "He rearranged the lives of his enemies," the narrator remarks of Edgar, "their conversations, their relationships, their very memories, and he made these people answerable to the details of his creation" (*U* 559). Hoover isn't alone in his paranoia, of course; he stands side by side with his namesake Sister Edgar and the baseball collector Marvin Lundy. The characterization of these figures

---

[15] On conspiracy in DeLillo and in postwar literature generally, see Timothy Melley, *Empire of Conspiracy: The Culture of Paranoia in Postwar America* (Ithaca: Cornell University Press, 1999); Samuel Chase Coale, *Paradigms of Paranoia: The Culture of Conspiracy in Contemporary American Fiction* (Tuscaloosa: University of Alabama Press, 2005); Peter Knight, ed., *Conspiracy Nation: The Politics of Paranoia in Postwar America* (New York: New York University Press, 2002).

may seem confusing, even worrying, since it seems to blur any relevant distinction between paranoia and creativity, obsession and invention. Nick Shay criticizes what he calls *dietrologia,* "the science of what is behind an event" (*U* 280), which he sees as engendering "cheap and easy delusions" (*U* 336). But the search for the wholes expressed by parts is not something unique to the paranoiac. Compulsive characters like Hoover show the same basic "artistic" habits of mind, the same weaving together of disparate items and narratives, exhibited by Klara, Eisenstein, and all the other creative characters—and, ultimately, by DeLillo himself.

DeLillo himself has done little to dispel such analogies. In the same essay where he imagines the neural strands of *Underworld,* he claims that fiction-writing involves the very impulses motivating the religious quests of Sister Edgar and the more profane ones of Hoover: "At its root level, fiction is a kind of religious fanaticism, with elements of obsession, superstition and awe" ("History" 62).[16] Many critics have gone along with DeLillo's self-description, although they have drawn differing conclusions from it. Timothy L. Parrish, for example, has said that DeLillo shows an "aesthetic sympathy with the 'creative' work of J. Edgar Hoover," co-opting the Director's "astonishing imaginative power" and narrative techniques. He does so, says Parrish, not because he wants to condemn Hoover as "some sort of terrible cultural presence," but to show how Hoover was simply "capitalizing on possibilities inherent in the culture and therefore available virtually to anyone." James Wood, by contrast, has criticized *Underworld* for being "complicit with the paranoia it describes." The "*form* of *Underworld,*" says Wood, "is paranoid," a "dogmatic occultism" built upon "an infinitely extendable mystical spectrum" of connections. Clearly anyone in the postwar period could grow paranoid, but clearly, too, far fewer people could "capitalize" on this fact with the kind of massive technological and institutional power that Hoover quite deliberately, and quite viciously, wielded. Fiction's attention, Wood claims, "is toward what is tangible," and to forget this, as DeLillo does with his immaterial "connections," is to legitimate the habits of mind driving Hoover. A genuine critique of the FBI Director, in other words, should question the very idea of a coherent mass history. It should question not just—to use a distinction Parrish makes—Hoover's "politics," but his "aesthetics" as well.[17]

---

[16] In the *Rolling Stone* piece that became the origin of *Libra,* DeLillo similarly claimed that researching the Kennedy assassination made him conclude that "paranoia in some contexts is the only intelligent response." See "American Blood: A Journey through the Labyrinth of Dallas and JFK," *Rolling Stone,* December 8, 1983, 22.

[17] Parrish, "From Hoover's FBI to Eisenstein's *Unterwelt,*" 706–7; James Wood, *The Broken Estate: Essays on Literature and Belief* (London: Jonathan Cape, 1999), 201–2.

But analogies between paranoia, on the one hand, and fiction, on the other, are perhaps less persuasive than these readers, and DeLillo himself, assume. To equate the paranoiac and the writer is to overlook the specific *kinds* of creations that these different types of figure make. Hoover works primarily in the genre of the FBI dossier, which he considers "a deeper form of truth, transcending facts and actuality": "The second you placed an item in the file, a fuzzy photograph, an unfounded rumor, it became promiscuously true" (*U* 559). And his criteria for deciding what enters the file become clear in a remark attributed to Clyde Tolson, his assistant, when Tolson reflects on what has taken place in the 1960s. It is a period, thinks Tolson, when "well-founded categories began to seem irrelevant," when "a certain fluid movement became possible," and when "sex, drugs and dirty words began to unstratify the culture" (*U* 571). Next to this constricted and overdetermined conception of creativity, the leading characteristic of the artworks in the text is the way they defy easy classification. The Watts Tower, again, appears for Nick as "a rambling art that has no category" and leaves Klara thinking she "didn't know what this was exactly"; the Eisenstein's film is "some ambiguous filmscape"; Lenny Bruce's routines occupy some place between the raunchy joke and sharp-eyed political editorial, just as Klara's works move somewhere between recycled waste and conceptual art; the letters and numbers of Moonman's graffiti "fairly exploded in your face and they had a relationship, they were plaited and knotted, pop-eyed cartoon humanoids, winding in and out of each other and sweaty hot and passion dancing" (*U* 395). It is this rambling and unclassifiable quality of the artworks that allows them both to incorporate and to capture the messy, untamable aspects of postwar life, the underbelly that is either anxiously ignored by characters like Erica Deming or trivialized by repetition in the mass media, as with the Texas Highway Killer or the Zapruder film. Oppenheimer, notes Klara Sax, referred to the nuclear bomb as "merde," shit, because it "eludes naming" and had "brought something into the world that out-imagined the mind" (*U* 76–77). Brian Glassic has a similar insight into the unnamable when he visits the Fresh Kills landfill on Staten Island, where he feels he must become a "member of an esoteric order" in order to "penetrate the secret" of the massive heap (*U* 184–85).

With this we come to the full force of the term "heap," which I have been applying to DeLillo's particular aesthetic. Fluid movement, the breakdown of well-founded categories, the unstratification of the culture: these are the tendencies that Hoover's dossiers struggle to curtail. This reaction is part and parcel of Hoover's effort to cordon off waste, contain it, as befits a man who is said to have an air filtration system in his house to vaporize specks of dust (*U* 50). Such containment is precisely what the works of Lenny Bruce, Klara, Ismael, and all the other artists of *Underworld* eschew. They make the wilderness no longer wild, but the orders they build are not well-regimented; they include both the handsome and the hideous, and aren't assembled according to pre-established ground rules. Like Father Paulus, the artists name the world, categorize it, and work, as Paulus says in one of his talks with Nick, with an intense and persevering will, a sense of constancy and purpose (*U* 539). But like Paulus, they do so with a full awareness of the frailty of the names and categories they establish. Hoover surreptitiously watches Clyde undress in the mirror and Sister Edgar devours gossip magazines in the closet, but Paulus the priest doesn't deny the existence of his desires just because he avoids acting on them. He freely confesses to lusting after buxom movie stars.[18] In a similar vein, the bricolage of the artists' works accommodates rather than suppresses the competing forces of the world and human existence.

The artists work in "heaps" in precisely the sense proposed by Francisco Varela, Luhmann's guide, in his account of autopoiesis and cognition: they break down distinctions between higher and lower processes, are resonant patterns in one moment of emergence, aggregates involving back-and-forth activity among all participating local elements, never reducible to the parts constituting them.[19] The unities they exhibit model exactly the sort of self-organizing, self-maintaining processes that Luhmann claims characterizes contemporary social life. The largest of all these self-referring heaps is, of course, *Underworld* itself, with its semi-discrete paragraphs and chapters, its back-and-forth movements across space and time, its desire—to adapt Marvin Lundy's thoughts on his quest for the Thomson baseball—to record a culture's forward motion while simultaneously tracking it backwards to the distant past (*U* 318).

 THE UNDERCURRENTS OF THE OBVIOUS

I want to back up now and consider these observations about *Underworld* in light of DeLillo's work more generally, before returning to the novel in

---

[18] See *U,* 672. Here I am disagreeing somewhat with Osteen's comparison between Paulus and Hoover in *American Magic and Dread,* 220–21. Osteen is right to read Paulus as claiming that virtue requires experiencing all passions in order to contain them, but Hoover's "rejection of unacceptable principles" (*U* 573) seems to me simply to deny passions more than contain them.

[19] Francisco J. Varela, Evan Thompson, and Eleanor Rosch, *The Embodied Mind: Cognitive Science and Human Experience* (Cambridge: MIT Press, 1992), 98. With the metaphor of the heap Varela and his co-authors are drawing an analogy between neural networks and Buddhist philosophy, in which the image of a heap—*skandha*—plays a significant role.

my last section to suggest a few qualifications and complications. There are
several reasons for widening my frame of reference here. One is to head off
a suggestion that may seem to follow from my remarks above about Hoover
and paranoia. As I noted earlier, DeLillo's novels are often cited as evidence
of postwar fiction's preoccupation with paranoia. But while it may be true
that conspiracy theories arise from the belief that the threat to society is less
a specific agent or group than a system of ideas and discourses,[20] it is also
true that such systems are not the exclusive purview of the paranoid. And in
the case of DeLillo, I would argue, an interest in conspiracy emerges from a
more far-reaching interest in the ontological status of supra-personal systems
generally, not the other way around.

One expression of this larger interest is the recurrent appearance in
DeLillo's fiction of tight-knit communities existing on the margins of society. His 1982 novel *The Names,* for instance, is in part the story of a small,
dangerous cult that is said to act with "one mind, one madness," "part of some
unified vision," and the book speaks often about the "collective identity" or
"single living voice" of a city, and about "yielding" or "losing" oneself in
a larger body.[21] In *Americana,* DeLillo's first novel, a young white man who,
along with some others, has rejected the "death machine" of American society in order to join a small group of Apaches explains why the members of
the group dress identically: "But it's not like uniforms. It's just part of the
single consciousness of the community. It's like everybody is you and you are
everybody" (*A* 356). The terrorist hijackers hiding out in Hamburg in *Falling Man* are described as "strong-willed, determined to become one mind,"
"[b]ecome each other's running blood" (*FM* 83), and *Mao II* opens with a
striking account of a Unificationist Church wedding in Yankee Stadium,
a gathering that appears to one character as "a mass of people turned into
a sculptured object" (*Mao* 7). Comparable concerns are expressed in the recurrent tableaux of crowds in DeLillo's work, where particular persons go un-
named and unnoticed. Think here, again, of the Moonie wedding of *Mao II's*
prologue, which ends with the ominous sentence, "The future belongs to
crowds" (*Mao* 16); or the multilingual groups who enter the Parthenon at
the end of *The Names,* "people in streams and clusters, in mass assemblies"
(*Names* 331); or the "huge stadium filled with wildly rippling bodies" in which

---

[20] This is Melley's useful formulation in *Empire of Conspiracy,* 2.

[21] Don DeLillo, *The Names* (1982; New York: Vintage, 1989), 116, 146, 190; henceforth *Names.* Other
DeLillo texts will be cited as follows, using the abbreviations indicated parenthetically: *White Noise*
(New York: Viking Penguin, 1985) (*WN*); *Americana* (1971; New York: Penguin, 1989) (*A*); *Great
Jones Street* (1973; New York: Vintage, 1983) (*GJS*); *Cosmopolis* (New York: Scribner's, 2003)(*C*); *Fall-
ing Man* (New York: Scribner, 2007) (*FM*).

Bucky Wunderlick appears in *Great Jones Street* (*GJS* 2); or the street protests and seamlessly orchestrated Sufi funeral that interrupt Eric Packer's limousine journey in *Cosmopolis;* or the nameless New Yorkers fleeing the ash and smoke of lower Manhattan at the start of *Falling Man,* "thousands, filling the middle distance, a mass in near formation" (*FM* 5). These throngs are all cousins to the remarkable panorama that opens *Underworld,* with its "assembling crowd" arriving at the Polo Grounds, generating "some vast shaking of the soul" and expressing "the unseen something that haunts the day" (*U* 11).

Cults and crowds are important for DeLillo for much the same reason that Dionysian rituals and Attic theater are important for Nietzsche. They complicate our intuition that ascriptions of intentionality follow some principle of equal enfranchisement: one person, one mind. Of interest to DeLillo is how the masses gathered before a great leader or at a public event can make the boundaries of individual persons less consequential than the boundaries of a larger whole. But these crowds and cults are not included in DeLillo's work because they are anomalous. They simply make manifest the "neural linkages" (Hoover's phrase) or "neural strands" (DeLillo's) that are expressed by, yet go unnoticed in, the culture as a whole. The groups are heaps, distributed agents operating according to the kind of coherent and self-organizing "inner natures," "forces," and "unknown energies" that govern all larger social bodies, but of which we are usually unaware.

Which helps explain a further feature of DeLillo's work, namely, its emphatic contemporaneity. The Bronx of the early 1950s is as far back in time as DeLillo has ever reached, and the plots of his novels often depend upon the reader's having kept up with recent events in the news: the Iranian Revolution (*The Names*), the civil war in Lebanon (*Mao II*), the stock market boom and bust (*Cosmopolis*), the attacks of September 11, 2001 (*Falling Man*). The resolutely contemporary nature of DeLillo's writing implies a strong sense of historical epochs as discrete wholes, self-contained units distinct from other epochs. To be sure, the tight-knit cults in his work often represent an older sense of experience. Their atavistic hierarchies and blood rituals, their—as *Cosmopolis* puts it—"olden soul of awe" (*C* 9), are absent from our flattened and media–numbed current-day existence. But these groups are never the center of the books in which they appear, and they surface chiefly to play the role that Nietzsche ascribes to his own untimely study of the Greeks: not to showcase lost ideals, but to act counter to our time and thereby act on our time, possibly for the benefit of a time to come.[22] The very unfamiliarity of

---

[22] See Friedrich Nietzsche, *Untimely Meditations,* ed. Daniel Breazeale, trans. R. J. Hollingdale (Cambridge: Cambridge University Press, 1997), 60.

these groups reinforces the sense that the "style" and "self-organization" of our postwar *we* have virtually nothing in common with the styles and self-organization of any previous *we*. In interviews DeLillo has expressed doubts that his novels "could have been written in the world that existed before the Kennedy assassination," and has claimed that his work resists the comforts of fiction which "suggests that our lives and problems and our perceptions are no different than they were fifty or sixty years ago." The novel has changed since Balzac, he says, "because *we* have changed, because our consciousness has changed as a result of wars and other phenomena of the twentieth century" (*Conversations* 77, 107, 159). The idea that, beyond some antediluvian fringe groups, we have changed in some unalterable way, that the experiences of earlier human civilizations is incommensurate with what we now know and do, is something that separates DeLillo not only from a contemporary such as Toni Morrison, who often works as a historical novelist, but also from Pynchon, to whom he bears more obvious resemblances. Pynchon's fiction is set in turn-of-the-century Egypt, eighteenth-century Pennsylvania, and other places just on the verge of modernity. But DeLillo's work begins from an assumption that the shift into a culture of technology, media-saturation, and bureaucratic rationality has already occurred, and that, as a result, we have become entirely closed off from earlier forms of experience. Only once does the paranoid thought "everything is connected" occur in *Gravity's Rainbow,* but in *Underworld* it becomes a mantra dispersed throughout the entire society.[23]

This exclusive focus on our contemporary *we* has a bearing not only on DeLillo's selection of topics, but even on the style and tone of his sentences. Consider two passages, the first of which is the opening paragraphs of *Underworld,* and the second of which comes from DeLillo's response to the 2001 terrorist attacks on the World Trade Center and Pentagon, published under the apocalyptic title "In the Ruins of the Future."

> He speaks in your voice, American, and there's a shine in his eye that's halfway hopeful.
>
> It's a school day, sure, but he's nowhere near the classroom. He wants to be here instead, standing in the shadow of this old rust-hulk of a structure, and it's hard to blame him—this metropolis of steel and

---

[23] Parrish makes this point and develops this contrast along the lines I've suggested here in his "Pynchon and DeLillo," *UnderWorlds,* ed. Dewey, 79–92. DeLillo's stated reason for not writing historical fiction is not irrelevant in this context: "I haven't been there" (*Conversations* 158). One could develop this contrast more with discussion of contemporary experimental historical novelists such as Ishmael Reed, John Barth, and E. L. Doctorow.

concrete and flaky paint and cropped grass and enormous Chesterfield packs aslant on the scoreboards, a couple of cigarettes jutting from each.

Longing on a large scale is what makes history. (*U* 11)

Today, again, the world narrative belongs to terrorists. . . . Technology is our fate, our truth. It is what we mean when we call ourselves the only superpower on the planet. The materials and methods we devise make it possible for us to claim our future . . . We like to think America invented the future. We are comfortable with the future, intimate with it . . . This time we are trying to name the future, not in our normally hopeful way but guided by dread . . . What has already happened is sufficient to affect the air around us, psychologically. We are all breathing the fumes of lower Manhattan. . . .[24]

A simple question about all these sentences should be raised: who exactly speaks them? In the first case, we obviously don't hear the voice of the boy Cotter Martin, or a transcription of his thoughts via free indirect discourse. Cotter would not likely be conscious of his voice having an "American" quality (whatever we take this to mean), nor is he likely to come up with the subsequent description of the Polo Grounds, with the lyrical assonance and sibilance of "rust-hulk of a structure" and the polysyndeton trailing the dash. It is even less likely that Cotter would self-reflexively implicate the anonymous reader with the second-person pronoun, and still less probable that he could formulate the declaration about "longing" and "history." But if the voice of *Underworld*'s opening sentences isn't Cotter's, it also isn't that of a classic realist text. The narrators of, say, George Eliot wield a remarkable degree of omniscience and authority, but even at her most generalizing, Eliot's tone is typically that of a wise elder. Analogous questions arise from the sonorous essay on September 11. Critics have sometimes complained that the most prominent word in James Baldwin's essays is the pronoun "I," which takes precedence over everything the "I" describes and analyzes.[25] In DeLillo's prose, one detects a similar self-regard, but the pronoun is bloated into a first-person plural. The presumption is not that a particular someone will inherently interest readers, but that a particular someone will speak *for* readers. But just who is this being? Ellison's narrator asks whether he "speaks for" us, but only after we have accompanied him already over several hundred

---

[24] Don DeLillo, "In the Ruins of the Future," *Harper's Magazine,* December 2001, 33–40.

[25] See Marcus Klein, *After Alienation: American Fiction at Mid-Century* (Cleveland: World, 1964), 154.

pages of memoir. How, by contrast, are we supposed to trust DeLillo's claim to have identified the "world narrative" of which we are now a part? Who exactly is this "we" that, he says, is usually comfortable with the future but is now naming it full of dread?

Again, DeLillo's narrators speak not with the wisdom of historical hindsight; they are our contemporaries. The best way to characterize these sentences, then—and here we return to a term that has appeared a few times over the last several chapters, in connection with Stein, Robbe-Grillet, Houston Baker, and Ellison's Brotherhood-intoxicated narrator—is to say that they are uttered by a *prophet,* someone giving voice to "the culture and its loaded words" and, through them, revealing ourselves to ourselves. Implied in these passages is a speaker who can encompass all reaches of society and can see past and future (which is "white hot," according to the essay on September 11), much in the way that *Underworld* as a whole seeks to trace the connection between characters that they themselves, scattered across space and time, are incapable of ever perceiving. To repeat an earlier point, the narrator of *Underworld* can know the full history of the Thomson ball, including its early hours, even if nobody else in the text can, and we as readers learn the role of the Texas Highway Killer in the ball's journey, even if Nick never does. DeLillo's predilection for such Olympian vantage points may explain why some readers have felt his work is "impersonal." "DeLillo does not sound like anyone else," remarks James Wood about *Cosmopolis,* "but often he does not sound like a human being, either."[26] True enough, but leaving the matter here suggests that this "sound" is simply unmotivated. DeLillo's voice is frequently loosened from ordinary speech situations, assuming some higher or broader perspective. And such aspirations may engender what to some readers will seem like presumptuousness or ungainliness. But in its basic impulse, it is not markedly different from what Nietzsche and Luhmann do in their respective accounts of modern social and cultural life. Nor, to invoke Americans whose affinities with German intellectual traditions are no secret, is it much different from the kinds of things that Emerson and Whitman do in their own visionary moments.[27]

---

[26] "Traffic," review of *Cosmopolis, New Republic,* April 14, 2003, 31.

[27] Tanner has suggested that DeLillo is a "kind of latter-day American Transcendentalist" ("Afterthoughts," 67), a tradition evoked as well by Michael Ondaatje's blurb on the back cover of *Underworld:* "It contains multitudes." Two recent books have drawn out the Romantic and religious underpinnings of DeLillo's work at length (albeit with strongly different evaluations): Joseph Dewey, *Beyond Grief and Nothing: A Reading of Don DeLillo* (Columbia: University of South Carolina Press, 2006); Paul Maltby, *The Visionary Moment: A Postmodern Critique* (Albany: State University of New York Press, 2002), chap. 4.

It is partly from this prophetic mode that DeLillo's work gets the oppositional edge that it has. Readers are sometimes left unsure what kind of stance his novels take on the world they dissect, and certainly his prophetic voice is seldom as heated and denunciatory as Nietzsche's. In his self-descriptions DeLillo has sometimes adopted a coolly analytical perspective reminiscent of Luhmann: "I don't think in terms of optimism or pessimism" (*Conversations* 166). But as with Luhmann, the abstracted perspective of so much of his fiction is itself a symptom of a certain dissatisfaction with the society he describes, or at least with the level of self-awareness among most of its members. It expresses the same sort of buried impatience toward contemporary American culture that Luhmann expresses toward sociologists who have remained mired in outdated ideas about motive and action. This dissatisfaction and impatience is what places DeLillo's books within the tradition of what is sometimes called bourgeois self-hatred, a tradition that descends, among novelists, from Flaubert: a sense that, for all of its obvious material and scientific successes over the last few hundred years, modern bourgeois culture is deceptive and open to parody, flattening the depths and heights that are uniquely human, driving us toward (as one character in *Americana* says) "the world's longest march of vulgarity" and "the destruction of everything which does not serve the cause of efficiency" (*A* 118–20).[28] Not for nothing are the most heavy-handedly satiric moments in *Underworld* the segments focused on the pedestrian suburban housewife Erica Deming and the equally pedestrian business executive Charles Wainwright, which are almost Juvenalian in their aggression. (Charles is said to believe, implausibly, that the express train to the suburbs is "the evolutionary climax of the whole human endeavor" (*U* 535).) "I long for the days of disorder," thinks Nick as he considers the new shelves and carpets of his comfortable suburban home. "This is what I long for, the breach of peace, the days of disarray when I walked real streets...." (*U* 810). What Nick rejects here is not so overtly disdained in a book such as *White Noise,* the DeLillo text that is perhaps most unresistingly saturated in contemporary consumer culture. But even in that 1985 novel, bourgeois modernity is justified not as Adam Smith might have, as an effective way of distributing wealth or encouraging fluid and temperate social relations, but only as it provides signs of spiritual and metaphysical wonders. On the whole, DeLillo's novels pay as little attention as Luhmann's work to the modern public sphere; no newspaper editorial or public debate in his

---

[28] On the tradition of bourgeois self-hatred, see François Furet, *The Passing of an Illusion: The Idea of Communism in the Twentieth Century,* trans. Deborah Furet (Chicago: University of Chicago Press, 1999), chap. 1.

work looks anything like a piece of Habermasian deliberation. And, on the whole, his novels take as little serious interest in bourgeois love and marriage as they do in school board meetings and city elections. When such humdrum affairs do appear, they are usually treated as epiphenomenal, evidence perhaps of an overly privatized age, but in any case secondary to the larger powers surrounding us.[29] "There's an entire school of American fiction," DeLillo has remarked, summing up this attitude, "which might be called around-the-house-and-in-the-yard," and which deals in people's "marriages and separations and trips to Tanglewood." Readers are drawn to such writing, he claims dismissively, "because it adds a certain luster, a certain significance to their own lives" (*Conversations* 18).

DeLillo has been assailed by critics of various political stripes for this prophetic stance. One critic has complained in the *New Criterion* that it is better to be a "marauding, murderous maniac" in DeLillo's fiction than to content oneself with the air conditioners and credit cards of American life, because "when you're living the life of primitive violence, you're closer to the mystery at the heart of it all." Recent critics on the Left have similarly complained that DeLillo's work represents a high-minded commitment to irrationalism and ineffability that is at odds with "mundane political efforts to work toward imperfect justice."[30] Less frequently observed, however, is that DeLillo's prophetic stance often puts him at odds with the very genre in which he has made his name. "Fiction will always examine the small anonymous corners of human experience," he has written, as if such examinations were a routine or uncomplicated affair. "But there is also," he goes on in the passage I've quoted in part already, "the magnetic force of public events and the people behind them. . . . The writer wants to see inside the human works, down to dreams and routine rambling thoughts, in order to locate the neural strands that link him to men and women who make history" ("History" 62). DeLillo doesn't say why the anonymous corners of human experience don't themselves count as a part of social reality. But the argument seems to be that a novel quickly grows trivial not just when it recounts trips to Tanglewood, but

---

[29] For a reading critical of the metaphysical consumerism running through *White Noise,* see Hoberek, *Twilight of the Middle Class,* 125–26. Naturally I don't mean to imply here that bourgeois marriage is absent in DeLillo's work. It is important in *White Noise, Players, The Names,* and *Falling Man,* as well as *Underworld,* to name only the most obvious cases. But the marriages depicted in these novels occupy far less narrative space than they typically would in work by John Updike, Ann Beattie, or any number of DeLillo's postwar contemporaries. Still less, of course, do these books seem to lend much straightforward credence to bourgeois notions of romantic love.

[30] The first of these commentaries is from Bruce Brawer, "Don DeLillo's America," *New Criterion* 3.8 (April 1985): 34–42. The second is from Sean McCann and Michael Szalay, "Do You Believe in Magic? Literary Thinking after the New Left," *Yale Journal of Criticism* 18 (2005): 451.

even when it examines government offices, corporate headquarters, newsrooms, and underground bunkers. Only when a text attempts to trace the "deep mind" or "inner nature" of which all these things are expressions, the "inside of human works" that lies "behind" both public and private lives, does it begin to raise itself out of irrelevance.

Compare this with Nietzsche, whose hatred of the bourgeois led him to view the novel as a descendant of the Platonic dialogue, a symptom of modern Socratism. The novel, Nietzsche says, "may be described as an infinitely enhanced Aesopian fable, in which poetry holds the same rank in relation to dialectical philosophy as this same philosophy held for many centuries in relation to theology: namely, the rank of *ancilla*." Thus George Eliot is reduced to one of the "little moral females" of post-Christian Europe; thus Zola and the Goncourt brothers are enumerated among the "impossible ones"; thus Stendhal and Dostoevsky, the two novelists Nietzsche most admired, are usually praised not as fiction writers but as moral psychologists.[31] Luhmann's relation to the novel is more complicated than Nietzsche's, mainly because of the neutrality that he seeks to adopt relative to modernity. The eighteenth-century novel is sometimes lauded in his work for insights into modern experience that philosophers of the time were unable to achieve. Yet as I noted at the end of chapter 5, *Social Systems* praises the shift away from the "classical novel" toward more recent fiction in which motives are renounced, characters flattened, and stories "no longer carried forward" (*SS* xliii): with this, Luhmann suggests, we glimpse the proper model for future social theory. Reading these remarks, one is reminded how often DeLillo has cited the influence of the French *nouvelle vague* (one of whose earliest practitioners was, of course, Alain Robbe-Grillet), and how his earliest literary interests were piqued by Joyce and Faulkner. Clearly he is familiar with a range of pre-twentieth-century texts, but classic novelists like Dickens and Tolstoy simply don't engage his imagination. A novel such as *David Copperfield* is, as *White Noise* suggests, merely quaint, like whooping cough or old farm houses (*WN* 276).

A word about this term "novel," since it is relevant not just to DeLillo but also to the other literary texts that have been considered here. I mean by

---

[31] On the novel as Aesopian fable, see Friedrich Nietzsche, *The Birth of Tragedy*, trans. Walter Kaufmann (New York: Viking, 1967), 91. On Eliot, see *Twilight of the Idols*, trans. Richard Polt (Indianapolis: Hackett, 1997), 53. On Zola and the Goncourt brothers, see *Twilight*, 51. On Stendhal, see *The Gay Science*, trans. Walter Kaufmann (New York: Random House, 1974), 149. On Dostoevsky, see *Twilight*, 55; *The Will to Power*, trans. Walter Kaufmann and R. J. Hollingdale (New York: Random House, 1967), 392, 434–35.

it not so much any specific formal elements (prose/verse, long/short, etc.) as much as two related features long noted in commentary: its commitment to a critical scientific ontology and its concomitant concern for moral individualism. The common thread running through both post-Galilean natural science and post-Defoe fiction is the belief that what is most uncontrovertibly real is the extended physical universe, a universe that can be known only through the senses and that can be explained, predicted, and controlled though a handful of relatively simple natural laws. (Presumably something like this is what James Wood means when he says that fiction's "attention is toward what is tangible.") And if the universe is a calculable mechanism, and if "evidence" and "facts" are found primarily in the physical world, then what counts as worthy or base, friend or enemy, is no longer as clear as it may have been in the classical epic, Norse saga, or medieval morality play. Left in a world that no longer embodies a moral order, the novel's characters must ask not only how they can achieve a good life. They must also ask what achieving a good life would possibly mean, and how it could be identified amidst a swirl of local actions, non-intentional physical events, and specific circumstances. It is this ruthless absence of wider perspective that Lukács had in mind when he referred, in his ringing phrase, to the "transcendental homelessness" expressed by the novel tradition: "The novel is the epic of a world that has been abandoned by God."[32]

Such a tradition is of course embraced by Ellison and, with even more open arms, Bellow. *Augie March* is unthinkable without homey old *David Copperfield*. And for all the experiments with plot, character, time, and prose that make up the history of the novel over the last few hundred years, and for all the borderline cases we could name, any description that failed to cite the family resemblances I've named here—an attunement to naturalistic explanation and to secular individualism—would be eccentric indeed. Novels have typically been the kinds of texts that, as Ian Watt said many years ago, depict "a developing but unplanned aggregate of particular individuals having particular experiences at particular times at particular places."[33] And this fundamental concern for the particularity of persons and circumstances puts the novel somewhat at odds with the strong holism I've been associating with Nietzsche, Luhmann, and now DeLillo. This isn't to say that DeLillo's novels fail at what they do, *Underworld* least of all. Nor is to say that the novel tradition Watt describes should or will be cherished everywhere at

---

[32] Georg Lukács, *The Theory of the Novel,* trans. Anna Bostock (Cambridge: MIT Press, 1971), 41, 88.

[33] Ian Watt, *The Rise of the Novel: Studies in Defoe, Richardson, and Fielding* (London: Pelican, 1972), 34.

anytime. Nor is it to make the Thatcher Reduction that I noted at the start of chapter 5 and claim that "there is no such thing as society." But it is a way of explaining why DeLillo's books can often look less like novels than, say, religious texts, texts in which mental states are not restricted to human persons alone. My passing comparison between Lenny Bruce's strings of expletives and the books of the Old and New Testament was not accidental. And as with Nietzsche and Luhmann, such a picture raises important conceptual questions. Aren't the pre-eminent entities of DeLillo's fiction—cultures, systems, connections, history—manifest only through finite events occurring within finite contexts, and only to finite cognitive beings? Isn't even the most rudimentary form of *we* fraught with disjunctions and asymmetries, as when you use words in new ways in a conversation or I speak about concepts you don't understand? Moving into higher-level unities: isn't treating the Boston Red Sox as a coherent agent complicated by the pitcher and catcher mixing up their signals, much as governments are notoriously anxious about who "represents" them and who "leaks" information? From the point of view of the traditional novelist, it is persons who entertain thoughts, express hopes, feel disappointments, and find something funny. It is they who draw poor inferences, miscalculate the sum of 68 and 57, and fail to project *feed the kitty* into future contexts. Can the Culture also display all these talents?

Writing to a friend, D. H. Lawrence once said that E. M. Forster's *A Passage to India* is "good, but makes one wish a bomb would fall and end everything. Life is more interesting in its undercurrents than in its obvious; and E. M. does see people, people and nothing but people: *ad nauseam*."[34] As with Lawrence, another novelist-prophet, what matters most for De-Lillo are the continental drifts of *Geist* rather than "its obvious": what he calls the "hidden nature of things," the uncovering of which constitutes the "novelist's perennial effort" ("History" 62). Given such a stance, it is perhaps inevitable that he, like Nietzsche and Luhmann, grows weary with "the small anonymous corners of human experience," with stories showing people and nothing but people. Particular persons—persons with their endless train of reasons and confusions, local visions and revisions—are bound to seem merely by-products. As I'll argue in a moment, DeLillo concentrates on such extra-personal systems in more complex ways than Nietzsche and Luhmann. But in his narrative voice, his arrangements of plot, and his drawing of "connections," his career has pushed the novel form as far as it can go in its search for the "undercurrents"—or, better, the "underworld."

---

[34] Lawrence letter to Martin Secker, 23 July 1924; qtd. in Watt, *Rise of the Novel*, 200.

Leaping But Not Flying

The road back to *Underworld* is paved with a handful of sentences. Klara Sax in the early 1990s: "She wore a floppy orange T-shirt under the blazer and a necklace and several rings and one white running shoe and a sock the color of Kool-Aid grape" (*U* 67). Manx Martin, Cotter's father, the night of the Thomson homerun: "He is a man with high cheekbones sort of poxed in the hollows, rough-graded, and a thin mustache that he keeps well above his lip, tended and particular" (*U* 142). Ismael Muñoz in the late 1980s: "Ismael stood barefoot on dusty floorboards in a pair of old chinos rolled to his calves and a parrot-print shirt worn outside his pant, smoking a whopping cigar and resembling some carefree islander wading in happy surf" (*U* 243). And finally, Tanya Berenger, who makes the masks that Hoover and Tolson wear to the Black and White Ball: "She wore heavy makeup she might have poured from a paint can and cooked. And Clyde noted how one pocket on her dress drooped just a bit, becoming unseamed" (*U* 561).

I select these sentences in order to suggest a final direction of thought, one that goes somewhat against the grain of what has been said so far, and that will in turn make *Underworld* seem closer kin to the literary texts discussed in earlier chapters. We can agree, I assume, that these sentences describe public, common, and conspicuous objects; their dictionary definitions would say as little about cultures as they would about quarks. Moreover, the chief object identified in each sentence is a body: human faces, human limbs, the garments covering them. This perhaps obvious point is critical because up to now I have been describing *Underworld* as a book whose preeminent concern is with disembodied agents, variously referred to as forces, powers, energies—the culture and its loaded words. There is no reason to retract this basic claim. But I want to refine it now by suggesting that, while *Underworld* is indeed pulled toward non-novelistic forms like prophecy and theology, it also resists this movement. It resists it to the extent that the book registers disjunctions of intentional ascription—the difference between your words and mine, the pitcher and catcher—and to the extent that it identifies these disjunctions with distinctions between material bodies. For all the towering abstraction of the text, DeLillo dramatizes a tension between embodiment and disembodiment that is comparable to the one we have seen in Stein, Bellow, and Ellison. What gives the text its dominant character, its "feel," is indeed its attention to the sorts of disembodied entities that I've been describing. But this is not quite the end of the story. Kierkegaard once complained that, in constructing his System, Hegel was like a dancer whose singular abilities in leaping led him to believe mistakenly that he could fly—an ability reserved for winged creatures or residents of the moon, which is where Kierkegaard impishly suggested Hegel would eventually find his readers.[35] The picture I have given of DeLillo so far suggests that Kierkegaard might assign his books to a similar fate. But *Underworld* is not in fact as comically seduced by its own postulations as Kierkegaard claimed Hegel was. It does not wholly ignore the poor existent individual who belongs to the earth and respects the law of gravity.

To grasp the issue in a reasonably concrete way, consider how Michael Wood, reviewing *Underworld,* distinguished it from two other novels of 1997, John Updike's *In the Beauty of the Lilies* and Philip Roth's *American Pastoral.* In all three books, he said, public history plays a central role, but for Updike and Roth, it is a "speculative instrument," an "instigation" to develop character, plot, and other familiar ingredients of modern fiction. By contrast, says Wood, history appears in *Underworld* as a "named player": it "appears 'as itself,' the way famous movie stars appear in the movies 'as themselves'."[36] At first glance this sounds a lot like what I have been saying so far: history, the culture and its loaded words, exists as an entity in its own right, a being over and above particular characters and their actions. But Wood's account is in fact quite misleading. After all, we have well-known, if fallible, ways of identifying and re-identifying Marlon Brando. We can watch his films, look at photos, and if we were dogged enough, we could track the spatiotemporal coordinates of his body from birth to the grave. Doing these things wouldn't give us the *whole* of Brando, since a fuller picture would need to say how Brando's body expresses the dispositions, memories, and other things that in chapters 4 and 5 I was saying constitute a "self." But given the difficulty of decoupling self-properties from body-properties, turning to documents like films and photos would be a decent first step.

History certainly has an independent existence in *Underworld,* but the argument of this chapter should suggest why it is not independent in the way Brando's existence is independent. Wood's account of *Underworld* better fits a text such as Robert Coover's *The Public Burning* (1978), a book that DeLillo has sometimes praised but which actually presents a quite different set of conditions from that implied in his own epic text. Among the actors in Coover's novel, for example, is Uncle Sam, a "wily Yankee Peddler" superhero who fights evil around the globe, appears before Richard Nixon on

---

[35] Søren Kierkegaard, *Concluding Unscientific Postscript to* Philosophical Fragments, vol. 2, ed. and trans. Howard V. Hong and Edna H. Hong (Princeton: Princeton University Press, 1992), 124.

[36] "Post-Paranoid," review of *Underworld, London Review of Books,* February 5, 1998, http://www.lrb. co.uk/v20/n03/wood01_.html (accessed January 2, 2007).

the golf course, and eggs on the Vice-President to carry out the Rosenberg executions—eventually even raping him as a way of appointing him for the presidency (*"you're my boy!"* Sam declares while buttoning his striped pantaloons). Communism appears similarly as a villain called "The Phantom" who preys upon innocents, and *Time* magazine is the National Poet Laureate who anxiously tracks the Rosenberg trial, "less self-assured than his readers might suspect or hope."[37] This is all quite far from what goes on in *Underworld*. "History" in DeLillo's text may be "named"—"Longing on a large scale is what makes history"—but it is not a "player" in the way that Coover's cartoon characters are, and accordingly the text never approximates Coover's levels of allegory. The ontological commitments put into play within the world of Coover's text are different from what is demanded by our ordinary language and folk psychology; Uncle Sam obeys the laws of gravity neither literally nor figuratively. In *Underworld,* by contrast, all the forces, energies, and connections are *postulations,* in Sellars's sense—posits used to describe and explain the behavior of perceptible entities. History is the air the characters breathe, but not something they can point to or pick up. Only near the end of the text do we step out of this basically naturalistic frame, and this comes with the appearance of the World Wide Web, where Hoover and Sister Edgar are joined in virtual union. And even here, the fantastical space of the internet is visibly marked off from the world assumed in the rest of the text. Much as the phantasmagoric moments of *Invisible Man*—the narrator's reefer-induced dream at the beginning, the castration scene at the end—are designated by italics, the leap into cyberspace in *Underworld* is designated by the sudden appearance of an italicized web address: *http://blk.www./dd.com/miraculum,* and subsequently by *Keystroke 1* and *Keystroke 2* (*U* 810, 817, 824).

The fact that *Underworld* takes its bearing partially from an ontology of familiar material objects is one reason why DeLillo is occasionally described as a kind of realist.[38] We can hone this claim by looking at a few features of the text in particular. The first concerns the web address that I cited a moment ago, in particular its "dd." The effect of this self-reference is complicated. Again, the web address as a whole brackets cyberspace off from

---

[37] Robert Coover, *The Public Burning* (New York: Viking, 1978), 548, 320. For DeLillo's opinion about Coover's book, see "History," 62; *Conversations,* 96.

[38] See, e.g., John A. McClure, "Postmodern/Post-Secular: Contemporary Fiction and Spirituality," *Modern Fiction Studies* 41 (1995): 152. In *Don DeLillo's* Underworld: *A Reader's Guide* (New York: Continuum, 2002), John Duvall helpfully suggests that DeLillo is to Postmodernists such as Pynchon and Barthelme as Fitzgerald is to Modernists such as Joyce and Faulkner: not hitting "the high notes of ludic style" or pressing "the boundaries of representation," yet still powerfully showing "what it feels like to live in the contemporary moment" (21–22).

the world described in the rest of the text. But the inclusion of DeLillo's own initials allows it to do something more. The moment is an exemplary instance of what Joseph Tabbi, working in a Luhmannian framework, describes as a confrontation between literary and non-literary systems that is typical of recent literary fiction. In the early work of both Pynchon and Richard Powers, Tabbi claims, the narrative voice tends to seek a "planetary consciousness" and "get caught up in the millennial sweep" of its reading and theorizing, forgetting that all reading and theorizing is always the product of a particular reader and a particular theorizer. But in Pynchon's *Mason & Dixon* and Powers's *Galatea 2.2.* the narrators appear as observing minds *within* the narrative itself (Cherrycoke in the former, Rick in the latter), thus keeping the level of consciousness between them and the other characters on the same horizontal plane. These shifts in narrative strategy suggest for Tabbi a recognition, as he says of Powers, that "the author himself cannot write outside of frames." The only cognitive superiority these narrators have is the unspectacular kind accorded to any retrospective story-teller, and the limitations of this perspective draw attention both to what a speaker can know as well as to "the dimensions of our contemporary *unknowing*."[39] Something similar, I think, happens at the end of *Underworld*. By including his own initials in the web address, DeLillo not only marks off the world of the Web, but also situates his own novel relative to another representational medium. He draws attention, that is, is to the fact that everything we have read up to this point has been imagined by a particular mind, a literary author, "dd," and not, despite frequent appearances, the Culture as such. The text assumes that there are systems, to recall Luhmann's phrase, but here in its concluding pages, it suggests that the novel can itself be understood as a kind of system, with its own operating principles and sets of distinctions. The novel relativizes the very world that it has constructed, and implies that it is no longer possible to move up to an absolute level, to a place where an individual voice might be, as Tabbi puts it, "*incorporated* into some larger controlling presence," "an abstract agency."[40]

A second way that *Underworld* avoids flying to the moon is the character of Nick Shay, the closest thing in the novel to a protagonist. Nick refers to himself as "a country of one," and he attributes this solitude to his *lontananza*—an Italian term that for him designates his status as "a made man," a person who doesn't "need the constant living influence of sources outside" himself (*U* 275). In many respect he acts as *Underworld*'s Invisible Man,

---

[39] Joseph Tabbi, *Cognitive Fictions* (Minneapolis: University of Minnesota Press, 2002), 66, 59.
[40] Ibid., 37.

distinctly better-off in his finances and social status than Ellison's narrator, but like him, someone who has sought to "build an individual," someone who is uncomfortable with "blood beginnings" (*U* 502–3) and who eventually removes himself from the world in the face of its deformations.[41] Indeed, Nick's isolation goes much deeper than that of Ellison's character. Even in *Underworld*'s Epilogue, where he speaks of his growing intimacy with his wife and openly laments his unrecoverable past, he shows little clear sign that he seeks a *you* for whom and to whom he can speak. Through most of the novel he remains in what he calls "a state of quiet separation" from "the solid stuff of home and work and responsible reality," and from his "role as husband and father, high corporate officer" (*U* 796). If Ellison's chastened narrator eventually plans to rise from his lair to seek Deweyan associations or Cavellian friends, Nick remains by contrast a consistently stoical, consistently solitary figure, keenly guarding the distinction between his first-person perspective and the social roles he performs. Kierkegaard's poor existing individual indeed, or perhaps, to name an important American precedent—one resonant in Nick's name alone—a figure out of Hemingway.

Psychologists would likely, and perhaps rightly, say that Nick's detachment stems from his early abandonment by his father, whom he mourns unconsciously by purchasing the Thomson homerun ball. One might also ask if, in light of the systems and forces that spread over so much of the text, Nick's insistence on his own separateness is simply a case of damaging self-deception. What matters for us here, however, is how strongly Nick—again, like Hemingway's characters or Kierkegaard—identifies his spiritual separateness with the particularity of his embodied condition. Nick perceives a close tie throughout his narrative between personal identity and physical identity; the loss of the latter entails the loss of the former. His remorse in wandering his suburban home is expressed not in terms of a fading mental acuity, but of a diminished corporeal existence. "I want them back," he says in his final sentences, "the days when I was alive on the earth, rippling in the quick of my skin, heedless and real. I was dumb-muscled and angry and real" (*U* 810). The twice-repeated "real" here is primarily a bodily matter: Nick's youth consists entirely of demonstrations of physical power or prowess—playing pool, working as a delivery man, sex, street fights—whereas his later years are spent aloofly devoted to foreign languages and his work in

---

[41] We should note here that Klara Sax parallels Nick in this regard. She is a loner who also escapes the Bronx and who also works in her later years with waste, though she, like all the artists in the text, recycles this waste while Nick, like Hoover, "contains" it. Duvall takes this contrast in a somewhat different direction in *Don DeLillo's* Underworld, 47–48.

the bronze office tower. Physical sensations, accordingly, underlie virtually all the memories haunting him in later life, "something way back when" that evokes "a sense of heat and beach, the haze of slick stuff across the hair on my forearm and the way the tube pops and sucks when it goes empty" (*U* 807)—a remark that recalls a teenage visit to the beach briefly depicted in Part 6. The threat of disembodiment is likewise the source of Nick's startling capacity for physical violence. There is little of cool abstract justice about the vengeance he seeks after learning of Brian Glassic's affair with his wife. "It's the force of the body," the body that "crushes the other," he thinks before punching his terrified friend twice with an open hand (*U* 797). Father Paulus calls violence "an expanding force in a personality," a potential "source of virtue, a statement of his character and forbearance": "One way a man untrivializes himself is to punch another man in the mouth" (*U* 538–39). Nick's later life is experienced as the loss of "personality" understood precisely in these terms, and feels trivialized because it lacks the sense of "character and forbearance" that attends physical contact and confrontation. It is fitting that one of the first things he and Klara discuss is his effort to maintain his body: he drinks soy milk and runs the metric mile (*U* 72).

The "real" world for which Nick longs is the subject of Part 6, "Arrangement in Gray and Black," which is in many respects unique in the text. It isn't unique formally. As in the rest of the book, the section consists of chapters broken into subsections, and, as elsewhere, it shifts fluidly between semi-discrete narratives and a wide cast of interrelated figures, skipping forward over weeks and months irregularly. But the section is distinct in other ways. One is that, while the text here shifts from character to character, the stage on which these characters act consists of a small scrap of city blocks in the Bronx. The insularity of this world becomes clear when an employee in the local bowling alley is described as "about the only black person you could see, regular, in a radius of five or six blocks" (*U* 777). Confined to this limited physical space, relations between characters are radically different from those recounted in the rest of the book, where family, friends, and even neighbors are separated by alienating physical distances. Middle-aged Nick sees his brother and mother only briefly during business trips back east, and a simple visit to the condom store with Brian Glassic requires him to drive "out where the map begins to go white" (*U* 108–9). Teenaged Nick lives by contrast in cramped quarters with his family and the only car he drives is a stolen one that he and his friends use chiefly with their girlfriends in lieu of a bedroom. Relationships in Part 6 are unavoidably, often brutally, face-to-face, conducted between persons who are often all too familiar with one another's family sagas. Beyond the Soviet nuclear test—the news of which barely registers among the residents—little beyond this patch of the Bronx seems even to exist. This is the world inhabited and consciously embraced by Albert Bronzini, who, as Klara thinks to herself, has a "sense of earth and our connection to it" that is visible even in the way her husband savors his food and sips his wine (*U* 748).

The physical intimacy of this world has, in turn, a strong influence on the narrative perspective of Part 6. Though the scenes continue to shift in abrupt montage-like ways across space and time, the text has no need of insisting, as it does in every other section, that the events recounted are connected, linked, matched, and so on. Indeed, Klara's use of "connection" as she watches Bronzini sip his wine is one of only three appearances of the word in the entire 120-page section. Its other two appearances are equally telling. Having slept with an older woman, Nick returns to her house to spy on her, and gradually begins "to make the connection" that she is the wife of Bronzini, his former science teacher (*U* 741). Later, when Nick meets someone in the pool hall who knew his father, he notes that the man "wanted to make a connection and get his point across" (*U* 765). These are three markedly different ways of using "connection"—roughly, as moral and spiritual embedding, as logical inference, and as familiarity or camaraderie. But what is most important about them is that none are attributed to a paranoiac or to a prophet. The term is employed by no one standing beyond, above, or outside a specific situation. This is hardly to say that the "connections" displayed in the Bronx have less force than the ones postulated in other portions of the text. On the contrary: behavior in the Bronx is tightly scripted (consider, for instance, the repeated valediction "Be good") and there is much less room for the kinds of secrets that are hidden away everywhere else in the novel. Unlike elsewhere, however, the connections drawn in Part 6 are connections that most characters *in* the text can and sometimes do draw. When in Part 5 Nick meets Jerry Sullivan on the night of the New York City blackout, Jerry is said to want to "recite the destinies of a hundred linked souls" from the neighborhood (*U* 620), and these "links" would not be "beyond" Jerry in the way that (to recall a remark from the end of my last chapter) the financial, artistic, or political systems of modernity might seem "beyond" me. And what is true of the links Jerry wants to make in 1965 is still more true of the links displayed in Part 6 generally. They are all wholly unlike the connections implied between Erica Deming and the civil rights protesters in Mississippi, who can be linked only by DeLillo's magisterial narrator. History is described in the opening page as "longing on a large scale." But for the residents of the Bronx in Part 6, history is, more modestly, Nick Shay being taken away in a police car, "here in their own remote and common streets" (*U* 781).

I am arguing, then, that the claims made both inside and outside of *Underworld,* namely, that "everything is connected," are not so much wrong as they are overly broad. The text in fact describes two fundamentally different types of "connections." Again, the distinctiveness of *Underworld* as a whole lies in the weight it gives to connections discernible only from a higher standpoint, the attenuated kind recognizable only from an elevated perspective. The "dd" of the web address appears only in passing, and only in the final pages; Nick Shay is merely one character among dozens, and Part 6 is merely one of many other regions in the book. But the more local "connections" implied by these earthbound features of the novel remain. And the differences between these distinct types of connection correlate, of course, with different conceptions of agency. In its histories, cultures, energies, and forces, *Underworld* evokes the presences of Nietzsche and Luhmann; in its story of Nick Shay and the Bronx, it approximates the persons of Bellow and Ellison. The backward-tending narrative of *Underworld* may undercut some of the dramatic movement that readers typically expect from fiction. But this does nothing to diminish the deeper drama of the text, the one that emerges in the interaction of levels that I'm identifying now. Its different ideas of agency attract and repel one another, touch and come into tension, and the conflicts between them persist through the whole of the text.

They persist to the very end, right through to *Underworld's* extraordinary final pages. The bodies and objects of Part 6 don't eradicate the forms of disembodiment so dominant elsewhere in the book. Indeed, after Nick shoots George Manza, the Epilogue stretches further into the present day than the novel has ventured anywhere, and the text grows even less tethered to any single location than it was in earlier sections. In a mere forty pages it moves swiftly between Kazakhstan, Arizona, and the Bronx, as well as between first- and third-person points of view. "Everybody is everywhere at once," says Nick of this world, quoting his son (*U* 805), and he repeats the dictum when describing what is perhaps the most revolutionary technological achievement of this contemporary world, the Internet (*U* 808). Here the two Edgars of the text, the FBI Director and the nun, are at last joined together, "hyperlinked" into "a single fluctuating impulse now, a piece of coded information" that expresses, one last time, the mantra of so many of the novel's characters: "Everything is connected in the end" (*U* 826). Suddenly the novel takes on the cartoonish character of Coover's *The Public Burning,* and Bronzini's effortless intimacy with the sights and smells of his neighborhood is replaced with a more chilling directive: "No physical contact, please." The hyper-modern Web cancels the familiar ontology of material objects and biology much as the Wariri's pre-modern beliefs about reincarnation do in *Henderson the Rain King:* "A click a hit and Sister joins the other Edgar. A fellow celibate and more or less kindred spirit but her biological opposite, her male half, dead these many years" (*U* 826). Within the space of the Web, the laws of gravity no longer have any hold at all.

Yet as I noted earlier, this venture into the Web is all undertaken within an italicized frame, and this other-worldly image of the two hyperlinked Edgars appears just sentences before the most extended, concentrated, *this*-worldly description of the material world offered in this extremely long book. The penultimate paragraph finds the reader—addressed, as in the opening sentences, in the second person—looking out the window at children playing some kind of kickball (an image that harkens back to many other such games in the novel), and in a sentence that lasts over half a page and that recalls the heaping catalogues of text assembled throughout the book, "you" are said to observe a series of objects in the room, "offscreen, unwebbed,"

> the tissued grain of the deskwood alive in light, the thick lived tenor
> of things, the argument of things to be seen and eaten, the apple core
> going sepia in the lunch tray, the monk's candle reflected in the slope of
> the phone, hours marked in Roman numerals, and the glaze of the wax,
> and the curl of the braided wick, and the chipped rim of the mug that
> holds your yellow pencils, skewed all crazy, and the plied lives of the
> simplest surface, the slabbed butter melting on the crumbled bun, and
> the yellow of the yellow of the pencils.... (*U* 827)

The lyricism of this winding sentence, the gathering of noun phrase upon noun phrase, the care with which it deliberates over the physical things on the desk, gives a weight to these mundane objects that they otherwise might seem to lack. These pieces of ordinary matter are meant to matter. They matter precisely because they are so ordinary, they are so unordered, so lacking in deep metaphysical "connection." They are pieces of an unheroic world "linked" only by the most common and precarious powers of perception, and the slow, deliberate attention devoted to them expresses a commitment to *this* time and *this* world—a commitment that would be unachievable in a world where "everybody is everywhere at once." The entire passage is written with an attunement to, to recall Cavell's remark about "form of life," the specific strength and scale of the human body and the human senses, to the way human beings characteristically sit and the specific ways and distances our eyes and ears perceive. It is as if Albert Bronzini, fresh from his dinner and glass of wine, had sat down in the writer's chair and paused to look outside before composing the book's final sentences.

And yet this, too, is not the end; these words are not the final words. After its sympathetic, careful appraisal of the objects in the room, the narration moves back to the computer screen, where a word has now appeared, and in the concluding sentences of the book, "you" are described as wondering how this "sequence of pulses on a dullish screen" can be transformed into "a thing in the world," how it can extend "itself ever outward" into the physical surroundings that you have just observed so intensively. The novel ends, that is, by posing precisely the questions that have been asked throughout this and all my preceding chapters. How do immaterial things—in this final image, a single word—relate to the embodied, perceptible world of candles, apple cores, pencils, and human bodies? How do semantic items, expressions of intentionality, fit into or influence or become part of the non-intentional universe? When do we apply meanings to the things of the material world, and when do these things express meanings? The final paragraph of *Underworld* suggests that you "try to imagine" an answer to these questions, but nowhere does it finally say that you are able to do so. Nowhere, too, does it say that the word onscreen—"Peace"—will eventually extend itself through "the raw sprawl of the city and out across the dreaming bourns and orchards to the solitary hills" (U 827). In the ambivalent position of this *you,* in the uncertainty of its imaginings, we recognize DeLillo's own ambivalence. *Underworld* is a text that lavishes attention at great length upon the world of material objects, the cars and architecture and landscapes of the postwar American world. Yet this physical world is something with which the text is never wholly at ease. Such ambivalence is, as I've been arguing, hardly unique to DeLillo. The particular terms are his—the specific places where agency is located, the particular movements between embodiment and disembodiment. But in its encyclopedic breadth, and in the hesitation of its final "you," *Underworld* crystallizes one of the central tensions marking the literature of the last century. It speaks of both the loss and the rescue of the person, the erasure and recovery of bodies, the persistence and fragility of worldly acts, the ability to leap and the longing to fly.

Conclusion
Person and Presence, Stories and Theories

At one of the many bustling parties depicted in William Gaddis's massive mid-century novel *The Recognitions* (1955), Esther, one of the main characters in the book, is introduced by someone named Buster Brown to someone named Mr. Crotcher, who describes himself as a writer.

—My book has been translated into nineteen languages.

—I must know it, Esther said.—I must know *of* it.

—Doubt it, said the modest author.—Never been published.

—But you said . . .

—I've translated it myself. Nineteen languages. Only sixty-six more to go, not counting dialects. . . . It's Celtic now. . . . It took me only eight months to learn Celtic. It ought to go in Celtic.

—You mean be published?

—Yes, published in Celtic. Sooner or later I'll hit a language where they'll publish it. Then I can retire to the country. . . .

—It must be an awfully dirty book, said Buster.

Mr. Crotcher gave him a look of firm academic hatred which no amount of love, in any expression, could hope to erase.—It is a novel about ant life, he said.[1]

---

[1] William Gaddis, *The Recognitions* (1955; New York: Penguin, 1993), 582–83.

Mr. Crotcher doesn't say what he means by "a novel about ant life." As entomologists know, a drone's memoir would have a different plotline than that of a queen, and the story of a South American bullet ant would look quite different in setting and atmosphere than the tale of a common wood ant in southern England. This is to say nothing of the possibility that by "life" Mr. Crotcher means the life of an entire colony. The behavior of an ant colony can often seem the stuff of great fiction, not least in the spectacular nests and bridges that many colonies build, accomplishments that go well beyond the rather predictable capacities of any single organism.[2]

Mr. Crotcher is as egoistic and absurd as most of the party-goers in Gaddis's novel, but whatever "a novel about ant life" means, the preceding chapters are meant to suggest that his book may have more appeal to publishers than Gaddis's satire implies. Modern and contemporary literature, I've been arguing, is filled with a remarkable range of sentient things, purposive speakers and actors, and in this gallery Mr. Crotcher's ants would not look badly out of place. By no means have I tried to offer an exhaustive list of such entities, and along the way the reader will probably have thought of other anomalous agents who appeared in the decades both before and after *The Recognitions:* the Upanishads' thunder sounding in *The Waste Land,* the judging eyes of T. J. Eckleburg in *The Great Gatsby,* the malignantly hissing hair-spray of *The Crying of Lot 49,* the Kafkan breast of Philip Roth's *The Breast,* the dogs of Russell Hoban's *Riddley Walker,* the vengeful winds and storms of Louise Erdrich's *Tracks,* Toni Morrison's numerous ghosts. On offer have been classifications more than catalogues. The basic taxonomy I have outlined—embodied persons, presences within, presences without—gets us to the heart of much recent literature and philosophy, and gives us some of the broad strategies at our disposal for describing ideas of meaningful action generally.

At different points I have suggested that the variety of things to which literary and theoretical texts have attributed beliefs and desires is expressive of a great uncertainty about how to describe both ourselves and the world. Something animate and sapient under one description may be a mere huddle of atoms, cells, or organs under another; Mr. Crotcher might appear wholly ridiculous to one editor and wholly brilliant to another. In recent decades, and in varying tones of delight and scorn, theorists have talked much of the notion of the cyborg, a being that is both animal and machine, populating

---

[2] For some reflection on ant colonies as intentional systems, with a "life" over and above that of any individual ant, see Donald R. Hofstadter, *Gödel, Escher, Bach: An Eternal Golden Braid* (New York: Vintage, 1979), 311–36.

worlds ambiguously natural and crafted, problematizing the line between human and artifact, blurring identities, categories, and relationships.[3] From the point of view of the preceding chapters, however, such instabilities were common well before and well beyond debates about posthumanism. There are no facts of the matter about where to locate minds and meanings, and this can make it difficult to know always just what we are talking about and how best to do it. And this situation raises a couple questions that we would be remiss for not acknowledging. One concerns the explanatory force of my two key concepts, "person" and "presence." The other probes the relative merits of literary and theoretical texts as ways of coming to terms with these concepts—a question that takes us deep into the thicket of the ancient quarrel between poetry and philosophy. Both questions require far more space than we can give them here, but we can at least clear some of the ground upon which sturdier responses could be built.

The first question I envision coming from a critic impatient with my apparent unwillingness to champion one idea of agency over all of the others. We have circumnavigated an array of claims and opinions, this critic may point out, but where do we anchor? Which of these claims and opinions is *true?* Are these various stories about "persons" and "presences" merely that—*stories?* Or are there arguments to be made for seeing one of these terms as more basic, lucid, and explanatorily powerful than the other?

Such philosophical questions aren't inappropriate, but they run the risk both of misdescribing me and of missing the point. For starters, the charge that no assertions have been made here isn't completely true. My main traveling companions throughout all the preceding chapters have been Wittgenstein and Sellars, who develop the framework within which many of the themes of this book have emerged. Common to Wittgenstein, Sellars, and their descendents is an awareness of a point cited earlier from Austin: if ordinary language isn't the last word, it *is* the first word.[4] Moreover, both Wittgenstein and Sellars recognize that among these first words are those designating what I have called persons, and that this conceptual preeminence entails the particular understanding of meaning and behavior that I described

---

[3] To paraphrase Donna Haraway's seminal essay, "A Cyborg Manifesto: Science, Technology, and Socialist-Feminism in the Late Twentieth Century," in her *Simians, Cyborgs, and Women: The Reinvention of Nature* (New York: Routledge, 1991), 149–81.

[4] Austin, *Philosophical Papers,* ed. J. O. Urmson and G. J. Warnock (Oxford: Oxford University Press, 1961), 185.

at some length in chapter 2. Accordingly, it is these figures who lie behind many of the doubts that have periodically been raised about alternative conceptions of agency, be they from James, Pinker, Nietzsche, Luhmann, or their literary and critical counterparts.

One virtue of working with this framework is conceptual clarity. If we accept the heart of the Sellarsian and Wittgensteinian claims about agency, then we may be less impressed—enchanted or terrorized—by the various efforts over the last century to eradicate it. Theories trying to match minds and actions one-to-one with neural firings and brain chemistry, or announcing the elimination of meanings and intentions on historical or political grounds, can be made intelligible only when they make heavy use of the intentional terms they call into question. And given the kind of biological creatures we are, given the sorts of perceptual capacities that are typical of the human organism, given the way evolution has equipped us to perceive and grasp middle-sized bodies rather than molecule- or continent-sized ones—given all this, our paradigm of a purposive agent is most persuasively regarded as a human person. Which is to say that there are limits to anti-intentionalist revolutions. Whether they transfer meanings to mini-agents in the head or to macro-agents in the world, thinkers wanting to get rid of purposes will usually tell you their purposes in throwing out the term—to cite the witty observation from Kenneth Burke that we heard at the start.

As I've noted in a few places—so my response to this critic continues— there are important practical consequences to giving conceptual priority to the manifest image and the objects of our ordinary perception. For it is only at the level of persons that the idea of a *practical agent* makes sense. Ghosts and spirits are, as Sellars puts it, "truncated" persons at best, and a similar thing could be said about the specific sorts of extra-personal agents that have been considered here. Presences within and without are not ascribed an important range of predicates, most obviously those designating arms, eyes, and other physical attributes. But an inability to ascribe physical attributes makes it difficult to ascribe what are often regarded as "non-physical" attributes, including the capacities to make judgments and come to decisions—preconditions for a moral and political life on virtually anyone's reckoning. How do I raise my child? What are the limits of my loyalty to an old friend? Does this institution continue to deserve our respect? Is this war unjust, and why? Questions like these make little sense apart from specific settings and specific embodied persons. And even if we believed that judgments and decisions were made below, in a Cartesian ether, or above, by an omniscient universal God, their effects would be recognizable to us only among the goings-on of the perceptible material world. Thus for much the same reason that we can't say whether a Steinian "inside" experiences sunburn or sleepiness, it would be difficult to know in what contexts we could say it had mistreated someone or had behaved courageously. The same goes for the supra-personal systems filling DeLillo's novels and the theories of Nietzsche, Luhmann, and others. History, Culture, and the Social System are not the kinds of things that can easily be ascribed laziness or perseverance, for many of the reasons they cannot easily be ascribed ears and noses.

Two philosophical addenda should be added here. One follows from what I have just been saying: our embodiment makes our ordinary practical vocabularies as justifiable as our ordinary psychological vocabularies. Any theory that dismissed the "reactive attitudes" of our everyday lives, that denied how routinely we deem actions to be worth doing or not, that ignored how often (this hardly means always) we take ourselves to be free and thus responsible, would no longer be a theory about *us*.[5] To say that a person never *really* acts deliberately—never *really* reaches for the orange juice, never *really* signs the petition—is to pretend to occupy a position that is unavailable to embodied speakers. Our lives always take place in midstream, within a language and the judgments constituting it. This is the case as much when we apply terms like *justice* or *injustice* as it is when we apply terms like *belief, hope,* and *wish*. Such a claim isn't meant to console, let alone justify a smug sense that we have made past practical vocabularies otiose in the way chemists have done to alchemy. For if it is true that we're always embedded in our ordinary practical vocabulary, we should also acknowledge how mottled, how full of ruptures, this vocabulary is today. Knowingly or not, most of us speak a curious mishmash of Judeo-Christian pieties, Greek virtues, Kantian dicta, Romantic poems, and Benthamite calculations, and this makes agreement about the meaning of terms like *just* and *unjust* hard to find. Indeed, this lack of shared criteria leads to much disagreement about what exactly counts as an "ethical" or "political" matter—statement, text, action, institution—in the first place. And such disagreement often causes deep suffering, both within and between individuals. The criteria we share for knowing the chemical composition of zinc oxide are largely absent for arguing about a good society and a good life, and our *ad hoc* arrangements may make us yearn for a past or future where values-talk vanishes and responsibility is palmed off onto extra-personal agents.[6] From the point of view of a Sellars or Wittgenstein,

---

[5] The phrase "reactive attitudes" is from Peter Strawson's "Freedom and Resentment," *Proceedings of the British Academy* 48 (1962): 1–25.

[6] For a recent discussion of this in a non-literary and largely non-philosophical vein, see Michael Walzer's contrast between the moralizing contemporary American Left and the morals-free Old

however, such a yearning is a sign of philosophical mystification, a symptom of the wish to escape the everyday practices within which our words have their home.

A second philosophical codicil is that grasping the priority of the manifest image makes it difficult to understand claims occasionally heard about non-human subjectivity. Such a concept may have been what Jacques Derrida had in mind when, at the end of the "Structure, Sign, and Play" essay, he referred to the "unnameable which is proclaiming itself...under the species of the non-species, in the formless, mute, infant, and terrifying form of monstrosity." It was less ambiguously what he meant when he later questioned Heidegger's denigration of the animal that is "poor in world" and spoke of the "absolute alterity of the neighbor" that arises whenever one sees oneself "under the gaze of a cat."[7] In a very different register, Thomas Nagel has famously asked what it is like to be a bat, a creature that perceives the world not with any human-like sensory repertoire, but with echolocation. The radically different perceptual capacities of the bat, claims Nagel, means that its "subjective" experiences must also differ radically from ours, a fact that for Nagel pulls the rug out from reductionism generally.[8] As Cary Wolfe has argued, such thinkers challenge us to consider how we might stand toward a consciousness that is entirely "beyond" or "outside" our own, what Wolfe calls the "inhuman," "infra-human," or "nonhuman," "the most different difference." This challenge, Wolfe notes, is implicit as well in Wittgenstein's famous remark in the *Investigations:* "If a lion could talk, we could not understand him" (*PI,* p. 223).[9] It is not entirely clear, however, that we really know what we mean when we talk about this sort

---

Left and current-day Neoconservative Right, in "All God's Children Got Values," *Dissent* (Spring 2005): 35–40.

[7] Jacques Derrida, "Structure, Sign, and Play in the Discourse of the Human Science," in *Writing and Difference,* trans. Alan Bass (Chicago: University of Chicago Press, 1980), 294. Derrida's comments on Heidegger and the cat appear in various later essays, which are cited and discussed at length in Cary Wolfe, *Animal Rites: American Culture, The Discourse of Species, and Posthumanist Theory* (Chicago: University of Chicago Press, 2003), chap. 2. Readers familiar with Wolfe's book will recognize my partial disagreement with him here, but I'm indebted to his work for provoking me into further thought on these themes.

[8] Thomas Nagel, "What Is It Like to Be a Bat?" in *Mortal Questions* (Cambridge: Cambridge University Press, 1979), 165–80.

[9] See Wolfe, *Animal Rites,* chap. 2, entitled "In the Shadow of Wittgenstein's Lion." As I'm implying here, Wolfe's use of Wittgenstein's sentence is appropriate within his own overall argument. Unfortunately, however, this is the only remark he discusses at any length, a fact that makes his picture of Wittgenstein too one-dimensional. The sentence about the lion is certainly one of the pithiest and well-known in Wittgenstein's writings, but it is also one of the least persuasive, for reasons I sketch here, and not wholly consonant with the rest of the *Investigations.*

of incommensurability. If, after all, we couldn't translate at least a good portion of what the lion were saying, we would have little reason to say that it was "talking" at all—talking as opposed to shooing away flies or moaning from an upset stomach. Claims about forms of consciousness that are *in principle* "beyond" us, wholly non-human, are simply more dramatic versions of the claim that we could never interpret human beings like the Hopi or the ancient Greek scientist. Such assertions betray a residual faith in what Davidson has called the "third dogma of empiricism," the distinction between mental scheme and unconceptualized content.[10] An entity—including the sorts of disembodied entities that have interested me most here—may indeed make very different sorts of discriminations and decisions than humans typically do, and may indeed have radically different beliefs and desires. And these intentional states may be notably less fine-grained than ours (as, say, a bat's would likely be) or remarkably more (as with, say, a race of genius Martians). But if, with Davidson, we fully abandon sharp distinctions between "mind" and "world," we notice something important: a non-human mind could hardly be recognized *as* a "mind" if it didn't share at least some of our responses to the world and if we couldn't thereby recognize some similarities between us. If, that is, we had no grounds for attributing a basic capacity like "discrimination" or "decision" to a non-human thing, we would have no way of saying how these discriminations and decisions are radically *unlike* our own. Ascribing mental capacities and intentional states is always fallible, but without at least some of these states, the very idea of a "consciousness" is without content, mere hand-waving. If the lion (or the dog, or the Steinian inside, or the DeLilloan Culture, or the super-robot, or the genius Martian) could speak, we could indeed understand it, at least it in part, and if it conceives of the universe in ways radically unlike ours, then we would certainly have a lot to say to one another.

So there are arguments to be made for and against the various ideas of agency that have been presented here. At the same time, however, straightforward philosophical argument is not the only level at which the preceding chapters have attempted to operate. Here we come to the ancient quarrel question. For all the force of the arguments I've just reviewed, they remain, we might say, *merely* arguments. Calling them "mere" arguments is a way of suggesting that

---

[10] See Donald Davidson, "On the Very Idea of a Conceptual Scheme," in *Inquiries into Truth and Interpretation* (New York: Oxford University Press, 1984), 183–98.

the critic I have imagined just now does get something right about my way of proceeding. Part of my goal here has been to locate some shared space between different theoretical positions and different literary texts, identifying points of contact and divergence. But I have tried to resist "applying" a single theory everywhere, and this has caused my philosophical claims to be more muted than they would be in a more straightforwardly philosophical book. Much of what I have done here is to give descriptions of descriptions. Why?

A full answer would be complicated, but a starting point is a simple observation about the kinds of visions that have occupied us here. The notion of a disembodied agent is not like a phony courtroom story that will crumble in the face of a prosecutor's searing questions. We won't see through the idea once we know the knock-down arguments or have compiled the right evidence. To adapt a remark from the end of chapter 5, the "presences" that have been identified here in both fiction and theory can seem to explain something important about who we are, about who we have become. So it has certainly appeared for many intelligent thinkers over the last century. Seeking to stamp out these visions once and for all is to leave unaddressed the question of their *appeal,* of why so many people would give their allegiance to these arguments and pictures. Surely there are moments when, with Stein and Robbe-Grillet, or with James and Pinker, we might feel some discrepancy between the way we think or feel, on the one hand, and the well-worn words given to us, on the other, some sense, as we search for the words on the tip of our tongues or listen to someone characterize us in public, that language can't capture the particularity of everything we think and experience. And surely, too, there are moments, as one learns about the massive shifts of geological history, or as one reads about unreported government actions in foreign countries, or as one sits in the roaring crowd at a rock concert, when one senses that a person's actions have only the slightest effects, and that as single bodies we matter far less than, in DeLillo's words, the "streams and clusters" of "mass assemblies." The force of these different intuitions is what makes them the starting point for so many powerful literary texts and philosophical theories. These intuitions are not necessarily the seed of despair or fear. Belief in private inner agents might, as with Bellow's Dahfu, affirm a sense of personal integrity and uniqueness; belief in outer agents might, as with Ellison's Ras or Brother Jack, strengthen our sense of a shared fate with others. Nor need we, to repeat my arguments a moment ago, see such non-human entities as lying wholly beyond human understanding. The point is simply that, however such extra-personal agents are conceived, and whether we embrace or eschew them, they won't simply vanish in the face of well-tuned arguments about the incoherence of disembodied voices, the non-relationality of pain-reports, and so on.

The reasons for this persistence can be suggested by placing a handful of sentences from Wittgenstein and Sellars next to a handful from Bellow and Ellison, and using them to amplify a point that has been noted in various places before. The work of Bellow and Ellison, I've argued, arises from an attention to our first words that is also characteristic of their philosophical contemporaries. And the fact that their novels are most obviously the biographies of persons, rather than disembodied presences, is an expression of an important impulse, a sense, again with Wittgenstein and Sellars, that it is only here that the notion of a practical agent is intelligible. I don't mean to rescind this basic analogy between these writers and these philosophers. Yet it would be a mistake simply to note this family resemblance without also noting the distances separating them. Consider, then, the following four brief passages:

The impression that we wanted to deny something arises from our setting our faces against the picture of the "inner process." What we deny is that the inner process gives us the correct idea of the use of the word "to remember." We say that this picture with its ramifications stands in the way of our seeing the use of the word as it is. (*PI* §305)

Thus, to complete the scientific image we need to enrich it *not* with more ways of saying what is the case, but with the language of community and individual intentions.... We can, of course, as matters now stand, realize this direct incorporation of the scientific image into our way of life only in imagination. But to do so is, if only in imagination, to transcend the dualism of the manifest and scientific images of man-of-the-world. (*SPR* 40)

Laps and laps I galloped around the shining and riveted body of the plane, behind the fuel trucks. Dark faces were looking from within. The great, beautiful propellers were still, all four of them. I guess I felt it was my turn now to move, and so went running—leaping, leaping, pounding, and tingling over the pure white lining of the gray Arctic silence. (*HRK* 340–41)

"Ah," I can hear you say, "so it was all a build-up to bore us with his buggy jiving. He only wanted us to listen to him rave!" But only partially true: Being invisible and without substance, a disembodied voice, as it were, what else could I do? What else but try to tell you what was really happening when your eyes were looking through? And it is this which frightens me:

Who knows but that, on the lower frequencies, I speak for you? (*IM* 581)

What matters most about these passages is in many ways the most obvious. How do we go about making sense of them and how do we respond to them?

Both of the philosophical passages—even, here, that of Wittgenstein—come at the tail end of arguments, and we are encouraged to respond in the manner appropriate to such conclusions: assent or dissent, yea or nay. We're obliged to offer such a response in part thanks to the third-person perspective that each tacitly adopts. The authors aren't making avowals about their hunger or headache, nor are they recollecting joyful personal moments from childhood. Their arguments are intended to be valid for me and you and everyone else, and the royal *we* of the passages reflects the degree to which their claims are meant to apply across time and place. Moreover, the passages reiterate many of the concepts grounding the arguments that precede them, as if they want to finish off their opponents with one final thrust: *manifest image, scientific image, community intentions* in Sellars, *"inner process," the correct use of the word,* and *this picture* in Wittgenstein. Note, too, the categorical vocabulary: Sellars's *thus* (repeated no less than three times in the full paragraph), Wittgenstein's *what we deny* and *we say.* The two passages are not "complete" in the sense that nothing more could be said about the topics they address, but they do try to fix the boundaries of the playing field. Which leaves a reader with two sets of basic options. We can disagree in part or in whole, in which case we have to do the gritty work of exposing shaky premises or unwarranted inferences. Or we can agree in part or in whole, which means we can seek out further examples, restate or clarify some of the claims, or simply slap the table in triumph.

My own philosophical inclination, as I've suggested, is to side with the arguments that Wittgenstein and Sellars make. Set within their larger context, the passages from Wittgenstein and Sellars are persuasive and have profound consequences. When, however, we turn to the concluding sentences of *Henderson* and *Invisible Man,* a simple but unsettling fact confronts us, a fact so simple and so unsettling that readers often try to avoid it altogether: the very notions of *assent* and *dissent, yea* or *nay,* are without any clear application whatsoever.

The passage from Bellow recounts a series of baffling actions. En route from Africa to New York, Henderson leaves the airplane during a lay-over in

Newfoundland, walks outside with the Persian boy he has met on the plane and the lion he has taken from Africa, and begins to run around the resting airplane. Is this some kind of liberation or a moment of utter absurdity? How should we understand the presence of the boy or the lion? What is the significance, if any, of the "dark faces" peering out from the plane's windows? Is it important that the propellers are "great, beautiful," or that the final sentence uses no less than five different participles (running, leaping, etc.)?

The concluding sentences of *Invisible Man* are more meditative, but it would be similarly difficult to pinpoint a set of pronouncements. What kind of "social role" exactly will the narrator now play? Is he *still,* after all this time, "without substance"? Just what are "the lower frequencies"? *Does* he "speak for" us? The problem here isn't just that we don't have the information that would answer all these questions. It is the deeper problem that we don't know what kind of information we would need to answer them—and just as important, what kind of information we *wouldn't* need. Any claims about what Bellow and Ellison are "saying" or "denying" can therefore only be conjectural. Gone are the explicit intersubjective aspirations that we saw in the philosophical arguments; the Invisible Man wonders aloud if he speaks for us, but he doesn't stay to answer. And little is done in either case, particularly Bellow's, to reiterate and underscore keywords we've heard previously in the text. Beyond the dictionary definitions of the words on the page, it is unclear that the term "meaning" means anything here at all here. Bellow and Ellison may be "philosophical novelists" in some loose, literary-historical sense, but they are not unequivocal about the inferences they want us to draw. And this makes their work importantly different from the philosophical philosophers whom they otherwise resemble.

In my discussions of these novels, I have recommended ways of making at least some inferences and of approaching at least some of the interpretive questions the passages raise. But I have also tried to avoid purging these texts altogether of their uncertainties. That these uncertainties persist discloses some of the limitations haunting the philosophical arguments that have otherwise done so much to structure my discussions. The global assertions offered in Wittgenstein and Sellars are meant to justify the place of purposes, the space of reasons, in our conception of agency. Bellow and Ellison also imply that the capacity to give coherent reasons is in large part what distinguishes the minded from the mindless. In writing the kinds of stories they do, however, they place intentions and reasons within a far wider context—the context, that is, of an entire narrated life. After attending to Wittgenstein and Sellars, I feel fewer qualms about saying *I intend to raise my arm,* but I don't understand the larger intentions to which this arm-raising might be directed. Is it a military salute? Is it a pacifist's gesture of defiance? The philosophical defense of reason-giving explanations says little more than that these reasons are conceptually defensible. What are the ends not just of this or that action, but of my life? What would count not just as a *project*, but as a *life project*? About these questions it is difficult to know what to *say* or *deny*, and difficult to know where to claim *thus*. Recognizing ourselves as purposive agents is not the same as knowing what purposes we are to pursue.

This unknowing, this uncertainty, is brought to the surface in different ways by all the literary texts I've been discussing in this book. Next to them, the arguments of Wittgenstein and Sellars look merely formal. The philosophers largely inherit the Kantian account of judgment as the mark of the mental, but they cast off most of the larger moral drive that motivates so much Kantian theorizing about the mind. The casting-off of Kantian morals isn't itself to be mourned; there are reasons to be skeptical about the Moral Law and Kingdom of Ends. The point here is simply that the discursive self-assurance of Wittgenstein, Sellars, and many of their descendents is achievable only because their questions remain relatively specified, and only because their questions could, at least in theory, have agreed-upon solutions.[11]

Cavell has remarked that, for him, philosophy has always been "the achievement of the unpolemical, of the refusal to take sides in metaphysical positions."[12] This may be true of Cavell's philosophizing, but it is decidedly less true of most of his predecessors, and still less of most of his present-day colleagues. The unpolemical that is characteristic of literary works, including the ones I have examined here, arises not from the heightened moral sensitivity or ageless wisdom of their authors, but from these texts being the kinds of texts they are—fictions, stories, texts that recount actions and events rather than draw conclusions from premises, texts that remain silent, or at least quiet, about broad concepts like "the just society" or "the good life." Even Bellow and Ellison, who locate agency in ways so similar to Wittgenstein and Sellars, resist announcing what this agency exactly entails. Once we get past

---

[11] For a recent example of this inability to move from small-scale to large-scale purposes, see Daniel Dennett's response to T. Brian Mooney's proposal to weave some notion of virtue into Dennett's theory of mind, in Daniel C. Dennett's "With a Little Help from My Friends," *Dennett's Philosophy: A Comprehensive Assessment,* ed. Dan Ross, Andrew Brook, and David Thompson (Cambridge: MIT Press, 2000), 382–85. Not all descendents of Wittgenstein and Sellars have been as reticent to think about reasons on a wider scale, of course. Just think of Elizabeth Anscombe, Charles Taylor, Alasdair MacIntyre, Richard Rorty, and John McDowell, to note a few notable names.

[12] Stanley Cavell, *A Pitch of Philosophy: Autobiographical Exercises* (Cambridge: Harvard University Press, 1994), 22.

a certain range of purposive actions, once we move beyond raising my arm and opening the refrigerator, the best we can often do is to reflect upon the stories available to us or to tell new ones of our own.

The inconclusiveness of these practical questions is, of course, the source of the rickety values-talk that I noted earlier, and what gives rise to our hodgepodge of working practical vocabularies. It is also part of what engenders the different conceptions of disembodied agency that we have seen everywhere in this book. Uncertainty about what an agent *should do* can give rise to uncertainty about who or what an agent *is*, what its powers are and where precisely these powers lie. The accounts of presences within and presences without that have proliferated in the literature and theory of the last century is an expression of this unease, this sense that whatever happens in the world, including what seems to happen by virtue of me and you, it is not attributable to an embodied, perceptible agent alone. An embodied person can seem too fragile a being to bear full responsibility for a life, let alone for an entire culture or history. Yet responsibility seldom goes unassigned, and explanations rarely go unmade. Mr. Crotcher's novel about ant life may depict cathedrals, stalactites, and humans, and may evoke inner beings and outer forces. But while some of these entities will no doubt be deliberate doers and others will be mindless movers, we cannot assume ahead of time, before reading his published novel, which will be which.

INDEX

CPSIA information can be obtained
at www.ICGtesting.com
Printed in the USA
LVHW080741160122
708507LV00002B/91

9 781951 168742